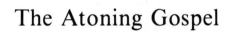

The Atoning Gospel

The Atoning Gospel

by

James E. Tull

Mercer University Press

All books published by Mercer University Press are produced
on acid-free paper which exceeds the minimum standards set by the
National Historical Publications and Records Commission.

Library of Congress Cataloging in Publication Data

Tull, James E.
    The atoning gospel.

    Includes bibliographical references and index.
    1. Atonement   2. Jesus Christ—Person and offices.   I. Title.
BT265.2.T84   232'.3   81-18732
ISBN 0-86554-029-2   AACR2

Contents

9. Christ the Living Lord   161

10. Atonement and the Church   181

Foreword

This book is not intended to be a history of the doctrine of the Atonement. It is rather meant to be a discussion, in topical form, of the relation of the Atonement to various segments and phases of Christian life and experience.

The organization of the material is determined by doctrines and concepts which are found in the Scriptures themselves. Each chapter attempts to show how large areas of the Christian faith are related to the Atonement—how the great doctrines of our faith are organically joined with God's atoning deed in Christ.

The first chapter considers the tremendous reality upon which atonement is based—the grace of God. A discussion of divine judgment follows in chapter 2, in order to point out that God's judgment is a correlative of divine grace. The next three chapters deal consecutively with the great Pauline trilogy which is identified in Paul's writings as justification, reconciliation, and sanctification. The position of these chapters is due to the fact that considering them in sequence offers the opportunity of bringing to light their separate and joint connection with the Atonement. Also, the position of the first three chapters—on grace, judgment, and justification—enables us to discuss these topics sequentially in close reference to the law of God, to which each one of these three topics is closely bound.

Chapters 6, 7, 8, and 9 deal with four great concepts in the New Testament which are profoundly associated with Christ's atoning life. These are: Christ as Deliverer, Christ as Representative of God and Man, Christ as Servant of God, and Christ as Living Lord.

The order of arrangement of these four chapters may be a matter of debate. I believe, however, that most thoughtful Christians would agree that they are all concerned with major topics which should be examined in a discussion of atonement.

The tenth and last chapter attempts to show that the meaning of the Atonement comes to a focus in the life and ministry of the Church. For the Church is the community of the redeemed whose life is redeeming in the world as it incorporates the atoning life of God in Christ.

While the substance and the methodology of the book are deeply involved with both biblical and historical materials, the discussion throughout deals with the *theology* of the Atonement. The fact that the first draft of the book was written during a personal crisis in the author's own life may account somewhat for the devotional tone that is evident, I trust, in many of the pages. The book comes out of some years of teaching courses on the Atonement in a theological seminary, and also out of the author's conviction that the atoning grace of God lies at the heart of the Christian faith and life.

The book is practical in its purpose. However deficient it may be in its interpretations, it deals with many of the great doctrines and realities of the Christian faith, and therefore with areas of that faith which are the common coin of the Christian pastor's preaching and of every Christian's daily witness. The deep wellsprings of the Christian life lie in the area of God's atoning work in Jesus Christ. It is hoped that this volume will be helpful to persons who want to have a deeper grasp of what our common faith is all about.

I wish to acknowledge especially the assistance of four of my colleagues at Southeastern Baptist Theological Seminary who have been helpful in the writing of this book: Dr. John W. Eddins, Professor of Theology, with whom for many years I have enjoyed exploring the broader ranges of theology, including the doctrine of the Atonement; Dr. Thomas A. Bland, Professor of Christian Ethics and Sociology, who has helped me to enrich my own insight into the ethical bearings of the Atonement; Dr. James H. Blackmore, Special Instructor and

Associate Director of Communications at the seminary, who read my manuscript carefully, and made many valuable suggestions; and Dr. Robert Culpepper, Professor of Theology, to whose book entitled *Interpreting the Atonement*, I am much more indebted than I fear I have explicitly acknowledged. While these and other persons have been greatly helpful, I cannot blame them for the book's limitations, which are my own responsibility.

James E. Tull
Wake Forest, North Carolina
September 1981

To Virginia

Chapter 1

Atonement and Divine Grace

Central to a Christian doctrine of atonement is an understanding of God as a God of grace. Atonement is provided by the grace of God.

In the Bible, the primary meaning of grace is that of a favor freely given. In the New Testament, grace has to do with the favor and kindness of God, extended freely to human beings in the life and death of Jesus Christ. Grace, then, is not only a divine "characteristic," or "attitude," but also has within it an active, outgoing, giving quality.

In this chapter, grace in its relationship to atonement will occupy our principal attention.

Grace and Salvation

Grace is a synonym for the love (*agape*) of God. Grace, however, emphasizes both the sheer gratuitousness of love and love's redemptive involvement in human life: "God shows his love for us in that while we were yet sinners Christ died for us" (Rom. 5:8, RSV). In brief compass, this verse sets forth the message of grace. The special quality of the divine love which is stressed by grace is indicated by P. T. Forsyth. "We make too little of the Father," Forsyth says, "when we do not rise beyond love to grace—which is holy love, suffering hate and redeeming it."[1] Grace demonstrates to us that God was not content to dwell "at ease apart" in some distant heaven. In Christ he came all the way to us to work mightily for our salvation. Forsyth expresses in a pungent exclamation the awesome wonder of this divine involvement: "Do not say, 'God is love. Why atone?' The New Testament says, 'God has atoned. What love!' "[2]

In a Christian context, grace is most searchingly illuminated when it is viewed against the dark backdrop of sin. Perhaps no capsule definition of sin is possible. Yet we point to the heart of its significance when we observe that sin is the worship of the self instead of the worship of God. "Our sin," says Edward Ramsdell, "is at bottom always the centering of life in our own little selves."[3] Sin manifests itself as a pride by which a person seeks to make himself self-sufficient, and therefore independent of God. It takes the form of a self-love, so concentrated upon one's own desires that the self is excluded from the fellowship of God and from true fellowship with other human beings. It discloses itself as a misuse of the freedom which God has given to us. We use this freedom, not to affirm him, but to deny and defy him. As a consequence, says John Whale, "Man is not at home in his Father's house, but a needy outcast in a far country."[4]

The alienating effect of sin is graphically described in a passage by Mendell Taylor:

> By yielding to temptation, disobeying the command of God, and raising a rebel flag into the face of the Creator, man became a sinner. The intrusion of sin into man's personality turned his existence into a seething mass of strut, artificiality, and confusion. He became a fugitive, running from the Lord, running from himself, and running from reality. Riddled by fears, overwhelmed by vagrant impulses, and driven by selfishness, man became morally helpless. He

---

[1]P. T. Forsyth, *God the Holy Father* (London: Independent Press Ltd., 1957), p. 7.

[2]Ibid., p. 4.

[3]Edward T. Ramsdell, *The Christian Perspective* (New York, Nashville: Abingdon, Cokesbury Press, 1950), p. 170.

[4]J. S. Whale, *Christian Doctrine* (New York: The Macmillan Company, 1941), p. 45.

was victimized by mixed motives, divided loyalties, and conflicting purposes.[5]

Sin, however, is not only the act of an individual person. The person does indeed sin as an individual, but nearly always in partnership with other persons. The doctrine of Original Sin has had many interpretations, not all of which have been enlightening or helpful. Yet this doctrine has at least called attention to mankind's solidarity in evil. As Reinhold Niebuhr acutely and repeatedly observed, man collectivizes his idolatries, and worships *his* class, *his* race, *his* nation. "There is in the world," says John Whale, "a kingdom of evil by which the evil acts of each individual are inspired, sustained, and reinforced."[6]

No depiction of how God deals with our sin can be adequate which does not include the element of grace. "The saying is sure and worthy of full acceptance, that Christ Jesus came into the world to save sinners" (1 Tim. 1:15, RSV). God's sin-bearing for us was "incarnate in the passion of Jesus."[7] In Christ the gracious God identified himself so profoundly with our plight that he felt the weight of our sin as though it were his own.

On the other hand, God's condescension to our condition did not mean that he condoned our sin. He deals with us in a personal confrontation—judging, healing, and restoring. He saves us, but he does not compromise with our wrongdoing.

Salvation is a broad term which includes deliverance from the world's powers of destruction and the divine, unmerited bestowing of reconciliation, wholeness, healing, and life. A deliverance from sin and death, a giving of new life in Christ—these ideas summarize the New Testament concept of salvation.

The New Testament writers used a number of metaphors in pointing to the experience of salvation which had come to them in Christ. Salvation was a newness of life, a rebirth, a transference from darkness to light, a death and a rising, a cleansing and a healing, a

---

[5]Mendell Taylor, *Exploring Evangelism* (Kansas City, Mo.: Beacon Hill Press of Kansas City, 1964), pp. 584-85.

[6]Whale, *Christian Doctrine*, p. 45.

[7]D. M. Baillie, *God Was in Christ* (New York: Charles Scribner's Sons, 1948), p. 20.

forgiveness, a conquest of evil, a newly found freedom, a seal of the Holy Spirit. The list can be extended indefinitely, but the terms refer to the same experience which all Christians shared. This was the experience of the transforming reality into which God's grace had brought them through Christ's atoning work.

So comprehensive was the meaning of salvation conceived to be, that it embraced the present, the past, and the future. "We were saved," Paul says in Romans 8:24 (RSV). "You are saved," he says in 1 Corinthians 15:2 (RSV). "We shall be saved," he says in Romans 5:9 (RSV). In one passage, Paul's thought embraces all three tenses: "Therefore, since we are justified by faith, we have peace with God through our Lord Jesus Christ. Through him we have obtained access to this grace in which we stand, and we rejoice in our hope of sharing the glory of God" (Rom. 5:1-2, RSV).

The Grace of the Father God

When grace is conceived to be a force or a substance which is transfused into the human soul, or when God is thought to be an uncompassionate monarch whose dispensing of favor to his human subjects leaves him free from personal involvement in the plight of their sins and sorrows, the meaning of grace becomes greatly distorted. The grace terms of the New Testament are terms like *forgiveness*, *reconciliation*, *love*, and *fellowship*. These are terms of personal relationship.

God is Creator, King, Judge, Redeemer, Savior, and Lord. Yet we apprehend his grace most truly when we think of him in the relationship which appears to have been most precious to Jesus himself. He is *Father*.

By calling God *Father*, we may properly refer to his benevolent care of the world which he has made. More fittingly, we use this word in connection with his care of his human creatures. We do not honor the term, however, if we conceive of God's fatherhood as a relationship towards his children which is marked by sentimental indulgence. We should think of him, as Forsyth urges, as "God the *holy* Father." He is a Father whose love makes demands on us, a Father who cannot be cajoled, manipulated, or intimidated.

The New Testament has taught us to think of God first as "the God and Father of our Lord Jesus Christ" (Eph. 1:3, RSV). Certainly in the view of the New Testament writers, Christ's relationship to the Father was special and unique. He was "the only begotten Son, which is in the bosom of the Father" (John 1:18, KJV). God's grace is so extended to us that we see with Christ's vision those fatherly qualities in God which Christ himself saw, and receive adoption by grace into a sonship with God which Christ enjoyed by right. In giving us this access to sonship, Christ has become "the first-born among many brethren" (Rom. 8:29, RSV). Therefore, we can say, "See what love the Father has given us, that we should be called the children of God" (1 John 3:1, RSV).

In all his relationships with his children, we should think of God as Father. He is King, but he is a king who rules as a father. He is Judge, but it is as a father that he judges. If God were merely the Moral Governor, says David Smith, "He would resent our sin as a violation of the moral order; were He merely the Judge, He would condemn it as a crime and exact a legal penalty; but because He is our Father, it pierces His heart. The sin is ours, but because He loves us, the sorrow is His."[8]

Electing Grace

Intrinsic to the Christian conception of grace is God's initiative in his dealings with the human family. God's grace is prevenient in the sense that it goes before anything that we can do for ourselves. A gracious God planned for us, made provision for our needs, sustains us with loving care, woos and wins us, fights for us, and suffers for us and with us. He does this because he loves us, and because he is *able* to do it. Grace would mean little if it were merely benevolent but impotent goodwill. God is a God of sovereign grace.

Election is a term which conveys the truth that God's power to save is joined with his steadfast purpose to save. Karl Barth could call election "the shining center of the gospel" because election directs attention to the fact that the choice and call of God to salvation is a primary factor in God's redemptive action. The following passage by Rudolph Otto points out the initiative of grace while acknowledging that its workings transcend our understanding:

A man who is the object of grace, when he looks back on himself, feels more and more that he has become what he is by no act or activity of his own, that grace came to him

---

[8]David Smith, *The Atonement in the Light of History and the Modern Spirit* (London, New York, Toronto: Hodder and Stoughton, n.d.), pp. 167-68.

without his own will or power, that it took hold of him, drove him, led him on. Before any act of his own, he sees redeeming love seeking and choosing him, and recognizes an eternal decree of grace on his behalf.[9]

From a conviction like that expressed above by Otto, it would seem to be but a short step to a belief in what strong Calvinists have called "irresistible grace." The meaning of this term is that, if God intends to save a person, his sovereign grace overcomes all obstacles—God's grace cannot be defeated. Since not all persons are saved, it is argued, God must therefore intend to save some, and *not* to save others.

It is difficult to see how this doctrine can be held without denying human freedom at the same time. The hyper-Calvinists, indeed, have come very near to making this denial. Moreover, if God's sovereignty overrides human freedom, the missionary outreach of the Church would appear to be a futile enterprise. Why bother to evangelize, we may ask, if God, before the beginning of time, determined the fate of each individual person by consigning him either to salvation or to damnation? The anti-evangelistic stand of the hyper-Calvinists has been a logical outcome of this theological position.

Both the Old and New Testaments contain repeated warnings and admonitions for persons to *decide* to do the will of God. The appeal to decide presupposes the *freedom* to decide. In the Old Testament, the elect nation, Israel, was warned not to presume upon her election. In Exodus 9:4-5, for example, God says to his people: "You have seen what I did to the Egyptians, and how I bore you on eagles' wings and brought you to myself. Now, therefore, *if* you will obey my voice and keep my covenant, you shall be my own possession among all peoples" (RSV, italics added).

The New Testament also shows clearly that one's freedom to affirm or reject God's will for his life is decisively real. For example, Paul said to the Corinthians: "We come therefore as Christ's ambassadors. It is as if God were appealing to you through us: in Christ's name, we implore you, be reconciled to God!" (2 Cor. 5:20, NEB).

Election is "in Christ." To say this is to affirm that God focused his sovereign and gracious purpose in Christ, in whom he was personally

---

[9]Rudolph Otto, *Das Heilige*, p. 109; cited in A. M. Hunter, *Interpreting Paul's Gospel* (London: S.C.M. Press Ltd., 1954), p. 137.

present, and that this purpose "finds us" in Christ. "He chose us in him [Christ] before the foundation of the world, that we should be holy and blameless before him. He destined us in love to be his sons through Jesus Christ, according to the purpose of his will" (Eph. 1:4-5, RSV). Again: "For those whom he foreknew he also predestined to be conformed to the image of his Son, in order that he might be the first-born among many brethren. And those whom he predestined he also called; and those whom he called he also justified; and those whom he justified he also glorified" (Rom. 8:29-30, RSV).

While these passages, taken by themselves, seem to argue for the kind of deterministic foreordination considered above, they do not so appear when they are seen in the context of the writings in which they are incorporated.[10] The discussion in the book of Ephesians says nothing about what has been called *double predestination*. The writer is arguing, rather, that the blessings of God are not blessings that we can merit or demand. They are free gifts. The way to obtain salvation is gratefully to receive God's gift of grace. The way to lose it is to try to earn it, or to demand it on the basis of one's imagined merits. "For by grace are ye saved through faith; and that not of yourselves: it is the gift of God: not of works, lest any man should boast" (Eph. 2:8-9, KJV).

In Romans, Paul shows that salvation is not bought, earned, or deserved; it comes to us only by God's grace. The opposite of election is not a divine consignment to damnation; it is unbelief. And the refusal to believe, to accept God's offer of salvation in Christ, is not God's decision, but *ours*.

God's purpose to save is incorporated in Christ. God, says Paul, "chose us in him" (Eph. 1:4, RSV). God's electing love has drawn near enough to us to become "bone of our bone and flesh of our flesh." Moreover, we are chosen, Paul says, "to be conformed to the image of his Son" (Rom. 8:29, RSV). We encounter the love, mercy, and judgment of God in Christ, and thereby are shaped into Christ's own image.

Christ was not merely a witness of God's grace. He was the presence and the embodiment of that grace in the world. He was the grace of God "in person." This truth receives eloquent expression in a statement by James Smart:

---

[10]Hunter, *Interpreting Paul's Gospel*, pp. 136-39.

> The heart of Jesus' mission and of his gospel . . . was the incarnation of divine love. In him the love of God came out of the distant heavens, and while still remaining the infinite compassion of God, became a love that spoke with a human voice and reached out to men with human hands . . . . Through the centuries men had sought and found forgiveness in God, and it had seemed that God had to wait for man to seek him. But now the forgiveness of God walked the earth in search of men.[11]

Election is misunderstood if it is conceived to be only God's choice of individuals for salvation. Actually, election is a social conception, which in the Old Testament centered upon God's choice both of the nation Israel and of Israel's Messiah-King. These two factors flowed together, because Israel as a whole appears to have been represented in the person of the Messiah. The election of individuals was less accentuated. And election first of all was not election to salvation; it was election to service.

In his book entitled *The Biblical Doctrine of Election*, H. H. Rowley has called attention to several aspects of God's election of the nation of Israel.[12] The first feature of Israel's choice was that she should receive and cherish the revelation of God given to her in history and experience. In the second place, she was chosen to reflect the will and the character of God in her life. In the third place, she was chosen to be a witnessing nation—to proclaim to the world her faith in the true God. A passage in Isaiah throws a beam of light upon this witnessing vocation of Israel: "I the Lord have called thee in righteousness, and will hold thine hand, and will keep thee, and give thee for a covenant of the people, for a light of the Gentiles; to open the blind eyes, to bring out the prisoners from the prison, and them that sit in darkness out of the prison house" (Isa. 42:6-7, KJV).

Rowley's analysis shows that the election of Israel was not to special privilege, but to special service. Moreover, as Israel was chosen to be a witnessing nation, so in the New Testament era a *new* nation,

---

[11]James D. Smart, *The ABC's of the Christian Faith* (Philadelphia: Westminster Press, 1968), p. 127.

[12]H. H. Rowley, *The Biblical Doctrine of Election* (London: Lutterworth Press, 1950), p. 165.

composed of redeemed individuals, became the elect community. This community was and is the church.

As Israel was chosen to disseminate the knowledge of the true God to the nations of the world, so the mission of the new nation is to proclaim the gospel of Christ to all people. Perhaps the purpose of the new nation is delineated in the New Testament nowhere more definitively than in 1 Peter 2:9: "But you are a chosen race, a royal priesthood, a holy nation, God's own people, that you may declare the wonderful deeds of him who called you out of darkness into his marvelous light" (RSV).

In the New Testament, of course, election applies to individuals as well as to the Church, but to individuals as they witness in and for the Church. Christians are corporately the elect because they are one body in Christ. Individuals are called to serve the Lord of the Church, and to serve the Church's larger mission. In this light, for example, Paul's call to his apostleship is to be seen: "Unto me, who am less than the least of all saints, is this grace given, that I should preach among the Gentiles the unsearchable riches of Christ" (Eph. 3:8, KJV). As the Apostle to the Gentiles, Paul was not assigned to a mission separate from that of the Church. He was rather an extended arm of the Church and, therefore, the Church's representative.

Grace and Covenant

The grace of God is also a covenant grace. The people of God are a covenant people. While the origins of the covenant idea in the Old Testament are obscure, the principal tradition indicates that the Horeb-Sinai covenant, described in Exodus 24, is the original covenant between God and Israel. To this covenant the great prophets—Hosea, Jeremiah, Amos, and Ezekiel—look back. The covenant established on Mount Sinai was a constant and principal reference-point in the history of the Hebrew people. It was considered to be the basis of their continuing relationship to God. Whenever the people kept the terms of the covenant, they were blessed; whenever they disobeyed these terms, disaster followed.

Those who receive and affirm God's electing grace are bound together in covenant with God. So important is the covenant relationship that Christians have seen the Scriptures in terms of an *old covenant* and a *new covenant*.

In Old Testament history, the constant danger of the covenant association was that it would degenerate into a legalistic connection between God and the nation, for the covenant involved commandment as well as mercy, obedience as well as gift. However, the covenant was basically one of personal rather than of legal relationships with God:

> Through His *Word* and in His *Acts* God has established with His chosen people a permanently binding personal relationship whose fundamental truth is "steadfast love." From the time of our father Abraham (Gen. 12; 15; 17) to the consummation of the Church in the New Jerusalem (Rev. 21), the Word by which God announces His steadfast love and sovereign righteousness is the same: *You* shall be my people, and *I* will be your God.[13]

In the Old Testament period, God's deliverance of the people of Israel from Egyptian bondage was a permanent strand in the covenant tie. This truth is beautifully expressed in the sixth chapter of Deuteronomy: "When your son asks you in time to come, 'What is the meaning of the testimonies and the statutes and the ordinances which the Lord our God has commanded you?' then you shall say to your son, 'We were Pharaoh's slaves in Egypt; and the Lord brought us out of Egypt with a mighty hand." (Deut. 6:20-21, RSV).

In the covenant relationship, God takes the initiative. It is he who has accomplished the deliverance of his people, and upon whom they utterly depend for life and salvation. The covenant involves duties and responsibilities, but it effects an order of life whose terms are laid down by God. The covenant means, therefore, that the redeeming purpose of God is carried on in a fellowship of persons, a fellowship in which God is the principal partner, but a fellowship in which there is mutual trust, mutual love, and a freely acknowledged mutual obligation.

As the apostle Paul saw keenly, a great danger of the old covenant was the danger of exteriorization, in which fellowship gave place to law, and the letter was exalted above the spirit. Jeremiah also saw this danger: he envisioned a new covenant and prophesied that a day would come when God would say,

> I will put my law within them, and I will write it upon their hearts; and I will be their God, and they shall be my people.

---

[13]Marvin Halverson, ed., *Handbook of Christian Theology* (New York: Living Age Books, 1958), p. 63.

And no longer shall each man teach his neighbor and each his brother, saying, 'Know the Lord,' for they shall all know me, from the least of them to the greatest, says the Lord; for I will forgive their iniquity, and I will remember their sin no more (Jer. 31:33-34, RSV).

The fulfillment of Jeremiah's vision of a new covenant, written on men's hearts, occurred in the establishment of this covenant by Christ. As the key to the meaning of covenant in the Old Testament was deliverance, so the new covenant is concerned with deliverance from sin and death, by a gracious God, through Christ.

At the Last Supper, Jesus spoke of "the new covenant in my blood" (1 Cor. 11:25, RSV). The symbolism of this occasion was beautiful and powerful. In a deep sense, Jesus appears to have looked upon his little band of disciples as a covenant community. He had called them to share his sufferings, his disgrace, and his triumph, and to perpetuate his ministry. In the final hours before his death, he ratified this relationship by establishing a new covenant. From that time forward, to the ends of the earth, and to the end of time, there would live in the world a community bound together with God in Christ by covenant love, and dedicated to the task of bringing men and women of all nations to stand together before the throne of God's grace.

Christ, says the writer of the epistle to the Hebrews, was "the mediator of a better covenant" (Heb. 8:6, KJV). This better covenant did not require the perennial offering of the blood of animals by high priests, who themselves were sinful men and whose ministry was ephemeral and ineffectual. Christ, the High Priest of the new covenant, himself sinless and eternal, offers his own blood for our deliverance from sin and death. "How much more," says this writer, "shall the blood of Christ, who through the eternal Spirit offered himself without blemish unto God, cleanse your conscience from dead works to serve the living God?" (Heb. 9:14, ASV).

Grace and Faith

Faith is one of the elemental ingredients of Christianity to which, in various contexts, we shall need to refer many times in the following pages. At this point, a brief discussion of faith in relation to grace is in order.

A person's positive response to the grace of God is faith. "By grace are ye saved through faith" (Eph. 2:8, KJV). The paradox of faith may be seen in the recognition that faith is both a gift of God and a free human response. The devotion of faith and the commitment which it entails are free human decisions and replies to the divine overtures of grace. Yet Christian insight discerns that what appears to be the result of human resolution and dedication is at the same time the merciful working of God.

Both faith and repentance have reference to the beginnings of the Christian life. Together they form an open door through which God's grace enters. Together they also characterize the continuing Christian style of life. The Christian's life-style is a repentant life in which he turns from his own will and way. It is also a life of faith in which he turns to God and walks in God's way.

The essential meaning of faith is stated by Paul when he affirms, "For me to live is Christ" (Phil. 1:21, RSV). Paul's understanding of faith has often been described as that of a *faith union* with Christ. So comprehensive is this union that all of life for Paul becomes a life "in Christ." Faith involves dying with Christ: "I have been crucified with Christ" (Gal. 2:20, RSV). Faith includes being buried with Christ: "We were buried therefore with him by baptism into death" (Rom. 6:4, RSV). Faith involves rising and living with Christ: "As Christ was raised up from the dead by the glory of the Father, even so we also should walk in newness of life" (Rom. 6:4, KJV).

Faith's dedication to Christ is, in the Pauline sense, of profound significance, because it is devotion to the Person in whom and through whom God has disclosed his redemptive activity, and in and through whom he has wrought that activity into the texture of the world. Faith is therefore free and glad involvement in God's task of world redemption; it is both a reception of and a participation in God's atoning action in Christ.

Grace and Law

The relation of grace to law is a vexing problem, especially in the light of the New Testament message. In the Old Testament era, the Mosaic law was considered to be a divine gift. The law given to Moses at Mount Sinai was a part of the covenant which God established with his people. The law expressed the will of God for the nation, and marked out a way of life by which his people were to live in his service. Israel was a nation set apart by virtue of her possession of the law. The law was a precious legacy which was remembered by the pious with thanksgiving and joy. Many of the psalmists sang their love of God's law. The Feast of Tabernacles was an annual celebration in which the Hebrew people rededicated themselves to a love of, and an obedience to, the law.[14]

The law, centering in the Decalogue and contained in the Pentateuch, was understood originally as divine instruction given to God's people for their good, and in the tutelage of which they had the way of service to him made plain. The law, when received in this sense, was gratefully observed in the context of God's covenant of grace with his people. In the course of time, however, the law was subjected to a misguided interpretation and application. For many Hebrews it became a system of rules, the faithful observance of which was esteemed to be a means of securing God's favor. Loyalty to the law became loyalty to precept rather than to the gracious God who had given it. Legal observance crowded out personal devotion. In much of postexilic Judaism, the way of salvation tended to be equated with a rigid obedience to the requirements of the law.

Jesus' attitude towards the law may be described as one of loyalty, and yet one of discriminating independence. His occasional criticisms of the law showed him to be far from a slavish legalism and literalism. In the Sermon on the Mount, Jesus said, "Think not that I have come to abolish the law and the prophets; I have come not to abolish them but to fulfil them" (Matt. 5:17, RSV).

The fulfillment which Jesus intended was in no sense a lowering of God's claims or demands upon his people. But Jesus saw the law principally in terms of the claims of fellowship and reconciliation. All commandments were gathered into the obligation to love, with a love that was spontaneous and free, a love which was directed towards God with all one's heart, soul, mind, and strength, and towards one's neighbor. Love, not legalistic observance, was the fulfillment of the law. By love, Jesus fulfilled the law, and by love he expected his disciples to do the same.

The most extensive discussion of the law in the New Testament is found in the writings of the apostle Paul. Paul has been criticized by some modern scholars because they assume that he understood the

---

[14]Cf. Iris V. Cully and Kendig Brubaker Cully, *An Introductory Theological Wordbook* (Philadelphia: The Westminster Press, 1963), pp. 109-10.

Mosaic law only in terms of a legalistic demand. F. W. Dillistone, for example, sees Paul as arguing the superiority of the Abrahamic covenant to the Mosaic covenant. The first was a covenant of grace: "Abraham believed God, and it was reckoned to him as righteousness" (Rom. 4:3, RSV). The later Mosaic covenant was a covenant of law. When Paul, says Dillistone, "draws so complete a contrast between the Abrahamic and Sinaitic covenants as to make the former purely of grace and the latter purely of law he himself is guilty of doing despite to the highest truth of the Old Testament revelation."[15]

Whether this criticism is valid or not, it must be remembered that Paul, a profound student of the law, believed the law to be holy. The commandment, he said, is "holy, and just and good" (Rom. 7:12, RSV). Whoever loves his neighbor, he said, has "fulfilled the law" (Rom. 13:8, RSV). The whole law "is fulfilled in one word, even in this: Thou shalt love thy neighbor as thyself" (Gal. 5:14, KJV).

Paul, however, had a keen sense of the limitations of the law. The law, he thought, was powerless to give what it demanded. It was "weakened by the flesh" (Rom. 8:3, RSV). What the law could not do because of its weakness, God had done by sending his Son, thereby condemning sin in the flesh (Rom. 8:3). By itself, the law not only reveals but increases sin, either through provoking despair in the one who finds himself unable to meet its requirements, or through leading to a legalism which attenuates and trivializes its demands.

The Christian does not live under the law, but under grace. Rightly used, the law convicts us of our sinfulness, and points us to the life of love which is available to us in Christ. But when the law as *tutor* or as *slave-attendant* has brought us to Christ, it has finished its task (see Gal. 3:24). "Christ is the end of the law unto righteousness to every one that believeth" (Rom. 10:4, KJV). Salvation does not come by means of keeping the law. Paul refers the redemptive experience to the atoning grace of God in Christ, apart from the works of the law:

> For I through the law died to the law, that I might live to God. I have been crucified with Christ; it is no longer I who live, but Christ who lives in me; and the life I now live in the flesh I live by faith in the Son of God, who loved me and

---

[15]F. W. Dillistone, *The Structure of the Divine Society* (Philadelphia: The Westminster Press, 1949), p. 74.

gave himself for me. I do not nullify the grace of God; for if justification were through the law, then Christ died to no purpose (Gal. 2:19-20, RSV).

The legalists had a vested interest in their efforts to win salvation by a successful keeping of the law. For, they believed, if they kept the law they could win the favor of God by deserving it—perhaps by demanding it. An earning of merit could purchase God's favor. Paul's reply to this position was blunt: "By the deeds of the law shall no flesh be justified in his sight" (Rom. 3:20, KJV).

The belief that merit can be earned is illusory on two counts: it does not do justice to the mandates of the law, for no one can keep these mandates well enough to earn merit and demand reward for their observance; and the attempt to accumulate merit misconceives the nature of the relationship between God and human beings. The pursuit of merit denies that fellowship of love which allows opportunity in abundance for labor and service, but which comes as a divine gift that no one deserves. The "last infirmity of the noble mind," says James S. Stewart, "is to think that the virtuous soul deserves something of God."[16]

Conclusion

The pinnacle of the New Testament understanding of grace is reached in its portrayal of Christ. The "grace of our Lord Jesus Christ" was known to be the highest expression of the love of God. Christ brought God's grace to the point of our human need. The light of the knowledge of the glory of God shone upon us, through the darkness, in his face. It was Christ, said Paul, "who loved me and gave himself for me" (Gal. 2:20, RSV). He died for the ungodly. Though he was rich, for our sakes he became poor. By the grace of God, he tasted death for every person. In him was life, and that life was the light of men. He was the great Shepherd of the sheep, who left the ninety and nine safely in the fold, and "dared the dark, the solitude, the mire," to find the sheep that was lost. He was the Good Samaritan, who traveled the highways and byways, who frequented the waysides and the hearthsides of the world, who visited the harvest-fields, the marts of trade, the centers of

---

[16]James S. Stewart, *A Man in Christ* (New York and London: Harper and Brothers Publishers, 1935), p. 251.

industry, to help and to heal those who had been bruised and broken by hardship and heartbreak. In all relationships he both bestowed and appealed to the human response of faith, which allowed him to make available the manifold resources of God's grace to human beings in their need.

Our inquiry in this chapter has been to relate God's grace to atonement. We must now consider the fact that God is not only a God of grace, but also is the Judge of all the earth. In the next chapter, we shall consider how the judgment of God affects the Christian doctrine of atonement.

Chapter 2

Atonement and Divine Judgment

Among many ancient peoples, the king was the supreme judge. Since Israel considered God to be King above all kings, the prerogative of judging was ascribed to him. The God who sits on the throne of the world is the Judge of men and nations. His righteous judgments establish the norms to which the lives of men must conform. The prophets constantly emphasized God's judgments and warned that a departure from God's will would bring deserved punishment. They also envisioned a future time, a Day of the Lord, when all people— both those of Israel and those outside Israel—would be confronted by the just judgment of God.

In the Old Testament, God delegates the coming messianic Prince both to exercise judgment on earth and to establish a messianic kingdom. Hence, the New Testament concept of Christ as messianic King enabled early Christians to associate Christ with the prerogatives and functions of divine judgment. While in the New Testament Christ is believed to be God's appointed agent who will "come again with glory to judge both the quick and the dead" in the final judgment at the end of history, a number of passages ascribe to him also the role of Judge during the days of his flesh. This is true particularly of the

Gospel of John.[1]

Now we shall take a closer look at what God's judgment means in relation to a doctrine of atonement.

Judgment and Grace

Those who attempt to interpret the judgment of God are exposed to at least two dangerous pitfalls. On the one hand, one is tempted to exalt the grace of God to such a degree that God's judgment is minimized. The tendency of this position is to emphasize so strongly the mercy of God that the divine love is degraded into a weak, indulgent goodwill. The judgment of God loses its severity, its sharp delineation, and its moral requirement. On the other hand, the element of judgment may be so exalted above grace that God is conceived to be an arbitrary tyrant. At least for those who are believed to be outside the scope of his redemptive purpose, he is esteemed to be lacking in love.

A Christian interpretation of God must reckon constantly with the question of what kind of God he is. If the judgment of God is divorced from his grace, God becomes a whimsical tyrant, or at best a supreme intelligent being whose power is devoid of compassion. If the grace of God is sentimentalized, it becomes what Bonhoeffer called "cheap grace," grace without cost and without requirement.

Grace and judgment belong together. Since God exercises his grace for the salvation of human beings, judgment must be an intrinsic part of his saving grace. Grace is extended as a redeeming love which has in it a divine requirement, but which at the same time may be rejected by human freedom. But to hold that God is love is not to say that he may be accorded with impunity either the hostility, the indifference, or the contempt of human beings. The judgment of God, we may well believe, has within it a retributive quality.

However, the caution of Gustaf Aulén here is well taken: "The idea of retribution," he says, "is dangerous whenever retributive justice is separated from divine love and is made the highest principle in the relationship between God and man."[2] In this relationship, love, not

---

[1]Alan Richardson, *A Theological Word Book of the Bible* (New York: The Macmillan Company, 1950), p. 118.

[2]Gustaf Aulén, *The Faith of the Christian Church* (Philadelphia: The Muhlenberg Press, 1948), p. 171.

retributive justice, must be given chief place. On the other hand, since God is love, we are likely to say that there is "nothing to be afraid of." Forsyth's warning is salutary: "There is everything in the love of God to be afraid of. Love is not holy without judgment. It is the love of holy God that is the consuming fire."[3]

The message of grace is a message of judgment, because grace summons us before a holy God, whose will for us is benevolent and redeeming, but who exacts from us a response in the freedom which he has given to us. To stand before God is to be judged. Whether this judgment is one of restoration or one of rejection depends upon our response. Paul admonishes those who refuse to repent in the face of God's offer of grace: "You are storing up wrath for yourself on the day of wrath when God's righteous judgment will be revealed" (Rom. 2:5, RSV).

The doctrine of judgment carries with it the idea of examination. Judgment is *crisis*, a time of testing. The divine Judge is the one to whom "all hearts are open and all desires known." His judgment involves a searching scrutiny of our lives, not only at the level of the deeds we do, but also at the level of the motivational springs of our being. He is a loving Judge, but nothing is hid from him, nothing escapes him, nothing deceives him. To be judged by God is to be "weighed in the balances."

The judgment of God is also vindicative. To say this is not to assert that his judgment is vindictive—a charge that is blasphemous when it is applied to God. Judgment is vindicative in the sense that it establishes and manifests the rightness of God's dealings with his creatures. It vindicates him by showing that man's willful rejection of him results in an inevitable separation from him. It vindicates those who embrace his redeeming grace, and who thereby are rescued from estrangement and are accepted into his favor and fellowship.

Since judgment in a sense stands for the requirements of grace, for the terms on the basis of which salvation may be received and fellowship with God and man enjoyed, judgment is concerned particularly with those violations of the terms of fellowship and salvation which we call *sin*.

---

[3]P. T. Forsyth, *The Work of Christ* (New York and London: Hodder and Stoughton, n.d.), p. 85.

Judgment and Sin

God both condemns and saves. God's judgment of sin is one of utter condemnation. Man's rebellion against God accents what W. M. Clow called "the dark line in God's face."[4] God will "by no means clear the guilty" (Ex. 34:7, KJV). The God who judges in no sense winks at sin, condones it, or excuses it. A famous passage by Forsyth, although perhaps overly rhetorical, nevertheless depicts with power the tendency of sin, and God's reactive judgment upon it. The mercy of God, Forsyth says,

> comes as no matter of paternal course, as no calm act of a parent too great and wise to be wounded by a child's ways. God is fundamentally affected by sin. He is stung and to the core. It does not simply try Him. It challenges His whole place in the moral world. It puts Him on His trial as God. It is, in its nature, an assault on His life. Its total object is to unseat Him. It has no part whatever in His purpose. It hates and kills Him. It is His total negation and death. It is the one thing in the world that lies outside reconciliation, whether you mean by that the process or the act. It cannot be taken up into the supreme unity. It can only be destroyed. It drives Him not merely to action but to a passion of action, to action for His life, to action in suffering unto death. And what makes Him suffer most is not its results but its guilt. It has a guilt in proportion to the holy love it scorns.[5]

Judgment and Christ

In the Old Testament, the judgments of God are judgments in the time-stream of history. In the New Testament, for the most part, statements about judgment refer to the judgments of God in Christ which will come at the end of history. The apostle Paul, for example, says, "We must all appear before the judgment seat of Christ, so that

---

[4]W. M. Clow, *The Cross in Christian Experience*, 5th ed. (New York and London: Hodder and Stoughton, n.d.), p. 28.

[5]P. T. Forsyth, *Positive Preaching and the Modern Mind* (London: Hodder and Stoughton, 1907), pp. 366-67.

each one may receive good or evil, according to what he has done in the body" (2 Cor. 5:10, RSV).

Only a superficial understanding of the New Testament, however, would permit us to claim that judgment in the New Testament refers only to a final judgment. On the contrary, the element of historical judgment is strongly accentuated in the New Testament. God's final judgment brings to light in open declaration the judgments which God is making of us every day of our lives. Two illustrations from Jesus' parables may suffice.

One day, Jesus says, the Son of man will gather before him all nations and, as a shepherd divides the sheep from the goats, so the Son of man will divide the righteous from the unrighteous. Those who have fed the hungry, shown hospitality to strangers, clothed the naked, and visited the sick, will be welcomed into the eternal home of the Father. Those who have lived and acted uncompassionately will be consigned to "eternal punishment" (Matt. 25:31-46, RSV). Obviously, this final judgment is made on the basis of how we treat our fellow human beings in this life.

Once more, those who wisely invest the talents which are entrusted to them will be esteemed "good and faithful" servants and will be welcomed into the joy of their master. But he who hoards and fails to use his talent will be adjudged a worthless servant, and will be cast into outer darkness (Matt. 25:14-30).

Perhaps both of these parables illustrate an important meaning of the doctrine of a final judgment. This meaning is that, though the judgments which we prepare for ourselves here may long be hidden, someday they will be summed up and openly declared by no less an authority than God himself.

Jesus' sternest judgments were directed, not towards publicans and sinners, but towards those who imagined themselves to be righteous—including many of the religious leaders of the nation, the exemplars of conventional piety. God's requirement of repentance they regarded unfeelingly, imagining that they needed no repentance. They were too sick with the disease of self-righteousness to know that they needed the healing medicines of a physician (see Mark 2:17). Their sins were not those of gluttony and self-indulgence like those of the prodigal son, but their self-centeredness, callousness, and lovelessness were like the failings of the elder brother. They prided themselves in keeping the letter of the law, but they neglected its weightier matters—such as love, forgiveness, and compassion.[6]

The warnings of Jesus were pertinent not only to the limited circle of persons whom he addressed day by day but also to all times and all people—including our time and ourselves. The wise and foolish builders, who constructed their houses on rock and sand, respectively, have their counterparts today among persons who choose to embrace or to ignore the gospel. We are told that it is difficult to enter the kingdom of God (Mark 10:23-24), that the gate is narrow and the way hard "that leads to life, and those who find it are few" (Matt. 7:13-14, RSV). We are told that "every tree that does not bear good fruit is cut down and thrown into the fire" (Matt. 7:19, RSV).

These warnings are as applicable today as ever. We worship pleasure, power, money, and worldly honor rather than God, as people did in Jesus' time, but we do not do so with impunity. The parable of the unforgiving servant, who was consigned to a well-deserved punishment, speaks to us across the centuries in the still relevant words of Jesus: "So also my heavenly Father will do to every one of you, if you do not forgive your brother from your heart" (Matt. 18:35, RSV).

Judgment and the Cross

In Christ the world conflict between God and the powers of darkness is most clearly seen. The gospels indicate that this conflict has its crisis and center, above all else, in the cross and resurrection. In this central drama of the world's history, not only the immediate personalities and forces which accomplished Jesus's death, but also all people and all times were judged.

In his analysis of the powers of evil which accomplished the death of Jesus, Walter Rauschenbusch concluded that Jesus felt the crushing burden of the six great public sins of organized society. These "great permanent evils which have blighted the life of the race and of every individual in it"[7] were: religious bigotry, the combination of graft and political power, the corruption of justice, mob spirit and mob action,

---

[6]Cf. Philip S. Watson, *The Concept of Grace* (London: Epworth Press, 1959), p. 271.

[7]Walter Rauschenbusch, *A Theology for the Social Gospel* (New York: The Macmillan Company, 1917), p. 247.

militarism, and class contempt. Jesus did not contribute to these sins, but he received their destructive impact upon his own body and soul. Since all of us have repeated the sins that slew Jesus, we are bound with all of mankind in a solidarity of guilt.[8]

Although it is not adequately comprehensive, Rauschenbusch's analysis is incisive and suggestive. Men of influence and power, on the basis of criteria sanctioned by the canons and mores of entrenched authority, judged Jesus worthy of a brutal death. William Manson has made this point in a vivid word-picture:

> Pass on now to the closing spectacle of the drama in which the Saviour is arraigned before His accusers in the trial-hall. All the world's worst is come upon Him and is loaded in accusation against Him. There is Caiaphas, head of the priesthood, chief of those ministers of religion who have received the law and the sacred oracles, the Urim and Thummim, to give to Israel. How does Caiaphas appear at this moment? As cynical head of a political party, that will callously extirpate the leader of a potentially dangerous Messianic movement in order not to risk a breach with the Roman authority! There are the Pharisees, the holiness party among the Jews, sanctimonious to a degree, and scrupulous for righteousness. But they have accused Jesus of blasphemy because of the personal authority which He claims to interpret the law and the tradition, and they have already proscibed Him as confederate with the powers of darkness. There is the Roman soldiery, set to act as guardians of the peace, but now venting on Jesus their sadistic malevolence against the Jews. There is Pilate, the man in authority, who despises the Jews, the priests and the truth. What is Pilate doing? Abandoning the innocent prisoner to His enemies on an unproved charge, and washing his magisterial hands of all responsibility in the matter. And there is the crowd that wants Barabbas. All forms of human iniquity have come together to point their arrows at the heart of Jesus.[9]

---

[8]Ibid., pp. 248-59.

[9]William Manson, *The Way of the Cross* (Richmond, Virginia: John Knox Press, 1958), pp. 179-80.

These central figures in the drama of Jesus' crucifixion did not realize that the right and power of judgment were in his hands, not in theirs.

The forces which accomplished Jesus' downfall and death were not those of unambiguous and unmitigated evil. The deed was done by people whose genuine righteousness was tainted, who were not able to understand or to bear a goodness which transcended their own—men who were honorable and capable representatives of a high religion, of an ordered society, and of a reasonably just government. But God, in the crucified Christ, judged them all.

Apparently, with reference to his sacrifice on Calvary, Jesus said: "Now is the judgment of this world; now shall the prince of this world be cast out" (John 12:31, KJV). God's purpose is to draw sinners to himself and to save them in Christ. If, however, they choose to love the darkness rather than the light, God's will of love interposes an objection. As men and women decide for or against him, they are judged: "They reveal themselves either as children of light or children of darkness."[10]

The cross of Christ shows that God is unalterably opposed to all that stands against his holy will. In the cross, as H. R. Mackintosh affirms, sin is condemned "because it there is permitted fully to expose its true nature."[*] There, more than ever before, it was forced into the light. Never before had the sin of men so starkly confronted unalloyed goodness and perfect love. Their rebellion against God, their cowardice in the face of challenge, their preference for expediency rather than for principle, their insensitivity, and their blind and ruthless hatred were forced into the open and judged for what they were.

In those who wrought the death of Jesus we see the mirror image of our own motives and our own deeds. We too were there when Jesus was crucified. We cannot blame "the Jews," the Pharisees, or the Roman soldiers by pointing at them a finger of self-righteous indignation. "What we are as sinners was lit up by a flash that told the whole and left nothing to be said."[11]

---

[10]E. F. Scott, *The Fourth Gospel* (Edinburgh: T. & T. Clark, 1908), p. 216.

[*]H. R. Mackintosh, *The Christian Experience of Forgiveness* (New York: Harper and Brothers, 1927), p. 200.

[11]Mackintosh, *The Christian Experience of Forgiveness*, p. 201.

Sin is exposed and judged at the cross, moreover, by the fact that Jesus turned his submission to the powers of darkness into a revelation of God's active and unrelenting opposition to those powers. By taking the hatred of sinners upon himself, Jesus delivered the counterstroke of divine love against our sin. Standing alongside the purity of divine love, sin showed itself in all its hideous guises and colors. Thus the cross is a standing monument in the world's history to the attitude of God towards sin, and to his undying opposition to it.

The judgment of God is not comprehended truly, however, until we recall the motivation of his judgment. A more extended discussion of this matter must be reserved until a later chapter. We must observe here, though, that God's judgment is not contrary to his love. It is in the service of his love. It is aimed at the salvation of sinners. "God must be inexorable towards our sins," says D. M. Baillie, "not because He is just, but because He is loving; not in spite of His love, but because of His love; not because His love is limited, but because it is unlimited."[12] The truth was put succinctly by George Macdonald: God "will forgive anything, but He will pass over nothing."[13]

Judgment and the Law

The law of God has been noticed in the previous chapter in its relationship to divine grace. The law is so closely joined with the concept of judgment, however, that we must give it some attention in this chapter from a somewhat different perspective. Here we must inquire more specifically what the law has to do with divine judgment.

The Goodness of the Law. In about the year 430 B.C., Ezra, "the high priest and scribe of heaven," appeared in Jerusalem. He persuaded his people to pledge their allegiance to the Book of the Law. On the basis of this pledge, he forbade the intermarriage of Jews and non-Jews in the land.

The Book of the Law appears to have been the Pentateuch. In any case, the Pentateuch soon became the Law of the Jewish people. Within the Pentateuch, the *priestly code* assumed a place of first importance. The ordinances and commands of God became the point of central emphasis. The religion of Israel thereby took the form of a

---

[12]Baillie, *God Was in Christ*, p. 173.

[13]Cited in ibid.

cult religion, and the life of the people was wrapped up in the observance of the ritual law.[14] After the time of Ezra, says Josephus, the Jewish people "made the observance of the laws and the piety thereunto appertaining the most necessary work of their entire life," and "even if we should lose riches, home, and all our goods, at least we still have the indestructible law, and no Jew can ever be so far from his fatherland or so intimidated by a bitter tyrant that he would cease to respect the law."[15]

The reassessment of the validity and value of the law by Christians in New Testament times is, of course, a well-known story. It caused considerable turbulence in the communities of the early Christians. As we noted in the previous chapter, even Paul, the strongest early opponent and the most trenchant critic of Judaistic legalism, acknowledged that the law was divinely given and was holy. From the vantage point of a later time, we can see that the law remained a guardian of monotheism among the Jews and of the divine revelation entrusted to Israel. It saved Israel from many of the idolatries and excesses of the pagans around them.

In the seventh chapter of Romans, Paul argues that the law drove sin from its hiding places, so to speak, and brought it out into the glare of daylight exposure. Also, he says, the origin of divine law was prior to the Law of Moses. Adam and Eve in the Garden of Eden came to know the will of God in a commandment which forbade their eating of the fruit of "the tree of the knowledge of good and evil" (Gen. 2:17, RSV). Paul confessed his own indebtedness to the law when he said, "If it had not been for the law, I should not have known sin" (Rom. 7:7, RSV). In Romans 7:22, Paul declared, "I delight in the law of God, in my inmost self" (RSV).

What was wrong was not the law itself. For the law was a chosen instrument of God to induce in the soul a consciousness of the need of salvation: "The law was our custodian until Christ came, that we might be justified by faith" (Gal. 3:24, RSV).

Martin Luther, one of Paul's greatest interpreters, remarked concerning the law: "The true function and the chief and proper use of

---

[14]Leonhard Goppelt, *Jesus, Paul and Judaism* (London, New York, Toronto: Thomas Nelson and Sons, 1964), p. 23.

[15]Cited in ibid., pp. 23-24; from Josephus, *C. Ap.* 1.60; 2.277.

the Law is to reveal to man his sin, blindness, misery, wickedness, ignorance, hate and contempt of God, death, hell, judgment, and the well-deserved wrath of God."[16] According to Luther, the law lights up the nature of sin, delineates its dimensions, and points out its consequences. This is an affirmative assessment of the law.

The Judgments of the Law. "The law always accuses." This remark by Philip Melancthon is true to the insights of the New Testament. It was a privilege belonging to the Jewish people that they had in the law an instrument of revelation which marked out for them the true relationship between God and his people. It was a fatal shortcoming of so many of the "righteous" among them that they imagined themselves to have kept the law.

As a matter of fact, the law served to arraign God's own people before the bar of his judgment. In this sense, judgment began at the house of God. The law warned its disciples and its custodians that they as well as the Gentiles had been guilty of transgression, idolatry, and hardness of heart. Paul wrote searchingly upon this theme as follows:

> But if you call yourself a Jew and rely upon the law and boast of your relation to God and know his will and approve what is excellent, because you are instructed in the law, and if you are sure that you are a guide to the blind, a light to those who are in darkness, a corrector of the foolish, a teacher of children, having in the law the embodiment of knowledge and truth—you then who teach others, will you not teach yourself? While you preach against stealing, do you steal? You who say that one must not commit adultery, do you commit adultery? You who abhor idols, do you rob temples? You who boast in the law, do you dishonor God by breaking the law? For, as it is written, "The name of God is blasphemed among the Gentiles because of you." (Rom. 2:17-24, RSV).

It was a signal irony that the keepers of the law did not obey the law themselves, even on *their own* terms. The promises of the law were applicable only on the condition of the law's observance. "I the Lord

---

[16]Cited in Paul Althaus, *The Divine Command* (Philadelphia: Fortress Press, 1966), p. 309.

your God. . . show steadfast love to thousands *who love me and keep my commandments*" (Ex. 20:5-6, RSV. Text slightly altered and italics added). If the law were viewed from the standpoint of a legal prescription, it coordinated precisely the threat of punishment with the promise of reward. He who observes the law may expect a due reward. He who fails to keep the law may expect the penalty of his transgression.

Even when viewed in the light of its true intention, the law accuses, because sin occurs much of the time beneath the level of consciouness. The human situation is not that of a person who is confronted by a choice between two divergent paths, as though he stood at a crossroads of decision—to keep the law or not to walk in the law's way. The real situation is that, by the time they are conscious that they are confronted by the necessity of a moral decision, all men *already* have transgressed the will of God. The Gentiles transgress without the Mosaic law, but violate instead the law of God written on their hearts. "Sinners" among the Jews break the law by seeking to live without the law. The "righteous" break the law in an even deeper way than do "sinners." They confess a meticulous adherence to the letter of the law, but they violate its spirit.

Outwardly they appear to be righteous, said Jesus, but inwardly they are full of hypocrisy and iniquity (Matt. 23:28). Their righteousness is not in accordance with truth but one to be seen of men (Matt. 6:1). Their outward show of righteousness does not take account of the fact that God discerns the secret intents of their hearts (Luke 16:15).

The law accuses because the advocates of the law fall short of keeping even the letter of the law. The true spirit of the law, on the other hand, brings upon them a far greater condemnation. For the judgments of the law must be seen to apply, not only to outward conduct, but also to inner motivation. The man who covets is guilty of stealing; the person who lusts is guilty of adultery; the one who hates is guilty of murder.

The Law Judged. The fundamental error of those who live by the law is their misconception of the decisive factor with which they have to reckon. The law is not the judge. The Judge is God. It is not the law with which one has to do; it is God. When the law is intruded between oneself and God, the law becomes an impersonal requirement by means of which one can achieve a status of independence before God. He then imagines that he can make claims upon God, that God is "obligated" to him.

The law was given as an expression of God's will; it was not meant to stand as an obstacle between God and the soul. It was not intended to be a substitute for fellowship between a person and his God. It was meant to guide man in the paths of obedience which spring from faith and devotion to God, not to be a set of rules by which one can earn a righteousness of his own. When one falls out of a relationship of love and fellowship with God, the covenant relationship becomes externalized, loving obedience gives way to legalistic observance, estrangement supplants community, egoistic self-righteousness subverts true communion, great horizons contract into selfish biases, and the adventurous lure of great mission is lost in small ventures.

The fatal weakness of the law is the frailty and perversity of human nature. Through the law comes the knowledge of sin, but the law cannot deliver from sin. Indeed, it more firmly tightens the shackles of our sin upon us. It is a curse because it accuses and condemns without redeeming or even alleviating our sinful condition. The state of man under the law, as Paul describes it, is one of slavery, abetted by anxiety and fear (Rom. 8:15). The law which is good thus becomes an instrument of death: "The very commandment which promised life proved to be death to me" (Rom. 7:10, RSV).

Judgment as Wrath

The *wrath of God (orge theou)* is mentioned many times in the New Testament. The phrase occurs sixteen times in the writings of the apostle Paul alone. Romans 1:18, John 3:36, and Revelation 19:15 may be cited as representative instances in which the term is used in the New Testament. The wrath of God is revealed against the ungodliness and wickedness of men "who by their wickedness suppress the truth" (Rom. 1:18, RSV). "He who believes in the Son has eternal life; he who does not obey the Son shall not see life, but the wrath of God rests upon him" (John 3:36, RSV). In the book of Revelation, the rebellion of men evokes the wrath of God and of the Lamb: "He will tread the wine press of the fury of the wrath of God the Almighty" (Rev. 19:15, RSV).

Although the New Testament unmistakably asserts the reality of the wrath of God, the meaning of God's wrath is not so clear. At least three options have been proposed by serious interpreters: the wrath of God means *personal vengeance, impersonal retribution,* or *angry love.*

To interpret the wrath of God as vindictive anger or personal vengeance poses serious theological difficulties for a Christian understanding of the character of God. If God's wrath is "the emotional reaction of an irritated self-concern" (William Temple), if we think of God as one who loses his temper and throws his love aside in violent reaction to our sin, we have, in our own minds, seriously compromised the character of God.

This kind of interpretation is a temptation to many who think of the doctrine of the Atonement in juridical terms. Seen in these terms, God is angry with us and demands that we be punished for our sins. The loving Christ steps between us and God's anger, and takes the blow of God's wrath upon himself. By venting his anger upon Christ instead of upon us, God's anger is appeased, and his demand for justice is satisfied.

Christian theology must never seek to impose a dichotomy between the character of the Father and the character of the Son. To think of the wrath of the Father in contrast or opposition to the mercy of Christ is fatal to a Christian theology of atonement.

In comparison with this untenable approach, a much more defensible position is to consider the wrath of God to be an impersonal retribution which the moral order of the world imposes upon those who offend and rebel against this order. Persons who hold this view concede that the term *wrath* is a troublesome anthropomorphism. However, it is difficult to speak of God in nonanthropomorphic terms. Indeed, the *love of God* is also an anthropomorphic expression.

In his book entitled *The Wrath of the Lamb*, A. T. Hanson has argued weightily that God's wrath is an impersonal retribution which people bring upon themselves. God, Hanson points out, is never spoken of in the New Testament, in contrast with the Old, as being personally angry with anyone. "The wrath of God," Hanson concludes, "is the punishment of God, and the punishment of God is what He permits us to inflict on ourselves. God loves the most obdurate infidel as much as he loves the most devoted saint. He permits wrath, but He is love."[17]

---

[17]A. T. Hanson, *The Wrath of the Lamb* (London: S.P.C.K., 1957), p. 198.

Again, Hanson says,

> The Cross was a manifestation not only of the love, but also
> of the wrath of God. Not that God was angry with men for
> crucifying his Son, but that those who rejected the love of
> God manifested in the life, death, and resurrection of Jesus
> Christ abandoned themselves utterly to self-destruction, to
> the process of wrath. God had spoken finally in Christ, so
> those who rejected God rejected Christ also. The wrath is
> closely related to the Cross, and will be to the end of history.
> When God's last word is spoken it is inevitable that at the
> same time there must be left to man the supreme
> opportunity of destroying himself.[18]

C. H. Dodd, whose position on this subject seems close to that of
Hanson, notes that Paul uses the terms *love, grace,* and *faithfulness* to
describe the personal attitude of God to men. However, Paul never
uses the verb *to be angry* with God as its subject. Paul, Dodd says,
constantly uses *wrath,* or *the wrath* "in a curiously impersonal way."[19]
The apostle, Dodd thinks, retains the term *wrath,* not to describe the
attitude of God to man, but to describe an inevitable process of cause
and effect in a moral universe."[20]

This kind of interpretation removes any vindictive element from
God's wrath. Not to speak of God's wrath at all is better than to depict
it in terms of a personal vengeance. God is not a cosmic Shylock,
demanding his pound of flesh.

The claim that the view elaborated above has deistic tendencies,
however, is a charge to reckon with. If God's love is personal, P. T.
Forsyth argues, his wrath is also personal.[21] Heinrich Ott urges the
same point as that made many years before by Forsyth. One cannot
really love who cannot really be angry. The concept of the wrath of
God, Ott feels, proves to be "a notable test of the personal
understanding of faith."[22] It may be true, as Hans Conzelmann claims,

---

[18]Ibid., p. 200.

[19]C. H. Dodd, *The Epistle to the Romans,* The Moffatt New Testament
Commentary (New York and London: Harper and Row Publishers, 1932), p. 21.

[20]Ibid., p. 23.

[21]Forsyth, *The Work of Christ,* pp. 239-40.

[22]Heinrich Ott, *Theology and Preaching* (Philadelphia: The Westminster Press,
1961), p. 140.

that "wrath is not an ingredient of the gospel." Love is what God is; wrath is what he does in history as he reacts to the rebellion of men.[23] It is a correlate of love, subordinate to love, not an element in God's being on a par with his love. We may add to this that God's personal involvement in his wrath does not seem to be precluded by Conzelmann's distinction between wrath and love.

That God's wrath is his "angry love" is an appealing interpretation. By his sin the sinner brings the destructive consequences of sin upon himself. However, God is not coldly indifferent to this situation, as the conception of wrath as impersonal retribution might seem to imply. Wrath is, says James Moffatt, "the reaction of [God's] holy love against the defiance of sin."[24] The wrath of God, says Henry W. Clark, is "the reacting action of God's conquering anger against sin. It is God putting His power against the power of the evil forces which have deranged His world."[25] God is angry towards the sinner, but the anger of God is not opposed to his love. Indeed, it is but another name for God's "resisted love."[26] When God's love is despised, then this love is felt by man as wrath, as an opposing and even a hostile influence. "God's anger is God's love reacting against man's refusal to receive it."[27]

A passage from James S. Stewart's book on Pauline thought is an eloquent statement of the position here under consideration:

> Had anyone suggested to Paul that God's wrath alternates with his love, that where one begins the other ends, that sometimes God acts out of character and needs to be won round from punishment to mercy, he would certainly have branded the idea as a deadly heresy: he would have declared that God's wrath is not understood until it is seen as the

[23]Hans Conzelmann, *An Outline of the Theology of the New Testament* (New York and Evanston: Harper and Row, Publishers, 1969), pp. 240-41.

[24]James Moffatt, *Grace in the New Testament* (New York: Ray Long and Richard R. Smith, Inc., 1932), p. 211.

[25]Henry W. Clark, *The Cross and the Eternal Order* (New York: The Macmillan Company, 1944), p. 281.

[26]Ibid., p. 285.

[27]Ibid., p. 286.

obverse of his grace. . . . God's wrath is God's grace. It is his grace smitten with dreadful sorrow. It is his love in agony. It is the passion of his heart going forth to redeem.[28]

W. J. Wolf agrees that the divine wrath is not opposed to love; it is, rather, the rejection of the rejection of love and, as such, a work of love. It is God's love rejecting our rejection of him. God's will is set against sin, and expresses itself as antagonism or wrath against the sinner.

Wolf believes that two considerations show God's wrath to be his love in action against sin. The first is that God takes the consequences of sin upon himself. He shows us that he does so in the cross of Christ. At the cross there is a personal absorption of the meaning of our sin into the heart of God. This is how love is affected by the wrongdoing of the beloved—personal involvement, compassion, and redemptive suffering.

Secondly, Wolf continues, the fact that wrath is love is shown in the fact that God's wrath does not seek to destroy the sinner as a person, but rather to win him out of his sin. The chastisements of God upon the sinner are corrective and redemptive in purpose, not vindictive.[29]

The debate as to whether God's wrath is impersonal retribution or "angry love" cannot be resolved here, although this writer inclines towards the latter interpretation. In either case, the wrath of God is the judgment of God. Every person, whether Jew or Greek, earns for himself, by the hardness of his heart, "wrath . . . on the day of wrath when God's righteous judgment will be revealed" (Rom. 2:5, RSV).

Christ is related to the wrath of God, as indeed he is related to the judgment, the kingdom, the life, the power, and the wisdom of God. The New Testament repeatedly shows that Christ administers God's judgment. By his symbolic curse of the barren fig tree, he pronounces the divine judgment against Judaism. He announces the doom of Jerusalem. He pronounces severe strictures against the hypocrisy of the scribes and Pharisees. Moreover, the cross of Christ is the supreme manifestation of God's wrath against the ungodliness and unrighteousness of human beings (Rom. 1:18; see 2 Cor. 5:21 and Mark 15:34).

---

[28]Stewart, *A Man in Christ*, p. 222.

[29]W. J. Wolf, *No Cross, No Crown* (Garden City, New York: Doubleday and Company, Inc., 1957), pp. 193-96.

The wrath of God is an expression of his judgment. This judgment is to be kept in the closest relationship to God's love. Christ has taken upon himself the weight of God's judgment, so that God may be shown to be righteous, even though he acquits sinners (Rom. 3:24-26). Although Christ bears for us the judgment of God, it is not a judgment that Christ bears apart from the Father. The Father himself bears this judgment in the Son.

The Last Judgment

The New Testament envisions a Last Judgment, in which God's judgments of the living and the dead will be brought to a decisive manifestation and cosummation. The final settlement will come at the end of history.

To what extent the language concerning the *second coming* and the *last judgment* is to be literally understood is a matter for legitimate argument. But whatever its attendant features may be, the final judgment will show the ultimate sovereignty of God over all things, and the accountability of individuals and nations to him.

The description of Karl Heim is striking and penetrating:

> The first thing that must happen when Christ makes His claim on all men who have lived so far will be that He will act as a householder who returns after a long time of absence and personally takes over his property the management of which he has entrusted to His servants. He will have to settle with all those who have managed His property for Him. "We must all appear before the judgment seat of Christ" (2 Cor. 5:10). "His eyes" are "like a flame of fire" (Rev. 1:14). From these eyes nothing can hide itself any longer. All things must be revealed. All dark designs and shady intrigues are mercilessly brought to light. Every concealed spell is exposed. The death-rattle of the innocent victim pierces the ears of the murderer. The inaudible sighs uttered in the dark dungeons are heard now. The innocent blood cries from earth to heaven. No one can think without trembling of this day which brings all things to light. And yet who could stand all the privations which have to be borne in silence, all the misrepresentations of the truth which have never been rectified, all the outrages to which an accused is exposed without any opportunity to reply—who could bear with all that without the firm certitude that the

day of the great exposure and final settlement is coming?[30]

The belief in the Last Judgment is a conviction that the great Judge of the world will make all things right at last. Justice will triumph over injustice, love over hate, humanity over inhumanity, peace over conflict, and the kingdom of God over the kingdom of evil. The world and all persons within it will come face to face at last, not with annihilation, but with God. To say that "we must all appear before the judgment seat of Christ" (2 Cor. 5:10) is to affirm that the Judge who meets us at the end of our earthly journey is the Savior who took upon himself God's judgment for our sins, and for the sins of all men.

The God of the Last Judgment will be the Christlike God, the God of grace and mercy whom we have met in Christ. The redeemed in Christ, we are told in the Scriptures, will enjoy the fellowship of God and his saints forevermore, while those who have rejected God's offer of mercy will be given over to perdition.

Reinhold Niebuhr reminds us that we cannot claim "any knowledge of either the furniture of heaven or the temperature of hell."[31] We must add that we cannot imagine a God of love who could abandon a single soul forever without the deepest anguish. We can believe in some kind of everlasting separation from God, which is designated "hell," only if we take with great seriousness the freedom which God has granted to human beings to pursue their own ways even to the point of ultimate ruin. Whether God will pursue his strategies of mercy and redemption beyond the borders of this life, we do not know. We firmly believe two things: first, that upon our decisions here on earth an eternal issue hangs; second, that the Judge of all the earth will do what is right with every human being.

---

[30]Karl Heim, *Jesus the World's Perfecter* (Philadelphia: Muhlenberg Press, 1961), pp. 190-91.

[31]Reinhold Niebuhr, *The Nature and Destiny of Man*, 2 vols., (New York: Charles Scribner's Sons, 1945), 2:294.

————————————Chapter 3————————————

Atonement and Justification

Justification is a Pauline term, drawn from law-court procedure. "To justify" means "to acquit," "to vindicate," "to reckon to be righteous." A person is "just" or "righteous" when he is so recognized by the judge who is the presiding authority. His acquittal comes not by virtue of his *being* righteous, but by virtue of his being *pronounced* righteous upon the authority of the judge. On lexical grounds, says Vincent Taylor, the Pauline verb "to justify" (*dikaioo*) means "to declare righteous," "to treat as righteous," "to vindicate." It does not mean "to make righteous."[1]

As we shall see, the meaning which is assigned to justification transcends that of a mere legal judgment. For by itself a legal judgment does not give the answer to an inevitable question, namely, "On what ground is the judgment of 'reckoning to be righteous' based?" A statement by N. H. Snaith indicates the decisive step which must be taken beyond both legal and lexical definitions. In both Testaments, he says, to be justified "means to be brought into right relations with a

---

[1]Vincent Taylor, *Justification and Reconciliation* (London: Macmillan and Company, Limited, 1948), p. 33.

person. . . . Justification is that immediate setting right with God which God himself accomplishes by his grace when man has faith."[2] In the New Testament, Christ is the executor and agent of God's justifying deed.

Some scholars (for example, W. D. Davies in *Paul and Rabbinic Judaism*, pp. 222-23) have claimed that Paul's use of the metaphor of justification is not only forensic but also polemical. Only in Romans and Galatians, where Paul is combatting the claims of Judaism, is the term *justification* emphasized. Justification, therefore, Davies thinks, is a "convenient polemic" rather than the "essential pivot" of Paul's thought.[3]

We may well believe that Paul emphasized justification by faith as a polemical weapon against the views of a hostile Judaism. This fact, however, in no sense detracts from the profound significance for the Christian faith of God's justifying action. In the development of the doctrine of justification, Paul recovers the Old Testament prophetic conception of the righteousness of God, which conception came to its clearest expression in Deutero-Isaiah. In line with prophetic thought, Paul gives powerful expression to the conviction that justification comes as a free gift from the outgoing righteousness of God. In contrast to the rabbinic view that salvation comes by the keeping of the law, "a righteousness from the law" (compare Phil. 3:9), he was championing the view that man is saved by the righteousness of God "apart from the law" (compare Rom. 3:21). Paul's answer was pointed: "If righteousness is through law, then Christ died for nothing" (compare Gal. 2:21).

The Problem of Justification

In advocating that justification is the acquittal of the guilty sinner by a righteous God, Paul appeared to be at a distinct disadvantage. The rabbinic view was that a person wins acquittal by becoming righteous himself. In a real sense, therefore, he *deserves* his acquittal. The problem of justification for Paul was that God pardons the sinner and pronounces him not guilty when the sinner really *is* guilty. In

---

[2]N. H. Snaith, "Just, Justify, Justification," in Alan Richardson, ed., *A Theological Word Book of the Bible* (New York: The Macmillan Company, 1951), p. 119.

[3]W. D. Davies, *Paul and Rabbinic Judaism* (London: S.P.C.K., 1948), pp. 222-23.

Romans 4:5 Paul wrote that God "justifies the ungodly." Can a judge pardon a proven criminal without cheapening the law and without impugning his own integrity? It is no wonder that Paul's doctrine of justification has been esteemed by many critics across the centuries to be an "immoral" doctrine. Justification on the terms which Paul sets forth has been called a "legal fiction." The criminal, still guilty, and still criminal at heart, is no less a criminal after being pronounced innocent. God may "impute" his own righteousness to the sinner, but to impute is not to "impart." It thus appears that God merely ignores sin, passes over it, "lets it go."

With these and with kindred considerations we shall attempt to deal in the discussion which follows.

Justification by Grace

"We are," Paul said, "justified freely by his grace" (Rom. 3:24, KJV). When grace is brought into the picture of God's justification of the sinner, the legal understanding of justification must be amended. The judgment of the sinner is to be seen not in terms of the judge's disinterested pronouncement of a verdict on the basis of an impersonal law. Grace, as we have seen, involves a personal relationship, in which God is a profoundly interested party.

This insight is by no means foreign even to the Old Testament. It is misleading to contend that the devout Jew of the Old Testament era was unacquainted with grace, that he thought of God only as a Judge, or that he conceived the Torah to be cast in merely impersonal terms. One need look no further than the Psalms and the prophets to see how untrue is this assessment of Old Testament thought. To say that justification comes by the grace of God means not only that God's law must be taken into consideration, but also that his unmerited favor and love form a part of the judgment which God pronounces upon the guilty.

Our point here is that the writers of the Old Testament were acquainted with this relationship between grace and law.

Moreover, it is doubtful that Paul, profoundly grounded as he was in the prophetic tradition of his own countrymen, would think of justification in terms of either Roman or late Pharisaic and rabbinic law. He would think of it, instead, primarily in terms of the *covenant* relationship between God and his people. As F. W. Dillistone says:

In the developed system of the Rabbis the means of atonement included penitence, fasting, the merits of the fathers, private and public sacrifice and much more. In other words it was by the offering of religious devotions believed to be acceptable to God and in some way compensating for wrong done. But Paul's movement of thought is in exactly the opposite direction. It is God Who comes forth to re-establish the broken relationship by fulfilling His own gracious commitment to men even to the limit of blood and by inviting all who will to accept by faith the atonement which He has made.[4]

Justification on Pauline terms assumes, not the priority of a legal requirement, but the priority of the divine mercy. Paul contends that the justification of the sinner is utterly undeserved. Our sinfulness leaves us without the slightest claim upon God's favor. In his grace God accepts the unacceptable, when men throw themselves without claims of merit upon his steadfast love. "The Hebrew conception of the function of a judge," says C. H. Dodd, "tends to be not so much to apply with strict impartiality an abstract principle of justice, but rather to come to the assistance of the injured person and vindicate him."[5]

Justification and the Righteousness of God

Most persons find it much easier to believe that God saves by his mercy than to believe that he justifies by his righteousness. The psalmist was extolling God's mercy when he wrote: "He does not deal with us according to our sins, nor requite us according to our iniquities. For as the heavens are high above the earth, so great is his steadfast love toward those who fear him; as far as the east is from the west, so far does he remove our transgressions from us" (Ps. 103:10-12, RSV).

In contrast to his grace and mercy, righteousness seems to us to be an austere and forbidding quality in God, because we associate it with his rectitude, holiness, and justice. Indeed, God *is* the Judge of all

---

[4]F. W. Dillistone, *The Christian Understanding of Atonement* (Philadelphia: The Westminster Press, 1968), p. 182.

[5]C. H. Dodd, *Jesus and the Greeks*, p. 46. Cited in D. E. Whiteley, *The Theology of St. Paul* (Philadelphia: The Fortress Press, 1964), p. 159.

people, and his righteousness involves the truth that he is right and that he puts things right. On the other hand, God's righteousness, stemming from Old Testament understanding, means also his saving and sustaining power manifested for the deliverance of his people. By his righteousness, God vindicates his purpose for mankind, and particularly for Israel. When his people experience defeat and disaster, the righteous God upholds them with his strong arm, and causes retribution to descend upon their enemies.

In the Old Testament, God's righteousness is frequently associated with salvation. "There is no other god besides me, a righteous God and a Savior" (Isa. 45:21, RSV). In the Old Testament, P. S. Watson observes, the righteousness of God can be synonymous with his saving acts (Isa. 46:13; 51:5), and in the New Testament it is identified with his saving activity in Christ (1 Cor. 1:30; Rom. 1:16).[6] "The righteousness of God," says Van A. Harvey, is "not so much God's abstract character of being but his redemptive, saving will as manifested in Christ."[7]

At the same time, God does not justify at the expense of his own integrity. His righteousness is retributive as well as vindicative. In his massive indictment of human wickedness in the first two chapters of Romans, Paul warns. "By your hard and impenitent heart you are storing up wrath for yourself on the day of wrath when God's righteous judgment will be revealed" (Rom. 2:5, RSV).

In Pauline thought, then, God's righteousness means not only an attribute of God's character, but also a divine act or activity. Righteousness is dynamic. When Paul says that in the gospel "the righteousness of God is revealed through faith for faith" (Rom. 1:17, RSV), he means that God is performing a work in the area of human experience. His righteous judgment rejects those who respond to him with hard and impenitent hearts, but he justifies those who have faith (Rom. 3:26).

For Paul, the years of Israel's military struggles against foreign political states were long past. The deliverance which the righteous God accomplishes for his people was not from destructive conflict with

---

[6] P. S. Watson, "Righteousness," in Alan Richardson, ed., *A Dictionary of Christian Theology* (Philadelphia: The Westminster Press, 1969), p. 296.

[7] Van A. Harvey, *A Handbook of Theological Terms* (New York: The Macmillan Company, 1964), p. 210.

alien political powers, but from the power of evil. The righteousness of God delivered men from their sin, giving them a standing of acceptance before God. "Always," says C. H. Dodd, "righteousness is not primarily an attribute of God or of His people, but an activity whereby the right is asserted in the deliverance of man from the power of evil."[8]

When we discern that the righteousness of God is God's activity in vindicating the right, overcoming wrong, and delivering man from the ruin of evil, it becomes apparent that there is no contradiction between God's righteousness and his love. It is in the love which proceeds into the human predicament, which proceeds for the purpose of saving from the oppression of sin, that the righteousness of God most clearly appears.

An element intrinsic to the righteousness of God, as to the grace of God, is the power of God. God is the living Power with which all of the forces of evil will have to deal (see Rom. 1:18 to 3:20). But just as the power of a righteous God is a threat to all the ungodliness and unrighteousness of men, it is also "the power of God for salvation to every one who has faith, to the Jew first, and also to the Greek" (Rom. 1:16, RSV).

God will be finally and completely victorious in the age to come, when he will set all things right. In that day, the arm of God will discomfit and defeat the forces of evil and will establish the good forever.

This vision of a future vindication of God's righteousness, says Dodd, was where Paul stood as a Pharisee. Where he stood as a preacher of the gospel, however, was in his understanding that "the righteousness of God" is being revealed *now*. In Christ, the age to come has arrived. The incursion of this age has not been completed, but even now it is real and in process of disclosure. Someday a final justification will occur at the bar of God's judgment (see Rom. 5:19 and 8:33). Those who receive by faith God's justifying righteousness look to the future in the light of this confident hope.[9]

---

[8]Dodd, *The Epistle to the Romans*, p. 12.

[9]Cf. Gerhard Kittel, ed., *Theological Dictionary of the New Testament*, Geoffrey W. Bromiley, trans. and ed., vol. 2 (Grand Rapids: Wm. B. Eerdmans Publishing Company, 1964), pp. 207-208.

Justification by the Redemption That Is in Christ

God justifies all who believe, Paul says, "by his grace as a gift, through the redemption which is in Christ Jesus" (Rom. 3:24, RSV).

Justification is Christologically centered. Both the grace of God and the righteousness of God find their focus in Christ. At this point it is appropriate to inquire more particularly what this means.

Justification Comes Not by the Works of the Law. In our attempt to understand the meaning of justification, we must look once more at Paul's understanding of the law. This is true because Paul's concept of justification was heavily involved with what he thought to be the relationship between law and salvation. Paul contrasts the "righteousness of God" or "righteousness based on faith" with "righteousness based on law" (Rom. 10:5-6; Phil. 3:6,9). Apart from the law, he says, the righteousness of God has been revealed through faith in Jesus Christ (Rom. 3:22).

Although the law was intended by God to lead people to him, the sinful hearts of men had used the law as a means of living apart from God. The law, therefore, did not bring men and women to the loving fellowship of God. Instead, they made themselves believe that this fellowship was unneeded and unnecessary. The law led to a bookkeeping introspection and practice rather than into the large horizons of wonder and praise in the presence of a God whose love was without measure. The law did not bring men into the liberty of the sons of God; it bound them with the shackles of burdensome rules and formulae. The zeal of the law did not inspire a compassionate concern for the weak, the lowly, the troubled, and the lost; it led, rather, to a hardhearted fanaticism which Paul knew only too well as a personal experience. The distorting vision which it had inspired had made him a persecutor of the Church.

The sin of legalism which preoccupied itself with observing the law was, then, in substance akin to all other sin. It attempted to establish one's own self-sufficiency apart from God. Legalistic observance was a desperate but futile attempt at self-justification.

Christ the End of the Law. Paul states that Christ is "the end of the law, that every one who has faith may be justified" (Rom. 10:4, RSV). To say that Christ is the end (*telos*) of the law means more than to say that the goal of the law has been reached in him. It means also that the law has been superseded by him. The pathway of a legal righteousness leads away from God, more and more deeply into sin. It thus becomes an enemy and a captor, in whose service is the reward of death. "When the commandment came," Paul confessed, "sin revived, and I died" (Rom. 7:9).

Christ saves us from the tyranny of the law. He has "cancelled the bond which stood against us with its legal demands; this he set aside, nailing it to the cross" (Col. 2:14, RSV).

In Christ, God has shown conclusively that his righteousness transcends the mandate of a legal requirement. The bonds of any merely "forensic" understanding of justification are decisively broken. In Christ's ministry and cross the righteousness of God stands revealed in its glory and its power. Here was the man who loved not only his friends, but also his enemies; who prayed to the Father for the forgiveness of those who nailed him to the cross; who, when reviled, reviled not again. His obedience was given not to the dictates of an impersonal law but to the will of the Father—an obedience even unto death.

Christ, the sign and embodiment of the righteousness of God, did not prescribe for us another law by which we might work to obtain a righteousness of our own. Rather, he died for our sins and was raised for our justification. In this deed he brought to our rescue the liberating righteousness of God. While the law condemns us as sinners, "there is therefore now no condemnation for those who are in Christ Jesus" (Rom. 8:1, RSV). By the law alone those who are guilty of transgression cannot be accepted by God. Through Christ, however, God shows us that he accepts the guilty.

The good news of the gospel is that God not only receives sinful men, but also seeks them out, like lost sheep, until he finds them and brings them into his fold. In Christ, he has proven himself to be greater than his own law. His way with people is not the way of law. We are justified, not by the law, but by forgiveness, mercy, and grace. Dillistone says:

> The atmosphere of Romans 5-8 is not that of a law court nor of an adjudication of penalties. Rather it is of an utterly new beginning in human affairs made possible by a refusal to be bound by the strict injunctions of any legal system. The whole emphasis is on man's helplessness, man's alienation, man's hopelessness. It is into this situation that God comes, revealing His love, offering His abundant grace, breaking

the bonds of death, establishing righteousness among men and opening the path to eternal life.[10]

Jesus believed, as did the Pharisees, in the righteousness of God. Yet for Jesus the way to righteousness was the way of the humble heart which gladly accepted the divine offer of mercy. This was the way to righteousness because it was the pathway to God. "For the Pharisees, the matter of righteousness rested with man. Man was to keep the law; that was righteousness. Meanwhile, the 'sinners,' responding to Jesus's message, were pressing into the kingdom, while the 'righteous,' satisfied, remained without."[11]

Justification through Faith

"Therefore, since we are justified by faith, we have peace with God through our Lord Jesus Christ. Through him we have obtained access to this grace in which we stand, and we rejoice in our hope of sharing the glory of God" (Rom. 5:1-2, RSV).

When the term *justified by faith* appears alone, it is subject to serious misinterpretation. Many persons have misconceived justification to be a reward which God gives to those who exercise faith. Even in Romans 4, where Paul argues the justifying effect of Abraham's faith over against the thesis of justification by keeping the law, some interpreters mistakenly have seen in the faith of Abraham a meritorious work.

This understanding was the opposite of that which Paul intended to convey. A more precise statement of Paul's meaning would be that we are "justified by grace *through* faith." Faith is never a deed of righteousness which we perform, and by means of which we earn salvation. Faith itself is a gift of grace, by which we receive the justification of God, not a meritorious action on the basis of which God awards salvation to us. "Faith," says Adolph Deissmann, "is not action, but reaction, not human achievement before God, but divine influence upon man in Christ . . . Faith is not the pre-condition of justification, it is the experience of justification."[12]

---

[10]Dillistone, *The Christian Understanding of Atonement*, p. 183.

[11]Harris Franklin Rall, *Religion as Salvation* (New York, Nashville: Abingdon, 1953), p. 115.

[12]Adolph Deissman, *Paul*, William E. Wilson, trans., 2nd ed. (New York: George H. Doran Company, 1926), pp. 169-70.

Faith is not just a subjective state of mind in him who exercises it. In the New Testament meaning, it is never simply "faith in faith." It is believing trust in, acceptance of, and commitment to an object. In the argument of Paul, faith is faith in *God* through Jesus Christ. The righteousness of faith is not determined by any intrinsic value which it supposedly has apart from its object. Faith is the conditioning medium by means of which the believer receives the righteousness of God as his own. It is the character and righteousness of God which determine the nature of faith in him.

The vital reality for which justification stands is a clear indication that the legal connotations of the term must be burst asunder if we are to apprehend its dynamic and profound essence. Here the work of Jesus must be taken into account. The ministry of Jesus enabled Paul to contend that God justifies "the ungodly." When we see how Jesus forgave the sinful woman (Luke 7:36-50), how he dealt with the publicans and sinners who show up all through the Gospels, when we read many of his parables, particularly those of the Pharisee and the publican, and of the prodigal son, we know that we have in his teachings and his life a paradigm of the Pauline doctrine of justification.

Justifying faith is a summons to live for God. But it is no longer a living by rules and ordinances which stultify the spirit. It is trust and confidence, not in articles and doctrines, no matter how true they are, but in God himself. It is not believing in the Bible, no matter how reverently we receive the truth of God which sounds through its pages. It is believing in God. It is not believing in "saving faith," but in the God who saves. It is "throwing oneself on God for life or death."[13]

Although justification calls attention primarily to the righteous standing which the justified sinner receives by the pronouncement of a gracious God, it is dangerously untrue to say that no communication of real righteousness occurs in the acquittal of the sinner. When God accepts us in Christ, we enter God's own way. The righteousness of Christ is not merely "imputed" to us; it is *imparted* to us. The verdict "not guilty" is no mere fiction. By God's justifying action, Christ's life becomes our life, his will our will, and his love our love.

---

[13]Cf. Shirley C. Guthrie, *Christian Doctrine* (Richmond, Va: C. L. C. Press, 1968), pp. 169-70.

Justification is therefore God's vindication and acceptance of those who leave an old life to take up a new one. The heights of Christian living lie far beyond us and rise high above us; but, if ours is a genuine faith in Christ, we are *on the way* to being what God wants us to be. The justification of God, that is to say, does not merely prepare us for the new life. It incorporates, conveys, effects, and establishes that life. Emil Brunner speaks with trenchant insight when he says: "The new life is not only one in which we believe, but in faith it is real. Indeed faith itself is this new reality. Man in faith *is* the new man, life in faith *is* the new life."[14]

The righteousness which God imparts furnishes no ground for boasting. Again and again Paul says that it is not a righteousness which one earns or which frees itself from Christ to go its own way. Its expression and its fruits are constantly just as dependent upon our steady engrafting in Christ as the fruit of the vine is dependent upon the branches remaining engrafted in the vine.

Justification by Christ's Blood

Paul affirms that God shows his love for us, in that, "while we were yet sinners Christ died for us. Since, therefore, we are now justified by his blood, much more shall we be saved by him from the wrath of God" (Rom. 5:8-9, RSV). Another great passage related to this theme is Romans 3:21-26. By justifying sinners apart from the law, Paul says, God shows us that salvation is a gift of his grace. This gift comes to us through the redemption that God has accomplished in Christ, "whom God put forward as an expiation by his blood, to be received by faith. This was to show God's righteousness, because in his divine forbearance he had passed over former sins; it was to prove at the present time that he himself is righteous and that he justifies him who has faith in Jesus" (Rom. 3:25-26, RSV).

Blood has an involvement in sacrificial meanings which we shall discuss in a later chapter. The emphasis to be made here is the grounding of God's justifying work upon the cross. As we have noted already, the righteousness of God is both a quality in the character of God and a saving grace which he bestows upon those who believe.

---

[14]Emil Brunner, *The Divine-Human Encounter* (Philadelphia: The Westminster Press, 1943), pp. 101-102.

Preeminently in the cross of Christ, God manifests his own righteousness.

But how does the cross do this? Does the righteousness of God stand for the justice of God which must be satisfied by the penalty of death, a penalty which Christ endured for us by taking the blow of God's wrath upon himself? According to this position, someone must pay the penalty for violating God's law. Either the sinner or a substitute for the sinner must pay this penalty, before the mercy of God can bestow forgiveness. Christ was that substitute.

A more acceptable view is that God's option was not that of punishing the sinner or of punishing Christ, the sinner's divine substitute; his option was rather that of *punishing* the sinner, or of *redeeming* him, in Christ. God, Paul insists, shows that in Christ's atoning work God could be a righteous God without exacting a legal penalty for sin. W. T. Conner's interpretation here is discerning. The way of faith, he says, "represents God as condemning sin in the cross of Christ by condemning it not as the law does, unto despair, but as the cross does, unto salvation."[15]

The cross, with all that it stands for of compassionate love and redemptive power, is what a righteous God has done to set us in a right relationship to himself, and through Christ to communicate to us his own saving life. If this action of God cannot reach us and redeem us, nothing can. Indeed the cross is God's chosen instrument for effecting our redemption.

Since all have sinned, the strict administration of the law would mean that all persons would suffer the condemnation of God. But the cross, as the supreme demonstration of God's righteousness, showed the length to which a loving and righteous God would go both to condemn sin and to save the sinner. The impression that God is "easy" on sin was forever refuted and nullified by the cross. Christ died for our sins, and in his death we see the divine condemnation of sin. We see there how seriously God regards it and how radically he deals with it. God will not come to terms with it, overlook it, or compromise with it. He will only destroy it. He will destroy it by absorbing its consequences into his own life. *He* takes the penalty, and lets the sinner go free. *He*

---

[15]W. T. Conner, *The Cross in the New Testament* (Nashville, Tennessee: Broadman Press, 1954), p. 85.

pardons the sinner of his sins and accepts him into fellowship with himself.

The message of the cross is not that Christ, a third party, stands between the sinner and God, and bears the penalty of the breaking of the divine law instead of the sinner. It is rather that God in Christ gets under the burden of sin and bears it for us.

This righteous act does not show a sentimental kind of God whose character is devoid of justice or of moral requirement. There is in this righteousness the strong moral fiber, the unbending rectitude, of the holy God. There are also in it the qualities of goodness, kindness, forgiveness, grace, and a vast compassion. In the cross, as nowhere else, we see and feel the very pulsebeat of God's great heart.

Conclusion

In the opinion of modern secular man, the doctrine of justification by faith is strangely archaic and irrelevant. Few persons are concerned with the meticulous keeping of the Mosaic law, or with what the relationship is between the observance of this body of law and the salvation of one's "soul."

When the "archaic" framework of the doctrine is removed, however, the meaning of justification still remains pertinent and disturbing. Most people are frantically eager to justify themselves—if not before God, then before their peers, or before their own consciences—by the keeping of a chosen code, by working hard at their jobs, or by amassing wealth, possessions, and power. They thereby earn "merit" for themselves; they furnish for themselves ample ground for "boasting" about their achievements; in their own eyes they win for themselves at least a relative, tolerable prestige and security.

They therefore have what Paul would call a works-righteousness— a righteousness of their own, an ostensibly defensible, creditable, if autonomous standing before themselves, before their community, or before "whatever gods may be."

If the Christian message is true, however, these persons' illusions about their self-justification are just as misguided as were those who sought salvation by keeping the Mosaic law. The gospel message to them is substantially the same message that Paul urged with power upon his own contemporaries. This message is that no one can be saved by his own righteousness, however noble; nor by his own work, however laborious; nor by the keeping of his own rules, however exacting. The God who lived two thousand years ago is the God of the ages who lives now and forever. His character is the character which was revealed in Jesus Christ. His righteousness, both as gift and as demand, shines upon us in the face of Christ, and commands our hearts and lives in the sacrifice of Christ's cross.

In Christ, we still experience both the judgment and the mercy of God. Life, health, peace, meaning, and salvation—for time and eternity—come not as the fruit of our own earning, but as a gift of God's justifying grace. We can receive this grace, accept it, live and die by it, and make it our hope and our home, just as our forefathers in the faith have done through many centuries. Or we can neglect and spurn it at our peril.

Chapter 4

Atonement and Reconciliation

In the New Testament the basic meaning of reconciliation is restoration to fellowship with God. While the Greek term for reconciliation is characteristically a Pauline word, the New Testament as a whole is permeated with the message of reconciliation.

Paul uses a number of *picture words* by means of which he attempts to express in common language the essential content of salvation. Of these, five probably are the most important: justification, reconciliation, forgiveness, redemption, and adoption. Together, they show different aspects of the Christian experience of salvation. They are synonyms, each a different gleaming facet of one precious stone.

In each of these "pictures" man stands before God in a different guise:

●He appears before God as an accused person; his acquittal is called *justification.*

●He comes before God as an enemy; his restoration to harmony and fellowship with God is called *reconciliation.*

●He stands before God as a debtor; the remission of his indebtedness is *forgiveness.*

●He appears before God as a slave; his purchase and liberation are *redemption.*

•The released slave is taken into the family of God; this elevation to God's family is *adoption.*

As Adolph Deissmann observes, the words which Paul uses to describe salvation are valuable, unless we attempt to make each one of them stand for an exclusive "doctrine."[1] That Paul himself did not do this is easy to determine by reference to his writings. If the above-mentioned terms, however, refer to the same basic experience of God's grace, this is not to say that they are simply interchangeable in meaning. It is more accurate to observe that they say "different things about the same thing."

There is a particular affinity between justification and reconcilation. Many Pauline scholars contend that reconciliation is but an alternative way of expressing the reality which has occurred in "justification."[2] There is a parallelism of the two words in Romans 5:9-10, for example. In 2 Corinthians reconciliation is described as God's "not counting" the trespasses of men against them — an idea which is virtually interchangeable with the meaning of justification.[3]

The advantage which the word "reconciliation" has over "justification" is that it lifts our relationship to God from the level of the law-court to that of personal association. It more easily allows us to think of our relationship to God in terms of His Fatherhood and our sonship, of love rather than of law, of fellowship rather than of legal acquittal. While Paul does not use the term "reconciliation" very often, his employment of it is extraordinarily pungent, for it takes us to the heart of the gospel. "This is the simplest of all the pictures," says William Barclay. "Reconciliation means bringing together two people who have become estranged, and Jesus Christ brought man and God together again."[4]

The four main passages in the New Testament which deal with the theme of reconciliation are as follows: Romans 5:8-11; 1 Corinthians

---

[1]Deissmann, *Paul*, p. 177.

[2]Victor Paul Furnish, *Theology and Ethics in Paul* (Nashville and New York: Abingdon Press, 1968), p. 149.

[3]Cf. Rudolph Bultmann, *Theology of the New Testament*, Kendrick Grobel, trans., vol. 1 (New York: Charles Scribner's Sons, 1951), pp. 285ff.

[4]William Barclay, *The Mind of St. Paul* (London: Collins, 1958), p. 81.

5:14-21; Colossians 1:20-22; and Ephesians 2:12-17. Since all of these passages are found outside the Gospels, however, perhaps we should begin our approach to the theme of reconciliation with the reminder that the portrait of Jesus which we see in the Gospels is that of one whose chosen vocation is preeminently that of reconciliation. Reclamation is the spirit of reconciliation; reclamation is at the center, both in word and in deed, of what Christ came to accomplish. He spoke of God as one who seeks to reclaim the lost son, the lost sheep, and the lost coin. God sends his servants into the highways and byways to find men and women to come to his feast, not waiting for them to deserve forgiveness and restoration to his fellowship. He seeks them out while they are still afar.

Jesus ate with publicans and sinners, sought out and befriended zealots, collaborationists, prostitutes, the destitute, the depraved, the defeated, the discouraged, the sick, the underprivileged. He served in order to reconcile; he suffered in order to reconcile; he died in order to reconcile persons to their Father, and estranged brothers and sisters to one another.

Much of the power of Jesus' reconciling ministry was due to a remarkable conjunction of teaching and action. He did not say one thing and do another. Not only did he teach reconciliation, but also he brought it about. Even so, there was in him far more than the fidelity of a good man to a noble and exemplary ideal. He was able to reconcile persons to God because he was one with the reconciling God. In his reconciling work, those who saw him with the discernment of faith saw that God was in him, reconciling the world unto himself. We do not best conceive of the person of Christ in terms of an abstract hypostatic union of divine and human elements in him but in terms of a person whose atoning and reconciling life and death show with unique illumination the gracious love of an atoning God.

God Was in Christ, Reconciling

We have fallen from our fellowship with God: this theme is repeated almost constantly in the Scriptures. Let us see how this estrangement is described in the Pauline writings.

Sin, the Cause of Our Estrangement. In close conjunction with the theme of reconciliation, Paul uses several terms which express the disruption of our relationship with God. All of these terms indicate that the fundamental human problem, sin, is a breach of fellowship with the God who loves us. In Romans 5:10, Paul says that "while we were *enemies* we were reconciled to God" (RSV, italics added). In Ephesians 2:14-16, he states that Christ's atoning sacrifice has broken down the dividing wall of *hostility* between Jew and Gentile. In Ephesians 4:18, he speaks of men who are "*alienated* from the life of God because of the ignorance that is in them, due to the hardness of their heart" (RSV, italics added). In Colossians 1:21, Paul addresses Christians who once were "estranged" and "hostile" to God, who now, however, have been reconciled by the death of Christ.

In these various references, to be in sin is to live in a state of enmity and hostility to God, of alienation and isolation from God. This alienation from and hostility to God has resulted in alienation from and hostility to one's fellows, especially those who do not belong to *our own* nation, race, class, or group. Sin thus sets up an estranging obstacle between God and men. It isolates them from their true home, makes them enemies of the Father who loves them, and alienates them from other persons with whom they should be bound by ties of closest brotherhood. God's reconciling work is that of rescuing us from the isolation of this terrible estrangement, of restoring us as loving children to the heavenly Father, and of binding us in ties of friendship and fellowship with our fellow human beings.

God's Act of Reconciliation.

1. *The Divine Initiative.* Reconciliation is an expression of God's grace. The barrier between men and God can be removed only by God. The problem which our enmity poses is beyond the solution of human resourcefulness and ingenuity. The overtures of mercy depend on the absolute priority of God. "For in him [Christ] all the fullness of God was pleased to dwell," says Paul, "and through him to reconcile to himself all things, . . . making peace by the blood of his cross. And you, who once were estranged and hostile in mind, doing evil deeds, he has now reconciled in his body of flesh by his death" (Col. 1:19-21, RSV).

It thus appears that a Christian concept of reconciliation must bring two truths to the forefront of consideration. The first is that the enmity is on our side, not on that of God. It is not God but ourselves who stand in need of reconciliation. The second truth is that the work of reconciliation is God's work. God is the subject of reconciliation. The object of reconciliation is the world (2 Cor. 5:19), and "all things." More particularly, God reconciles "us" (v. 18). "While we were enemies we were reconciled to God" (Rom. 5:10, RSV). Parallel expressions, like "while we were yet helpless" (v. 6), and "while we were yet sinners" (v. 8), show the magnitude of our estrangement and the necessity of divine action in overcoming it.

2. *Reconciliation Both Finished and Ongoing.* We were reconciled to God by the death of his son "while we were enemies" (Rom. 5:10). In a real sense, the reconciliation which God effects on our behalf takes place before either our own effort or our knowledge. It is not dependent upon what we do or upon how we "feel" about it. As Rudolph Bultmann remarks, it has taken place, not as a subjective process, but as an "objective factual situation brought about by God."[5] Reconciliation, then, is not something we do; it is something we receive: "We also rejoice in God through our Lord Jesus Christ, through whom we have now received our reconciliation" (Rom. 5:11, RSV).

To say that the reconciling action of God is "finished" is to affirm that reconciliation is a permanent ingredient in the divine order of reality. It looms as an everlasting fact and factor for man to reckon with and take account of, having within it the firmness and grandeur of the everlasting hills. It is not something that is here today and gone tomorrow, a divine "flash in the pan" which ignited and blazed two thousand years ago, leaving only the gray ashes of an empty hope behind. The reconciling act which God performed in Christ burns and shines forever. The Holy Spirit, who sheds the love of God abroad in our hearts, takes what God did in Christ and applies it with redeeming efficacy, and with undiminished power, to the lives of men and women. James Denney's grasp of reconciliation as something already accomplished prompted him to say, "Reconciliation is not something which is doing; it is something which is done."[6]

To say that God's act of reconciliation has in a sense been completed does not mean, however, that a personal response to this act is a matter either of divine predetermination or of divine indifference. When God established the reconciling action in Christ, he also set up the ministry and message of reconciliation. The "word of

---

[5]Bultmann, *Theology of the New Testament*, p. 286.

[6]James Denney, *The Death of Christ*, 2nd ed., (New York: Armstrong, 1903), p. 145.

reconciliation" is the proclamation of the reconciliation which God has already accomplished. Moreover, the proclamation of the word is an invitation to faith, without which personal response on our part the divine provision for us is ineffective. The reconciling work of God, which has become a reality in Christ, is not yet concluded, for men must still be exhorted to receive the reconciliation, and because the peace with which God intended to embrace the whole world (Col. 1:20) has not yet brought the world under its sway.

3. *Christ the Agent of Reconciliation.* "God was in Christ, reconciling the world to himself" (2 Cor. 5:19, RSV). This brief statement sets forth the essence of the Christian belief in the reconciling endeavor of God. The Pauline emphasis is that God in Christ reconciled the world to himself, not that Christ reconciled God to the world. The forensic theories of atonement affirm the opposite, namely, that God would not be reconciled until he was appeased by the death of his Son, who made a willing offering of himself on the cross in order that the Father's anger might be placated. The justice of God had first to be satisfied before his love could become operative. By stepping into our place, Christ paid the price for our sins, died the death that we should have died, and satisfied to the full the demand of God's justice for the payment of the debt which our sins had made to accrue against us. By the payment of our debt with his blood, Christ reconciles the Father to us.

The very reciting of representative Scriptural passages on this subject should be enough to establish the fallacious character of this argument. "If, while we were enemies, *we* were reconciled to God by the death of his Son, much more, now that *we* are reconciled, shall we be saved by his life" (Rom. 5:10, RSV, italics added). "All this is from God, who through Christ *reconciled us to himself* and gave us the ministry of reconciliation; that is, *God was in Christ reconciling* the world to himself. . . . We beseech you on behalf of Christ, *be reconciled to God*" (2 Cor. 5:18-20, RSV italics added). "For he is our peace, who has made us both one . . . [that] he might *reconcile* us both to God in one body through the cross, thereby bringing the hostility to an end" (Eph. 2:14-16, RSV, italics added.) "And you, who once were estranged and hostile in mind, doing evil deeds, *he has now reconciled* in his body of flesh by his death" (Col. 1:21-22, RSV, italics added).

Interpreters of the Atonement who think of Christ's work as one whose purpose is to propitiate the anger of God, or to satisfy God's demands for justice, do violence to the unity of the will of Christ with the will of the Father. In many instances, this type of interpretation exalts the justice of God above the mercy and love of God. For example, the American theologian A. H. Strong maintained that justice "is a principle of God's nature, not only independent of love, but superior to love."[7] W. G. T. Shedd, another American theologian, held that justice inheres in God's nature, but mercy is God's disposition.[8] In other words, mercy is a more or less capricious act after justice is done. Love serves the ends of justice. While God is a God of both justice and love, he is justice primarily, love secondarily. Justice is the higher principle.

In popular theology, at least, the interpretation of the Atonement in terms of satisfaction and propitiation has been attended by a conception which places Christ in a position inferior to the claims of justice. For if the work of the Son is that of appeasing the Father, it would seem to follow that the principle of justice is superior to Christ's work of love. W. J. Wolf's insight here is penetrating: "A God who forgives because His justice has been satisfied does not really forgive." This position makes "the grace of God of no effect."[9]

On the other hand, the history of the doctrine of the Atonement shows the danger of pressing the reconciling love of God in such a way that God's love is sentimentalized. This danger is the reason why the doctrine of reconciliation should always keep within its purview the correlative conception of the wrath of God. We live in a moral order, which we believe to be established, supported, and permeated by the living God. God is present in the moral order which he sponsors. Moreover, our relationship to him is much more personal than that which is suggested by the term *moral order*. If God is personal, and if reconciliation is personal, then wrath is also personal. It seems therefore much more feasible to view God's wrath as "angry love" than as an impersonal retribution.

God reconciles. *We* are reconciled. But to say this is not to signify that God is unaffected by our relationship to him, either before or after

---

[7]Cited in George Barker Stevens, *The Christian Doctrine of Salvation* (New York: Charles Scribner's Sons, 1905), p. 178.

[8]Wolf, *No Cross, No Crown*, p. 113.

[9]Ibid., p. 114.

we receive his reconciling act in Christ by faith. Terms like *anger, antagonism,* and *wrath,* are, with respect to our own interpersonal relationships, so loaded with the ambiguous and positively evil connotations which we associate with human alienation, that we may well hesitate to use them in speaking of our relationships with God. Yet the attempt must be made.

William Temple makes one such significant attempt. There is, says Temple, a real antagonism in God against the sinner so long as the sinner continues in his sin:

> So long as there is ill-will in me there is an antagonism on His side to be ended as well as on mine. It is of my making, but it exists in Him and not only in me. It is not anger, if by anger we mean the emotional reaction of an offended self-concern; it is anger, if by anger we mean the resolute and relentless opposition of a will set on righteousness against a will directed elsewhere. God must abolish all sinners, but He seeks to abolish sinners by winning them out of their sin into the loyalty and love of children in the Father's house.[10]

Wrath, says R. H. Strachan, is a manifestation of God's essential "incapacity to be morally indifferent, and to let evil alone. . . . No love can be called good which lacks the capacity for instinctive repulsion, in the presence of the mean and the base." Wrath and love comprise one divine activity, which Paul designates by the term *reconciliation.* "Together they are the complete response of Divine love to the tragic fact that men whom God created and loves, have become what they are through sinning."[11]

The wrath of God repels the charge that reconciliation is easy for God, that God regards man's sin without pain, and forgives with an almost jocular ease.

Many interpreters who press the idea of an easy reconciliation like to cite the parable of the prodigal son as evidence for their thesis. The

---

[10]William Temple, *Christus Veritas* (London: Macmillan and Company, Ltd., 1954), p. 259. Cf. Robert H. Culpepper, *Interpreting the Atonement* (Grand Rapids, Michigan: William B. Eerdmans Publishing Company, 1966), pp. 111-13.

[11]R. H. Strachan, *The Second Epistle of Paul to the Corinthians,* The Moffatt New Testament Commentary (New York and London: Harper and Brothers, Publisher, 1935), pp. 117-18.

Father who waited at home through the long months was always of a reconciling, forgiving spirit. It was only necessary for the wayward son to return home with a contrite spirit for the father to receive him with arms wide open in joyful forgiveness.

This parable, however, does not contain all of the elements necessary for an understanding of atonement. If the lesson of this parable were the only thing needful, P. T. Forsyth says, it is a wonder that Christ did not consider that his mission was discharged immediately after the parable was delivered. Then he could have returned to heaven without delay.[12] A ministry of self-denial, suffering, and service would have been unnecessary. Gethsemane and Calvary would have been superfluous.

The message of an easy reconciliation neglects the dimension of love which the father bore in his heart as he waited and longed in anguish for his son's return. It does not make plain that the father goes out to seek the son, as God has done in Christ.

The true situation, as indicated in the discussion which follows, is this: The reconciling act of God in Christ, in Christ crucified and risen, makes it possible for the prodigal to come home.

4. *The Reconciling Cross.* "We were reconciled to God," Paul says, "by the death of his Son" (Rom. 5:10, RSV). This means that we are reconciled, not by the fiat of a generous benevolence, but by the anguish of a costly grace. The "riches of his [God's] kindness and forbearance and patience" (Rom. 2:4, RSV) may convey the impression that God is indifferent towards sin, but this impression is utterly mistaken. God's forbearing kindness is intended to lead people to repentance. To a self-indulgent and self-excusing mentality, it appeared that God's attitude towards human wrongdoing was one of condonation rather than of condemnation. This attitude reached its disastrous nadir in the delusion of licentious pseudo-Christians who desired to continue in sin, that grace might abound (Rom. 6:1).

No one who looks at the cross of Christ with discerning eyes can ever believe again that God makes light of sin. Here is where the depths of human evil have the searchlight of reality thrown upon them with an all-revealing, searing illumination. Here, with poignant, stark, and

---

[12]Forsyth, *The Work of Christ*, p. 109.

unforgettable power, what God thinks and feels of our sin is revealed and demonstrated forever.

The reconciling act of God in the cross must be seen as the focal thrust of all that God has done and is doing to meet our human needs. The cross is the epitome, the consummation, of God's grace, brought to a radiant concentration. Christ made himself one with sinners. He entered into the "horror of thickest darkness" as the dereliction and godforsakenness of the cross overtook him. His identification with the needs of sinners was so intense that the shame and curse of sin became his portion.

All of this involvement in vicarious suffering must be seen in the light of the person who endured to the uttermost. He who was chastised for our peace was the Son of God. But it cannot be too strongly emphasized that, while he took away the barriers which kept us from God, the Father was not just an admiring and sympathetic spectator who watched this drama of suffering and sorrow from afar. It was God *in* Christ who bore the load of our sins, who paid the price of reconciliation, whose love went to the utmost length to restore us to his fellowship.

Reconciliation and the New Creation

"If anyone is in Christ, he is a new creation; the old has passed away, behold, the new has come. All this is from God, who through Christ reconciled us to himself and gave us the ministry of reconciliation" (2 Cor. 5:17-18, RSV).

The "newness of life" which comes to us through reconciliation is a "life in Christ." Paul accepted the Jewish doctrine of the *two ages*: the present age, which is under the rule of evil powers (2 Cor. 4:4; Eph. 6:12), and the age to come (Eph. 1:21; Luke 8:30). The present age is transient, and is filled with all kinds of immorality; it is ruled by sin and death, and is doomed to pass away.

The age to come stands in striking contrast to the present age. The age to come is an age in which God's power will summon into existence "things that do not exist," and will give "life to the dead" (Rom. 4:17, RSV). An unrelenting opposition exists between the powers of the present age and God's transcendent power in the coming age (2 Cor. 4:7). The conflict opposes the "spirit of the world" to the "Spirit of God" (1 Cor. 2:12), the "flesh" to God's Spirit (cf. Rom. 8:4-5, 12-13;

Gal. 4:29), sin to righteousness (Rom. 6:16-23), and life to death (1 Cor, 15:26).

We live now in the convergence of the two ages. The old age is still present, but the new age is beginning to dawn upon the world. In the meantime, the power of the world to come is already active in this present life.

The Christian is a "new creation" because the world of the Christian is under the domination of the "world to come" which reaches into the "present evil age." The work of reconciliation which God has performed in Christ constitutes for the Christian a new environment in which God "has delivered us from the dominion of darkness and transferred us to the kingdom of his beloved Son"(Col. 1:13, RSV).

The law, the flesh, the world, sin, suffering, and death continue because the Christian still exists in the present age. They continue, but they do not dominate and enslave anymore. They operate and influence, but they no longer have the last word. Tragedy and calamity may come, but they do not separate from the love of God. God works "all things" for good for those who love him.

The "new creation" is a new self. Wayne Oates shows how this new self differs from the old one:

> What were the characteristics of the "old self" as contrasted with the "new self" in Christ? The old self was *separated* from Christ, whereas nothing could separate the new self from him. The old self was alienated and isolated from the community of faith, whereas the new self was reconciled with God and the people of God. The old self was a *stranger*, but the new self was now a fellow citizen in the household of God (See Eph. 2:12-21). The old self was drained of hope, but the new self has hope "poured" into his heart "through the Holy Spirit . . . ."(Rom. 5:5). The old self was "enslaved to the elemental spirits" or "no-gods" of the universe. The new self in Christ was "no longer a slave but a son."The old self has been redeemed and adopted into the family of God as a son and an heir, not as a slave. For this freedom did the Christ set us free (Gal. 4:1-11). Finally, the old self lacked identity with a "people;" the Christians were, before encounter with Christ, "not a people." Now they were

"God's people." The decisive factor that made the difference between the old self and the new self was their encounter with Christ (1 Pet. 2:10).[13]

Reconciliation and Peace with God

The apostle Paul closely associated reconciliation and peace. The New Testament as a whole is filled with references to peace. Indeed, there are about ninety such references, including those in the gospels, and particularly in the fourth gospel, and in Acts, in Hebrews, and in First and Second Peter. If epistolary greetings are counted, then *peace* is found in most of the New Testament writings.

The Old Testament term *peace* (shalom) is one with rich and varied meanings. The fundamental meaning is *totality, well-being, harmony.* The well-being comprehended by the word included every kind of good, such as health of body, strength, security, long life, prosperity, and a community relationship marked by harmony and good fellowship. This harmony was enjoyed most intimately in the family, but was extended to others by a covenant relationship which might be designated "a covenant of peace."

Peace was central in the preaching of the prophets. Peace came after God's judgment. In Isaiah, the deliverance from Babylon brought glad tidings of peace (Isa. 52:7; 55:12; 57:19). Ezekiel announced that God would make a covenant of peace with the restored community (Ezek. 34:25-30; 37:26). Thus, peace is brought into a close relationship with salvation. It is associated with righteousness and truth, although the underlying meaning of prosperity is retained. The Servant in Isaiah brings peace to the nations. Peace has also, in some prophetic visions, an eschatological accent, as when it is seen as the end of war and the rule of the messianic king over the nations, or as an idealized existence in which conflict and strife of all kinds will be done away.

Of all the passages in the New Testament which deal with peace in relationship to reconciliation, perhaps the most striking is Ephesians 2:14-16:

> For he is our peace, who has made us both one, and has broken down the dividing wall of hostility, by abolishing in

---

[13]Wayne Oates, *Christ and Selfhood* (New York: Association Press, 1961), p. 25.

his flesh the law of commandments and ordinances, that he might create in himself one new man in place of the two, so making peace, and might reconcile us both to God in one body through the cross, thereby bringing the hostility to an end (RSV).

This passage speaks of the reconciliation of Jew and Gentile which is accomplished at the cross. The purpose in view, however, is that these old enemies might be reconciled "both in one body *unto God.*" The peace of Gentile with Jew was at the same time a peace of both of them with God. The peace which they were drawn into with each other, indeed, was founded upon the peace with God which they shared through the cross of Christ. Christ came to preach peace both to those who were afar off and to those who were near, "for through him we both have access in one Spirit to the Father" (Eph. 2:18, RSV).

Romans 5:1 also speaks of the peace which has been effected for us with God through Christ. This peace through Christ has given us "access to this grace in which we stand, and we rejoice in our hope of sharing the glory of God" (RSV).

This *access*, in which the enmity in our hearts against God has been eradicated, has enabled us to enjoy fellowship with him. It has brought us into this fellowship *together*—Jew and Greek, male and female, bond and free. The fellowship with God ends the enmity which we have had towards each other, and binds us into one body, in which all our differences of race, temperament, background, and points of view are transcended.

This fellowship of reconciliation and peace will continue, for it is founded upon the most solid and most permanent realities. God has established it in sending Christ to live and die for us. The power of God supports it. The Spirit of God makes this power ever-present and ever-sustaining.

Reconciliation and Forgiveness

While in the New Testament there is some variation in the understanding of forgiveness, there is basically the same understanding of its meaning as there is in the Old Testament. It means the covering or removal of sins and transgressions, of iniquity and impiety, so that reconciliation between God and men is effected.

The synoptics emphasize the bondage which sin brings. Christ is represented as being engaged in a mighty conflict with the evil powers which have enslaved mankind. Forgiveness appears as a release from bondage and a restoration to wholeness of life. The sick, the unclean, the blind, and the captives are freed from the powers that bind them. The case of the paralytic (Matt. 9:2-8, RSV) is a good example. He was forgiven of his sins, *and* he was made well. With his forgiveness there was a restoration to wholeness. In the fullest sense, he was a human being again.

Where sin is interpreted in terms of guilt, forgiveness is seen in a context of expiation or atonement. Forgiveness brings peace with God, release from anxiety and from a burdened conscience, and deliverance from guilt. This emphasis is found in the book of Hebrews, in the johannine letters, in First Peter, and in the writings of Paul.

Where sin is thought of as rebellion against God, the closest connection between forgiveness and reconciliation appears. Here forgiveness expresses the removal of enmity and alienation between God and man. Through forgiveness, fellowship is renewed with the Father, the repentant sinner is adopted into the family of God as a son, and God grants to his restored children the renewing and sustaining powers of the new age.[14]

Restoration to the fellowship of God may appear to be all too easy in some of the biblical teachings. God is ready, willing, and able to forgive. All that he asks is that we turn from our wicked ways and ask for his free pardon: "Let the wicked forsake his way, and the unrighteous man his thoughts; let him return to the Lord, that he may have mercy upon him, and to our God, for he will abundantly pardon" (Isa. 55:7, RSV). Also, in the New Testament, we find Christ saying to an adulteress, "Neither do I condemn thee; go, and sin no more" (John 8:11, KJV). To a paralytic he says, "Take heart, my son; your sins are forgiven" (Matt. 9:2, RSV). Once again we may notice that the classical teaching of Jesus concerning forgiveness is the parable of the prodigal son. The point of this parable is that God freely forgives all who repent. All of the teaching of Jesus seems to be in harmony with this teaching.

In these examples and teachings of forgiveness we see the expansive generosity of God, who forgives all who ask him for

---

[14]George A. Buttrick, ed., *The Interpreter's Dictionary of the Bible*, 4 vols. (New York, Nashville: Abingdon Press, 1962), E-J: 319.

forgiveness in a spirit of true repentance. We are wrong, however, if we think that the grace of God's forgiveness is cheap, or if we believe that there is no cross which is necessary to this forgiveness and which makes it possible.

In his great book entitled *The Christian Experience of Forgiveness*, H. R. Mackintosh describes graphically what takes place in a person's mind and heart when he forgives a great wrong which has been done to him by another person:

> It is an exacting thing to pardon a great wrong; assuredly it is not with a heart of stone that an act so brave and free and loving can be carried through. A man engaged in it is conscious of wrench and agony in proportion as on the one hand he feels the shame of his friend's evil and as on the other sympathy brings him close to the guilty life, actually by intense feeling putting him where the other is. To enter by passionate imagination and self-projection into the other's conflict, to hold by intercession his faltering hand, to weep with his sorrow, actually to think self still at the other's side in the misery and loneliness of guilt—all this is requisite; and how true it is that in heart and mind the forgiver must set out on "voyages of anguish!" It is an experience of sacrificial pain, of vicarious suffering. It is the state of a soul under great stress.[15]

When we ask how Jesus could bestow forgiveness during his earthly lifetime, if the cross is indeed the medium through which the mercy of God reaches us, we can only reply that the spirit that animated him as he ministered to sinful, battered, and beaten human beings along the roadway of life was the spirit which led him to Golgotha. "In spirit," Mackintosh says, "He went down to where they were, in their bitter, grief-stricken distance from God; and thus joining Himself to them inwardly He took hold of their hand, that He might raise them up."[16]

The depths and heights of forgiveness can be seen only as we see the cross at the heart of Christ's life, as well as at Golgotha. We see its

---

[15]H. R. Mackintosh, *The Christian Experience of Forgiveness* (New York and London: Harper and Brothers Publishers, 1927), pp. 190-91.

[16]Ibid., p. 216.

scope and outreach only as we see in Christ's forgiving ministry the love of the reconciling God. As we observe Jesus healing, forgiving, and dying, we discern, says William Temple, that "no further entry of the Supreme God into the tangle and bewilderment of finitude can be conceived."[17]

To the first Christians, the forgiveness which Christ brought was not only a sign of God's loving-kindness but also an eschatological event which ushered all believers into the beginning of the new creation. It was "the first of the last things." From their viewpoint, it meant virtually the same thing to believe in the forgiveness of sins, the resurrection of the body, and the life everlasting.[18]

We must be careful, however, not to consign forgiveness, by stamping an eschatological label upon it, to a place of irrelevance in the world. Indeed, forgiveness is a mark of the kingdom of God which exists here and now, not in some cloud-land of specious idealism far removed from the necessities and practicalities of our present life. Jesus' teaching that one must forgive, not seven times, but "seventy times seven," and his admonition that no one can obtain the forgiveness of God without forgiving his unreconciled brother, is all too painfully pertinent to the animosities, envies, and bitternesses of our daily lives.

The character of forgiveness refutes the charge that God cannot give it freely without violating the moral law. Forgiveness is not an obeisance to a legalistic requirement; it is the practice of the law that fulfills and transcends all law. This is the law of love. Forgiveness is not the parole of a criminal over whose head there hangs, like the sword of Damocles, the threat of retribution at the slightest additional offense; it is a pardon to a new life whose requirements are exacting, but whose exactions are the responsibilities of love and service in God's great fellowship.

Reconciliation and Sonship

Reconciliation with God brings sinners into a condition of forgiven sonship. It restores them to the full privileges of members of God's family, in a relationship which had been nullified by sin.

---

[17]William Temple, *Christus Veritas*, p. 270.

[18]Oliver Chase Quick, *The Gospel of the New World* (London: Nisbet and Co., Ltd., 1945), p. 57.

The sonship which Christians enjoy with the Father is derivative from and based upon the unique sonship of Christ. This unique sonship is mentioned in the synoptic gospels in events such as the baptism of Jesus, the transfiguration, and Gethsemane, as well as the cross. In the synoptics, perhaps no claim to a unique sonship is so sweeping as that recorded in Matthew 11:27: "All things have been delivered to me by my Father; and no one knows the Son except the Father, and no one knows the Father except the Son and any one to whom the Son chooses to reveal him" (RSV).

In the Gospel of John, the unique sonship of Christ is even more pointedly stated. The best beloved passage is "the gospel in miniature," John 3:16: "For God so loved the world that he gave his only Son, that whoever believes in him should not perish but have eternal life" (RSV). Three other examples may be cited. "The Father loves the Son, and has given all things into his hand" (John 3:35, RSV). "Shall I not drink the cup which the Father has given me?" (John 18:11, RSV). The discourse in the upper room, culminating in the prayer of John 17 shows the profound unity of will and purpose which existed between the Father and the Son. In this prayer, Jesus says, "I glorified thee on earth, having accomplished the work which thou gavest me to do; and now, Father, glorify thou me in thy own presence with the glory which I had with thee before the world was made" (John 17:4-5, RSV).[19]

The truth of these sayings was tested and verified in the entire ministry of Jesus, and supremely in his death. It was as God's unique Son that Jesus suffered, died, and rose again.

With a consideration of the unique sonship of Christ should be placed the question of whether all human beings are in some sense children of God. This question has been much debated in Christian thought. It is true that New Testament references concerning human sonship relate preponderantly to Christian believers. On the other hand, the issue between those who affirm and those who reject a universal fatherhood of God and a universal sonship of men is more than a semantic issue. It is because men are children of God that they can be sinners. It is because God is their Father that he always has claims upon them, wherever they are and whatever they do. The

---

[19]F. W. Dillistone, *The Significance of the Cross* (Philadelphia: The Westminster Press, 1944), pp. 107-109.

disquiet and the dispeace in the heart of the lost sinner is due to the fact that God is calling him to his true destiny, which is to be "conformed to the image of his son." St. Augustine's insight is a true one: "Thou hast made us for thyself, and our hearts are restless till they find their rest in thee." Sonship may be forgotten or denied, but it is still written indelibly upon the human soul.

On this subject, David Smith contends that the parable of the prodigal son is a decisive illustration:

> The Heavenly Fatherhood is as wide as humanity. The children of men are all children of God. A believer is a son of God, and so also is an unbeliever; and the difference, the radical and momentous difference, between them is that the latter is a son *still lost*, while the former is a son who *has returned home.* The believer too was once in the far country, and he is a son who "was lost and is found," whereas the unbeliever is a son who is lost and not found as yet, but still remembered and desired; and the Father's heart will never be satisfied until the wanderer is restored .... "A lost soul" is one who has gone astray, a wandered child whom the Father loves and yearns after, and has sent His Eternal Son . . . to seek and find and carry home.[20]

If we grant the thesis of a universal human sonship to God, we must at the same time emphasize that the true meaning of sonship is not realized until the sinner believes in God. The prodigal son did not know the true meaning of sonship until he returned to the home of a forgiving father. The elder brother, however, did not know the true significance of sonship, because by his hardness of heart he excluded himself from the father's fellowship.

Redeemed sonship is a radical restoration of a broken fellowship with God. It comes to us as a gracious gift of the Father. It requires repentance and faith, humility and trust, on the part of the estranged son, as the Father, through the agency of Christ, bestows a healing and forgiving mercy.

To indicate the difference between the estranged and the restored relationship, Paul sometimes uses the term *adoption* rather than the

---

[20]David Smith, *The Atonement in the Light of History and the Modern Spirit* (London, New York, Toronto: Hodder and Stoughton, n.d.), pp. 144-45.

term *sonship.* "For ye have not received," he says to the Roman Christians, "the spirit of bondage again to fear; but ye have received the Spirit of adoption, whereby we cry Abba, Father" (Rom. 8:15, KJV). God sent forth his Son in the fullness of time "to redeem them that were under the law, that we might receive the adoption of sons" (Gal. 4:5, KJV). Again, God "predestined us unto the adoption of children by Jesus Christ" (Eph. 1:5, KJV).

Although the term *adoption* may seem cold and formal in comparison with *sonship,* its use in the first-century context in no sense detracted from the warmth and privileges of the family relationship. By Roman law, anyone who was made a son by adoption severed all his former ties. Apparently, even his debts were cancelled. The person who was adopted was sold publicly to his prospective parents in front of witnesses. The adopted person then became just as much a member of the family as though he had been born into it. By law, he was a new person; he had a new family; all of his relationships were new.

McLeod Campbell expressed the essential meaning of adoption in a beautiful way:

> Let us think of Christ as the Son who reveals the Father, that we may know the Father's heart against which we have sinned, that we may see how sin, in making us godless, has made us orphans, and understand that the grace of God, which is at once the remission of past sin and the gift of eternal life, restores to our orphan spirits their Father and to the Father of spirits His lost children.[21]

In Romans 8:16-17 Paul writes, "It is the Spirit himself bearing witness with our spirit that we are children of God, and if children, then heirs, heirs of God and fellow heirs with Christ" (RSV). This passage calls attention to the liberty and the heritage into which the children of God are graciously brought by the Father. In fact, one may argue that the keynote of the theme of sonship is freedom. The restored son is redeemed from a life of slavery. He is adopted into a family in which he can claim and enjoy "the glorious liberty of the children of God" (Rom. 8:21, RSV). By the grace of the Father, he is now entitled

---

[21]Campbell, *The Nature of the Atonement,* p. 147. Cited in Stewart, *A Man in Christ,* p. 254.

to all the riches of the Father's estate and of the Father's glory. He is at peace with God, reconciled to his brother, and reconciled to himself.

This does not mean, of course, that the reconciled son is released from further battle and hardship. There are challenges to meet, difficult decisions to be made, a daily cross to bear, suffering to be borne. Yet he who enters into the meaning of sonship has come home. There is strength and grace for living each new day. There is hope and joy in the daily task. There is light for the darkest night; sustenance in the bitterest defeat; strength for weakness; zeal, vision, and insight for witness. Thereafter, one may travel far in the Master's service, but he will travel in the Master's company, and will always be at home.

The Ministry of Reconciliation

The message of the gospel is that God is a reconciling God. His reconciling ministry in Christ was not the beginning of his reconciling endeavor, but its consummation. Christ's life and death were a point of blazing light, in which God's efforts to redeem and to reconcile were concentrated into one radiant focus. All the strands of truth and fragments of revelation—the hopes, dreams, and visions of a people who had been chosen to be the bearers of God's redemptive purpose—reached their zenith and fruition in Christ. But there was a further quality in Christ, unexpected and unprecedented. Arnold Come calls attention to it:

> Here was no prophet who spoke for God; here God spoke for himself. Here was no priest who stood between God and men; here the encounter with a man proved to be encounter with God. Here was no king who ruled by laws dictated by God or by "nature"; here was God present in the immediacy of his creative power to restore and to perfect, to heal and to save, in a word, to reconcile. And all in the form of condescension and accommodation to man's lowly and needy condition, the form of One who comes to serve, moved by the love of compassion.[22]

The reconciling work of God, which he has manifested in Christ, is carried on in the world by a community of reconciliation.

---

[22]Arnold B. Come, *Agents of Reconciliation* (Philadelphia: Westminster Press, 1960), pp. 127-28.

Reconciliation to God brings the reconciled into the orbit and thrust of God's own reconciling endeavor. Paul reminded the Corinthians that Christ died for all men "that those who live might live no longer for themselves but for him who for their sake died and was raised"(2 Cor. 5:15, RSV). The "message of reconciliation" had been committed to them, as to all other Christians. In the light of this sacred trust, he told them, they were ambassadors for Christ. Through them God was making his appeal to those who had not accepted the gospel message (2 Cor. 5:20).

The reconciling community is made up of reconciled individuals, but it is a *community*, not just an aggregate of individual persons who, in a kind of flight of the "alone to the alone," have had an individual experience of reconciliation with God. A striking feature of Ephesians 2:11-22 is the emphasis placed on the unity of those who are engaged in carrying on Christ's ministry of reconciliation. The wall of hostility between Jew and Gentile has been broken down, so that their separation and alienation are done away. In Christ they compose one body, one "new man." They comprise the "commonwealth of Israel"; they are heirs of the "covenants of promise"; they are "fellow citizens with the saints" and "members of the household of God." They are to be a part of "a holy temple in the Lord," a "habitation of God in the Spirit."

There is no value in arguing whether the gospel of reconciliation is first social and then individual, or first individual and then social. It is first and always both individual and social, both social and individual.

Paul's letter to Philemon contains a small roster of principal personalities. There is a Jew(Paul), a wealthy Gentile(Philemon), and Philemon's runaway slave (Onesimus). Paul refers to the wealthy Gentile as "a beloved fellow worker"(v. 2), "my brother"(v. 7), and my "partner" (v. 17). He says to this Gentile brother, "Prepare a guest room for me, for I am hoping through your prayers to be granted to you" (v. 22, RSV). He speaks of the runaway slave as "my child, Onesimus, whose father I have become in my imprisonment"(v. 10, RSV). He urges Philemon to receive Onesimus back as "a beloved brother . . . both in the flesh and in the Lord"(v. 16, RSV). "Receive him," Paul says, "as you would receive me" (v. 17, RSV).

Here was the liberating ministry of reconciliation, not in theory but in practice. In this particular application, reconciliation involved only a handful of individuals. But the larger message—pertinent to the whole world and entrusted to the church for proclamation—was plain: "There is neither Jew nor Greek, there is neither slave nor free, there is neither male nor female; for you are all one in Christ Jesus" (Gal. 3:28, RSV).

Chapter 5

Atonement and Sanctification

In the New Testament a family of words is built on the root *hag*. *Hagiazein* is a verb which means to sanctify, to consecrate, to make holy. The nouns *hagiasmos, hagiosune,* and *hagiotes* signify holiness, consecration, and sanctification. *Hagios* is an adjective meaning holy, consecrated, sanctified. In the plural it relates to Christians as saints.

Several English words which stem from different etymological roots nevertheless translate the same basic Greek idea. Holiness, consecration, and sanctification share large areas of coextensive meaning. In the New Testament, *holiness* is a word which has a close kinship with *sanctification*.

When we reflect upon what has happened to these key concepts in modern Christianity, we may hesitate to use them at all. The talk of some Christian groups about "entire sanctification" and "sinless perfection"—as though these were attainable in this life, and as though they *are* attained, indeed, by certain spiritually superior individuals— has marked the terms with strongly sectarian connotations. On the other hand, the pessimism of some Christians who acknowledge God to be holy but who minimize man's ability to carry out the will of God has been just as destructive of a true Christian idea of sanctification.

Sanctification is both an indispensable Bible teaching and a teaching deeply pertinent to contemporary Christianity. Sanctification is both a divine gift and a human task. It is gift and task—not sequentially but simultaneously, not separably but cohesively and organically. It means being set aside for God's use and it means Christian growth. It means dedication and it means transformation. It is a work of God and at the same time it is a responsibility of the Christian believer.

In the biblical sense sanctification is a making or a being made holy. Here, however, we encounter a consideration of first importance. For, in biblical thought, only God is holy. Holiness is, indeed, the fundamental nature of God which distinguishes him from everything and anything that is not God. Nothing and no one can rival or challenge his prerogative as God. No force can unseat or dethrone him. He wills to be acknowledged alone as God. He is the Holy One.

A basic element in the idea of holiness is separation. God, the "Holy One of Israel," is "wholly other" than his creation and his creatures. God is separate and distinct from all else because he is God, and because no one or nothing else is God.

The separateness here envisioned is a transcendence of God above all else. This transcendence is not remoteness; it is otherness. It is supremacy without distance, indifference, or disdain. The "wholly other" God is not far away. He is very near.

Moreover, the holiness of God is communicative and communicated. It is a "transitive" holiness. God makes holy, says Emil Brunner, "that which in itself stands in conflict with (His) will, by taking it out of 'the world' and setting it apart for Himself, drawing it into His realm and claiming it for Himself, making it serviceable to His aim and purpose."[1]

The Old Testament Scriptures refer to God's "holy arm," his "holy word," and his "holy spirit." These are holy because they belong to God. The Sabbath is holy because it is God's. The Temple is holy because he owns it. He has a "holy nation," a "holy people," because they are his nation, his people. The heavens are holy, because he made them, encompasses them, and possesses them. Every item which has its

---

[1]Emil Brunner, *The Christian Doctrine of the Church, Faith, and the Consummation*, David Cairns and T. H. L. Parker, trans. Dogmatics, vol. 3 (Philadelphia: The Westminster Press, 1962), p. 290.

place in the sanctuary is holy: the shewbread, the oil, the clothes, the priests, the worshipers, the sacrifices are all holy, because they belong to him.[2]

Holy places, days, seasons, feasts, ceremonies, and persons are sanctified, not because they have any intrinsic quality of holiness, but because they belong to God. He has set them aside for his use. They are instruments of his purpose.

In the New Testament sense, a sanctified person is a *saint*. He is a saint not because he is intellectually superior to anyone else or even morally superior to anyone else but because he has been set aside for God's use. God has sought him out in the atoning love and sacrifice of Christ, has cleansed him by the blood of the cross, and has placed him on the pathway of Christian life and service. He is *God's* person.

Christ the Holy One of God

While only God is holy, it is Christ who, in a special and unique sense, is the "holy one of God." He is the one appointed of God, chosen and separated to bear away the sins of the world, to be the Savior of mankind, and to be the Lord of men and history. In his great prayer in John 17, Jesus says, "For their sake I consecrate myself, that they also may be consecrated in truth" (v. 19, RSV). By consecrating himself, Jesus has set himself apart as a willing agent to accomplish for mankind the redemptive purpose of the Father.

A close connection exists between sanctification and sacrifice. In the tenth chapter of Hebrews, the author says of Christ, "We have been sanctified through the offering of the body of Jesus Christ once for all" (v. 10, RSV). The giving of Christ's blood was the giving of his life in dedication to the will of the Father for the salvation of humanity.

Christ's followers are sanctified in him. What he has done for himself he has done for them; he has set them apart for dedication to God. For them, as for him, this means they must be willing and ready to be as grains of wheat that fall into the ground and die that they might live again in a different realm. This new life in a new realm is not a life of self-trust, self-love, and self-aggrandizement; it is a life of self-sacrificing service in the kingdom of God.

---

[2]Norman Snaith, *Distinctive Ideas of the Old Testament* (Philadelphia: The Westminster Press, 1946), pp. 51-52.

The Holy Spirit

Christ is the supreme standard and pattern of holiness. He is the holy one of God (Mark 1:24; Acts 3:14). The divine intention of our sanctification is that we might be conformed to the image of God's Son (Rom. 8:29). How this intention is accomplished we cannot fully understand. We do know, however, that it is not something we can do for ourselves. It is not something that is ever completed in this life, but it *is* something that is effected by the Holy Spirit. Sanctification is a Christlikeness into which the Holy Spirit shapes us.

C. F. D. Moule shows the New Testament identification of the presence of the Holy Spirit with Christlikeness:

> The diffused and little defined and fitfully manifested spiritual presence of God (viz. as we meet it in the Old Testament) becomes sharply contracted to a "bottle-neck"so as to be defined and localized in Jesus of Nazareth; God who formerly spoke at various times and in many different fragments has now spoken to us in one who is a Son. But the pattern, thus contracted to a single individual, widens, again, through his death and resurrection, to an indefinite scope, though never again to an undefined quality. However widely diffused, however much more than individual, it bears henceforth the stamp of the very character of Christ.[3]

The Holy Spirit sanctifies as the Spirit of Christ, and as the Spirit of him who raised Christ from the dead. To say that the Holy Spirit "witnesses to Christ" means that, in the sanctifying process, the Holy Spirit is dependent upon the death and resurrection of Christ, not only in the initiation of our sanctification but also in its continuation and completion.

The Spirit is therefore the agent of the exalted Lord who was crucified for us. His function is to glorify Christ by taking the things of Christ and showing them to God's people (John 16:14; 2 Cor. 3:17-18). He indwells his people as advocate, helper, and truth-bringer: "And I will pray the Father, and he will give you another Counselor, to be with

---

[3]C. F. D. Moule, in an unpublished lecture, "The Holy Spirit in the Church," p. 7; cited in E. M. B. Green, *The Meaning of Salvation* (Philadelphia: The Westminster Press, 1965), p. 176.

you for ever, even the Spirit of truth, whom the world cannot receive, because it neither sees him nor knows him; you know him, for he dwells with you, and will be in you" (John 14:16-17).

The Relationship of Sanctification to Other Christian Qualities

Sanctification is vitally related to the whole of the Christian life. It deals with Christian growth, Christian "perfection," Christian maturity. It is also vitally related to the initial act by which we become Christians. It is related to faith, because in sanctification the first act of trust in God is repeated again and again. It is related to regeneration, because it is the unfolding of the new life which was implanted in us in the regenerative experience. It is constantly related to the work of the Holy Spirit, whose regenerative power is carried forward from its beginnings in the heart of the believer until the Christian attains the fullness of the stature of Christ.[4] It is related to reconciliation, though not coextensive with it in meaning. The reconciling work of God is a sanctifying activity, in that it sets the believer apart for God's use, yet this initial divine hallowing has to be worked out and worked through amid the developing stages of the Christian life.

Although they have different shades of meaning, justification and sanctification are inseparable. In the aspect of sanctification which relates to the initial commitment of the believer to God, sanctification corresponds to the new status which God conveys by his justifying act.[5] On the other hand, while justification refers to a declaratory act of God made at the beginning of the Christian life, sanctification more clearly comprehends the whole of the Christian journey, and points to its goal.

Sanctification as Spiritual and Ethical Transformation

Justification and sanctification should not be identified with each other, because they bring out different aspects of the Christian life. If this identification is made, however, the harm done is not nearly so serious as when we distinguish them so sharply that we pull them apart so that each one stands isolated from the other. Justification and sanctification belong to God's one act of salvation. Justification

---

[4]E. Y. Mullins, *The Christian Religion in its Doctrinal Expression* (Nashville, Tennessee: Broadman Press, 1917), p. 420.

[5]Ibid., p. 420.

concentrates on the beginnings of God's act, while sanctification, although including this initial act, also points up the transforming effects of God's redemptive grace, as God, with the free cooperation of the believer, works out the results of grace in human existence.

Much damage to our understanding of the Christian life results if we conceive that we are justified without being sanctified. We are justified once for all, and in this declarative action of God we are set aside once for all to and for God's service. That is to say, we are justified and sanctified at the same time. We do not wait for some kind of "second blessing" in order to be sanctified, as though we should find it necessary to be a Christian for an indefinite amount of time before we start practicing our Christianity. To make this supposition is to tear justification away from sanctification, regeneration from ethical behavior. The action of God in our justification sets us on the pilgrim road, the road of service, the road of battle for the right, the road of fellowship with God and his people, the road of missionary outreach— in short, on the road of sanctification. The goal is not reached with justification, or with the initial step of sanctification, but, however inadequately, this goal is envisioned and its achievement projected.

Justification calls our attention to the fact that there has been "something accomplished, something done" for us by God in Christ. Sanctification reminds us that what God has done once for all is not a stopping-place, a terminus, but a starting-point. It calls attention to the open road ahead, the spacious horizon, the lure of the journey, the bugle call at dawn to be up and away on the journey towards tomorrow.

Theologians of an older time referred to sanctification as both "positional" and "progressive." Positional sanctification refers to God's initial act in saving us and setting us apart for his use. It refers to a new status which we have before God, a new spiritual environment in which we live, new tasks which we seek to accomplish, new goals which challenge us forward.

This new environment is life "in Christ." However imperfect we may be, every Christian in his act of faith is sanctified in the sense that he is dedicated, consecrated to God through the power of the Holy Spirit. He accepts Christ as Savior *and* Lord.

Paul said, "If any one is in Christ, he is a new creation" (2 Cor. 5:17, RSV). If we conceive of justification and sanctification apart from the vital reality of "life in Christ," the two concepts become formalized and empty. The declarative act of justification does not reach us at our center, but may leave us cold, isolated, and unchanged within. The Christian way ahead may see us embarked upon a lethargic journey in which neither the beauties nor the challenges of the road engage our interest or attention.

Our sanctification means in truth an active fellowship and communion, in which Christ's own life is unfolded within ours. Holiness, even in parts of the Old Testament, may have meant awe without genuine reverence, and possession by a deity whose character is unknown and perhaps unknowable. In the New Testament, however, the holiness of God is combined not only with a revelation of his sovereignty but also with a revelation of his goodness. These are declared and known in Jesus Christ, who, as the "pioneer of life," has led us into a pathway of both dedication and transformation. A passage from Paul is worth repeating again and again, for it shows with great illumination the scope and nature of God's sanctifying grace:

> But God shows his love for us in that while we were yet sinners Christ died for us. Since, therefore, we are now justified by his blood, much more shall we be saved by him from the wrath of God. For if, while we were enemies we were reconciled to God by the death of his Son, much more, now that we are reconciled, shall we be saved by his life (Rom. 5:8-10, RSV).

Sanctification as Growth in Grace

Growth in grace refers to the progressive character of sanctification. It may be true that in most New Testament references to sanctification, the term applies to a definite act of God at the beginning of the Christian life, rather than to the Christian's continuing growth. Nevertheless, the element of growth in Christian maturity is an essential element, and must be considered an important part of sanctification. Second Peter 3:18 is a fine statement of this aspect of sanctification: "But grow in grace and knowledge of our Lord and Savior Jesus Christ. To him be the glory both now and to the day of eternity" (RSV).[6]

---

[6]Cf. Georgia Harkness, *The Fellowship of the Holy Spirit* (Nashville, New York: Abingdon Press, 1966), p. 93.

In discussing sanctification as Christian growth, Emil Brunner makes the following observations:

> Sanctification stands alongside of justification as a second thing, which is not identical with justification. And this is the specific difference, that sanctification, in contrast to justification, is not thought of as a unique event which as such brings into being the new creature, but refers to the manner in which gradually, step by step, by those processes of growth characteristic of all things, a sinful, unsanctified man grows into a sanctified man. Sanctification then corresponds to the gradual growth of the new man as it proceeds under the progressive influence of the Holy Spirit. Thus the action of the divine Spirit within the temporal process in its human, temporal aspect is what is meant, in contrast with justification which declares man righteous as a totality and at one moment.[7]

No Christian disciple ever becomes completely sanctified in this life. Yet he moves towards the goal which God has designed for him, which is fellowship with God through Christ. The Holy Spirit gives enabling power and direction to this deepening fellowship, and to the continuing growth in Christlikeness.[8]

From the viewpoint of its character as Christian growth, the course of sanctification is uneven. The onward course is marked by struggle and failure, backslidings, discouragements, disappointments, bruises, and a tortoise-like slowness, many times, as well as by periods of joyous victory and measurable progress. Nevertheless, there is within the Christian's life a new principle of vitality and growth which was not operative in him before. "Our relation to God," says Harold DeWolf, "is not a static one in which we can rest. It is a dynamic relation in which we move ahead in spiritual growth or break ourselves off from him." Growth towards the goal "is possible only by the continual

---

[7]Emil Brunner, *The Christian Doctrine of God*, Olive Wyon, trans., Dogmatics, vol. 1 (London: Lutterworth Press, 1949), p. 291.

[8]Cf. Ralph E. Knudsen, *Theology in the New Testament* (Valley Forge, Chicago, Los Angeles: The Judson Press, 1964), p. 298.

renewal of faithful commitment, prayer, and the work of God in our hearts."[9]

Sanctification and Christian Perfection

Does a growth in Christian maturity sometimes eventuate in an attainment of Christian "perfection"? We all know that here we encounter a controversial subject. The problem which is posed is encountered in the New Testament itself. In 1 John 1:8, for example, it is said that if a person claims to be without sin, the truth is not in him. If we sin, the writer declares, we have an advocate with the Father (1 John 2:1). This affirmation certainly implies that Christian believers do commit sin.

On the other hand, in 1 John 3:6,9, we are told that if a man is born of God, God's seed abides in him and he does not sin. Those who have the Christian hope, this writer says, purify themselves as Christ is pure (1 John 3:3).

Some of the apostle Paul's comments have given many Christians a reason to believe that Christian perfection is attainable in this life. Since the Christian walks by the Spirit, Paul says, he is able to fulfill the law of Christ (Gal. 6:2). The law of the spirit of life in Christ, Paul affirms in the great eighth chapter of Romans, has made us free from the law of sin and death. Paul prays that the faith of the Thessalonians may be perfected, so they may increase and abound in love (1 Thess. 3:10-12; 2 Thess. 1:11). To the Roman Christians, Paul says, "We know that our old self was crucified with him [Christ] so that the sinful body might be destroyed, and we might no longer be enslaved to sin" (Rom. 6:6, RSV). Again, Paul says, "But now that you have been set free from sin and have become slaves of God, the return you get is sanctification and its end, eternal life" (Rom. 6:22, RSV).[10]

As far as Christian perfection is concerned, it would appear superficially that both Paul and the author of First John speak on both sides of the question. In my opinion, both of these writers are saying not that the Christian does not sin but that he is no longer under the

---

[9]L. Harold DeWolf, *A Hard Rain and a Cross* (Nashville, New York: Abingdon Press, 1966), p. 101.

[10]Cf. R. Newton Flew, *Jesus and His Church* (London: Epworth Press, 1951), p. 57.

dominion of sin. If he has been regenerated and united with Christ in the power of Christ's death and resurrection, sin has been dethroned in his life. The old self has been crucified. Sin no longer has him in its possession. Life is changed in its direction. The old house has a new occupant. The Holy Spirit now has taken up his residence in the personality's central citadel. He is now the controlling and directing agent of the Christian's life. The person is now "spiritual" in the sense that he delights in the law of the Lord in his inmost self (1 Cor. 2:15; Rom. 7:22).

This position would seem to agree not only with the position of Paul but also with that of John. The latter does not mean that the Christian is sinless, but that the Christian does not commit the sin unto death (1 John 5:16). He does not abandon himself again to sin.[11]

An important passage on this subject is Matthew 5:48, in which Jesus says, "You, therefore, must be perfect, as your heavenly Father is perfect" (RSV). It is probable, as Frank Stagg says, that this verse should be taken in its most obvious meaning: "This is our Lord's demand. What else should one expect? Does one expect him to say, 'Be nine-tenths pure'? God never compromises his standard; it is perfection. Jesus demanded absolute trust, obedience, love, loyalty. He gave his all, and he demands our all."[12]

The perfectionists, as John Murray points out, make three mistakes which distort the meaning of sanctification: They fail to recognize that victory over sin is the possession of every Christian, not of a spiritually elite class; they construe the victory over sin to be a state separable from the experience of justification; they depict the victory over sin as a cessation from sinning rather than as a liberation from the power and love of sin.[13]

Surprisingly, those who talk about sinless perfection virtually always speak of sin and sinlessness in a legalistic sense. Sin is the "transgression of the law," and sinlessness is making a perfect score in the keeping of a code of rules. Legalism is notorious for finitizing and

---

[11]John Murray, *Redemption—Accomplished and Applied* (Grand Rapids, Michigan: Wm. B. Eerdmans Publishing Company, 1955), pp. 177-78.

[12]Frank Stagg, *New Testament Theology* (Nashville, Tennessee: Broadman Press, 1962), p. 109.

[13]Murray, *Redemption—Accomplished and Applied*, p. 179.

trivializing the law of God. By its standards, sinlessness is negatively shaped into a series of don'ts having to do with moral conduct. But, if the summation and essence of the law is to love God with all one's heart, soul, mind, and strength, is there anyone in possession of his sanity and Christian sensitivity who would claim to have attained perfection in this kind of love? If the second great commandment, like unto the first, is to love one's neighbor as he loves himself, would any Christian have the temerity to claim that he has kept this law perfectly?

To claim a sinless perfection is not to follow the way of faith, which trusts in the grace of God alone, but to seek to supersede faith by a righteousness of one's own. It is not to follow Christ; it is rather to seek to rival him, to shoulder him aside by a claim that pronounces him unnecessary to and irrelevant to the attainment of Christian maturity.

With penetrating insight, P. T. Forsyth places the emphasis upon the right place. The emphasis, he claims with respect to sinless perfection, is not on sinlessness, but on faith: "Forever, faith is not the faith of the sinless but of the redeemed, not of the holy but of the sanctified, the faith and the love of those who have been forgiven much, forgiven often and long, forgiven always."[14] Love, says Forsyth, not sinlessness, is "the maturity of faith."

> There may be much sin tarrying in a man if there be but the love of God overriding it, and the love of man in God. Love is not a mere reduction of sin as an amount, but it is a life turned in a new way, tuned to a new key, vowed to a new Lord, and lived in a new spirit. The difference . . . is one of quality, not of quantity.[15]

If we are to think of Christian perfection, we must think of it first in terms of the acceptance of God's grace, response to God's love by our answering love towards him, communion and fellowship with him by faith, loving service to our fellowmen, faithful witness in the spirit of Christ, not as moral impeccability.

All of this is not to say, of course, that moral growth and attainment are unimportant in the Christian life. It is simply an

---

[14]P. T. Forsyth, *God the Holy Father* (London: Independent Press, Re-issued 1957), p. 101.

[15]Ibid., p. 105.

attempt to establish what the priorities are in that life. Christian activity becomes legalistic pharisaism unless it is a channel of God's overflowing grace, an instrument of love, an agent of justice and fellowship. Forsyth writes: "The error at the root of all false ideas of perfection is this: it is rating our behavior *before* God higher than our relation *to* God—putting conduct before faith, deeds before trust, work before worship."[16]

The primary concern of sanctification for faith, love, and fellowship towards God does not permit either abrogation of or escape from allegiance to the highest ethical ideals. Christian ideals and conduct are, indeed, inextricably bound up with the concept of sanctification. What is denied here is that the ideal is fully attainable, and that the standards of Christian conduct can be shunted off into the dead-end street of sinless perfectionism. "Ideals," says Carl Schurz, "are like stars; you will not succeed in touching them with your hands. But like the seafaring man on the desert of waters, you choose them as your guides, and following them you will reach your destiny."[17]

The Christian life is one of both grace and task. The Christian does not earn or deserve the gift of his salvation, yet this gift inevitably brings obligations in its train. The love of God has inescapable requirements. Citizenship in the kingdom of God has its privileges, not the least of which is the mandate of service which is both loving and ethically irreproachable. One does not become a child of God by deserving God's approval, nor cease to be a child of God by failing to attain perfection. Yet the demands of God are not lowered but rather are heightened by his grace. God's acceptance of us and his lofty requirements of us remain together, inseparably joined. The love and forgiveness of God sustain us in our failures, but they do not free us from God's exactions. They take away the bitterness of our guilt, they cheer and sweeten our daily walk, but they do not condone our sins nor relax our duties.

To claim that salvation comes by grace alone is not to minimize the importance and indeed the necessity of discipleship. To acknowledge

---

[16]Ibid., p. 121.

[17]Carl Schurz, Address in Faneuil Hall, Boston, 18 April 1859; quoted in John Bartlett, *Familiar Quotations* (Garden City, New York: Garden City Publishing Co., Inc., 1944), p. 580.

that we are utterly dependent on God's mercy is not to deny that the life of faith involves a cooperative relationship in which we become "fellow workers" with God (compare 1 Cor. 3:9). It is not depreciating the place of a Christian ethic if attention is called to the fact that the motivational springs of that ethic arise out of God's grace and the transforming experience which comes to us when we receive this grace by faith. Paul, in his preface to his discussion of ethics in the epistle to the Romans, exhorts his fellow Christians:

> I appeal to you therefore, brethren, by the mercies of God, to present your bodies as a living sacrifice, holy and acceptable to God, which is your spiritual worship. Do not be conformed to this world but be transformed by the renewal of your mind, that you may prove what is the will of God, what is good and acceptable and perfect" (Rom. 12:1-2, RSV).

In other words, dedication to the purpose and will of God precedes ethical conduct of a truly Christian character.

Paul reminds his Galatian brethren that the "fruit of the Spirit is love, joy, peace, patience, kindness, goodness, faithfulness, gentleness, self-control; against such there is no law. And those who belong to Christ Jesus have crucified the flesh with its passions and desires. If we live by the Spirit, let us also walk by the Spirit" (Gal. 5:22-25, RSV). Paul depicts Christ as one who took the form of a servant, who humbled himself and became obedient unto death, "even death on a cross" (Phil. 2:2-8, RSV). He enjoins the Christians of Philippi to "have this mind" in themselves, as it was also the mind of Christ.

In the dedication of ourselves to the will of God, in incorporating into our conduct, both personal and social, those qualities which stem from the character of God and which were exemplified in the life of Christ, in embracing the cross of daily service to God and to our fellow human beings, in loving one another as Christ loved us and gave himself for us, we are to embrace Christ's example and to "follow in his steps" (1 Pet. 2:21, RSV).

In following Christ, the Christian can spurn the question of whether he is in the process of achieving a self-centered, self-concerned "sinless perfection." His vision is concentrated on a far larger issue; his love is far deeper and more comprehensive in its sweep. He is constrained, not by a moralistic compulsion, but by the love of Christ.

This love is the "rule" of his faith and conduct, but it is the rule not of a heteronomously imposed law but of a law written by the Holy Spirit in his heart.

The Christian ethical imperative is world-affirming in the best sense. It is not "conformed to this world" in the sense that it embraces the world's values, standards, and mores as its own. To do this is to deny the Christian witness, not to practice it. It *is* world-affirming in that it is directed to the neighbor in the world, in order to serve the neighbor's true good by communicating the love of God to him— indeed, by *being* the love of God to him.

The doctrine of sanctification should remind us that the Christian faith is ethical to the core, because it worships a God whose character is ethical, and because the revelation which it has received of this God through Jesus Christ is the ground and inspiration of ethical conduct. No conduct is truly ethical, in a Christian sense, which is not consonant with the character of God as this character has been made manifest in Christ.

It is, however, naive and simplistic to think that, once we have been grasped by the grace of God in a faith experience, personal and communal behavior becomes, for Christians, automatically plain and clear. A part of sanctification is a Christian dedication to the task of wrestling, sometimes mightily, with ethical issues and decisions. It is a dedication to viewing both personal and social issues in the light of an informed intelligence. It is a hospitality to receive light from any source whatever. It is willingness to listen to and to learn from the "children of darkness" when, as it many times happens, they turn out to be wiser on specific issues than the "children of light" (Luke 16:8). It is dedication to the task of living with the best that one knows in the midst of ambiguities when clear light is not immediately given. It is a willingness to experiment responsibly by taking one's place at "the moving edges of change," and thus to have the courage to take the risk of being wrong. It is sitting by the world's bedside during all its desperate illnesses, pouring balm into the world's wounds, standing up to the hurricanes of the world's power, and refusing to be intimidated either by its glamorous allurements or by its nightmarish terror. It is a readiness to throw the stubborn ounces of one's weight onto the scales of right despite the myriad tons of opposition that make the situation seem hopeless. It is seeing each task, each day, and all tasks and all days, in the light of a central Christian vision which discerns God working in redeeming love at the heart of the world, and joining him in that work.

Sanctification is as radically social and communal in its meaning as it is individual and personal. Except for Christ, the "holy one of God," no individual in the New Testament is ever called "holy." "Holy people or saints," says Shirley Guthrie, "are found only in the plural, in the 'communion of the saints.' In other words, the gift of the Holy Spirit, who enables people to be holy people, is given in and with the *church.*"[18]

Sanctification and Eschatology

Sanctification is not completed in this life. What we have received here and now in our salvation is the seal of the Holy Spirit. "In him [Christ] you also, who have heard the word of truth, the gospel of your salvation, and have believed in him, were sealed with the promised Holy Spirit, which is the guarantee of our inheritance until we acquire possession of it, to the praise of his glory" (Eph. 1:13-14, RSV). *Seal,* a property word, signifies our ownership by the Holy Spirit. But more than this the Holy Spirit comes to us as the "guarantee," the earnest, the foretaste, the first installment, of the inheritance which will be given us in the future. Thus the Holy Spirit is the part of the age to come which is already present, the foretaste and guarantee of the blessedness which God has in store for us. Through him, as we live now in the world, we also stand, proleptically, at the *end* of the world.

This experience of the Christian in living at the overlap of the age to come with the present age, gives a paradoxical character to the Christian life. Here, as Cullmann says, the "ought" rests upon the "is":

The imperative is firmly anchored in the indicative. We are holy; this means that we should sanctify ourselves. We have received the Spirit; this means that we should "walk in the Spirit." In Christ we already have redemption from the power of sin; this means that now as never before we must battle against sin. This apparently contradictory joining of the imperative and indicative is nothing else than the application to ethics of the complexity, here shown in different ways, of the present situation in redemptive

---

[18]Guthrie, *Christian Doctrine,* p. 348.

history. We are dealing with the working out of what we have called the "tension between already fulfilled and not yet fulfilled."[19]

Sanctification, marked by struggle and incompleteness, awaits the consummation of God's kingdom, in which we shall be conformed to the image of God's Son, and in which sin, sorrow, and death will be no more. The victory of Christ over the powers of evil, which Christ accomplished at the cross (Col. 2:15), will then be made visible in a fullness of manifestation.

The present race, attended by "dust and heat," envisions the distant goal. So the believer does not lose heart. The spirit of the struggle—with its strain, zeal, and exultation—is enunciated powerfully by the apostle Paul:

> How changed are my ambitions! Now I long to know Christ and the power shown by His resurrection: now I long to share His sufferings, even to die as He died, so that I may perhaps attain as he did, the resurrection from the dead. Yet, my brothers, I do not consider myself to have "arrived," spiritually, nor do I consider myself already perfect. But I keep going on, grasping ever more firmly that purpose for which Christ Jesus grasped me. My brothers, I do not consider myself to have fully grasped it even now. But I do concentrate on this: I leave the past behind and with hands outstretched to whatever lies ahead I go straight for the goal—my reward the honour of my calling by God in Christ Jesus (Phil. 3:10-14, J. B. Phillips' translation).

Sanctification and Atonement

The link between sanctification and atonement is indissoluble. The atoning life which the Christian lives is based on the Atonement which Christ has made for us. Always we carry in the body "the death of Jesus, so that the life of Jesus may also be manifested in our bodies. For while we live we are always being given up to death for Jesus' sake, so that the life of Jesus may be manifested in our mortal flesh" (2 Cor. 4:10-11, RSV).

---

[19]Oscar Cullmann, *Christ and Time*, Floyd V. Filson, trans. (Philadelphia: The Westminster Press, 1950), p. 224.

The Christian is profoundly involved in Christ's death and resurrection. The old self has been crucified with Christ. The new self has participated in the resurrection of the Lord, and now lives with him in that "newness of life" which communion and fellowship with him gives. The cross and resurrection are not just events that happened to Jesus two thousand years ago; they are repeated constantly within our own lives; they are indigenous to the life of the church. Constantly, the Christian must put off the old man, which was taken to the cross by Christ, and put on the new man, who reflects the image of Christ, as Christ reflects the image of God. As Paul saw, the Christian must share Christ's sufferings, and become like him in Christ's death, if he is to know the power of Christ's resurrection.

A brief Pauline statement captures the essence of sanctification: "You are not your own. You were bought with a price" (1 Cor. 6:19-20, RSV). We have been bought with the price of Christ's own life, so that, ever after, we belong to God through him.

In a magnificent passage, John Calvin exposes the heart of what sanctification means:

> This is a very important consideration that we are consecrated and dedicated to God that we may not hereafter think, speak, meditate, or do anything but with a view to his glory, for that which is sacred cannot without great injustice toward Him be applied to unholy uses. If we are not our own but the Lord's, it is manifest both what error we must avoid and to what end all the actions of our lives are to be dedicated. We are not our own. Therefore, neither our reason nor our will should predominate in our deliberations and actions. We are not our own. Therefore, let us not propose it as our end to seek what may be expedient for us according to the flesh. We are not our own. Therefore, let us as far as possible forget ourselves and all things that are ours.
>
> On the contrary, we are God's. To Him, therefore, let us live and die. We are God's. Toward Him, therefore, as our only legitimate end let every part of our lives be directed. Oh, how great a proficiency has that man made who having been taught that he is not his own, has taken the sovereignty and

government from his own reason to surrender it to God.[20]

The Christian disciple is aware that the power for living which comes to him through the grace of God in Christ is not of his own deserving or doing, but is dependent upon the Holy Spirit, "the present tense of God," the indwelling God, who works to make the love of God a present and continuing power within us. The Holy Spirit works, in us who believe, the immeasurable greatness of God's power, "according to the working of his great might which he accomplished in Christ when he raised him from the dead and made him to sit at his right hand in the heavenly places" (Eph. 1:19-20, RSV).

---

[20]John Calvin, *Institutes of the Christian Religion*, 3.7.1; cited in Wilhelm Pauck, *The Heritage of the Reformation* (The Free Press of Glencoe, Inc., 1961), p. 193.

Chapter 6

Christ the Deliverer

In this chapter we shall examine three biblical themes pertaining to God's conflict with, and triumph over, the forces of evil which have challenged his saving activity. These themes are: redemption, ransom, and victory. The victory motif will receive our principal attention, not only because of its importance, but also because in recent years it has reemerged from a long period of relative obscurity.

Redemption and Ransom

The words *redemption* and *ransom* come from the same root. A *ransom* in the Old Testament sense is a sum used to free a prisoner of war. On the other hand, *redemption* is a term used to describe the liberation of a purchased slave. Redemption is the broader term.

> Originally "redemption" in biblical usage has behind it the particular and definite act of paying a sum of money, or its equivalent, for the restoration of property which has been lost or stolen. Thus "redemption" is related to buying back, setting free, paying a ransom price, deliverance (cf. Ex. 21:30; Lev. 25-27; Job 33:24; Mark 10:45; I Cor. 6:20; 7:23; I Peter 1:18-19). The suggestion of a financial transaction is

still retained in our secular vocabulary when we speak, for example, of the "redemption" of a corporation bond.[1]

The usage of the terms in both Old and New Testaments is demonstrably widened beyond the meanings cited above. Meanings which typically inform redemption and ransom in the biblical writings are, however, deliverance from bondage and the costliness of this deliverance.

In the Old Testament, the central focus of the redemptive activity of God in the history of Israel was the deliverance of his people from the bondage of Egypt. God was the Savior and mighty Deliverer of his people. Through many "dangers, toils, and snares" he led the children of Israel out of their affliction into a life of challenge and freedom.

The deliverance from Egypt was to the people of Israel a kind of polar star throughout their subsequent history. Many times they betrayed the covenant relationship between themselves and God, but always he remained faithful. When they were caught in the throes of betrayal and affliction, God again and again intervened on their behalf to rescue them and to guide them into a new life. Isaiah eloquently expressed the faith that the God who had redeemed in the past would remain Israel's redeemer:

> Break forth together into singing, you waste places of Jerusalem; for the Lord has comforted his people, he has redeemed Jerusalem. The Lord has bared his holy arm before the eyes of all the nations; and all the ends of the earth shall see the salvation of our God (Isa. 52:9-10, RSV).

A related emphasis in Hebrew thought was expressed in some of the later writings of the Old Testament and in the Hebrew literature of the two centuries immediately prior to the beginning of the Christian era. This emphasis derived from the apocalyptic tradition, whose advocates despaired of any partial restoration of the nation's fortunes through the return of the exiles from captivity. While the visions of the apocalypticists vary a great deal, a common feature concerns the coming of a messianic figure who will effect, on God's behalf, a final restoration. He will deliver his people from their foreign oppressors and will set up a righteous reign, not only over Israel, but also over the

---

[1]Halverson, ed., *Handbook of Christian Theology*, p. 296.

other nations of the world. Sometimes the evil powers which tyrannize mankind are compressed into a single figure, called Satan, or Beliar, or the Dragon. This evil sovereign, with his cohorts, will be defeated by the Messiah, and his captives set free.

While there is no explicit reference in the Old Testament to the sufferings of the Messiah*, there are repeated references to the sufferings of God's people. A logical inference, therefore, is that the Messiah would be involved in the sufferings of those whom he redeemed. These sufferings which they would endure together would be preliminary to the final overthrow of God's adversary, and the final establishment of God's righteous reign.

Despite the widely differing variations of interpretation, one pattern of imagery occupied a position of supremacy among Old Testament writers: the imagery of the exodus from bondage of the people of God. Israel had been formed into a nation when God led her out of slavery from Egypt, so that the Exodus, celebrated annually at the Passover, became the prototype of messianic deliverance. The messianic deliverer of the future would share the woes of his people as he led them to their divinely appointed destiny.[2]

The strong redemptive themes of the Hebrew people are continued in the Christian heritage. In the New Testament, however, the liberation of man from the powers of evil is accomplished by Christ in his redemptive sacrifice.

A prominent image of God's redemptive action in Christ is associated with the payment of a ransom. Jesus said, "The Son of Man came not to be served but to serve, and to give his life as a ransom [*lutron*] for many" (Matt. 20:28; Mark 10:45, RSV). In this saying there is an echo of the fourth Servant song (Isa. 53:11), which asserts that through his sufferings the righteous Servant will justify many. The ransom in this case means a price which is paid in exchange for deliverance. A related Old Testament notion is that of the *go'el* or bondsman, a role which God filled in his relationship to Israel (see Gen. 48:16; Ex. 6:6). In 1 Corinthians 6:20 Paul expresses the ransom idea when he says, "You were bought with a price"(RSV).

---

*See the section on "The Servant and the Messiah" in chapter 8 for a discussion of the relationship between the Suffering Servant and the Messiah.

[2]Cf. Dillistone, *The Christian Understanding of Atonement*, pp. 81-85.

Thenceforth, then, the redeemed belong no more to themselves, but to God. A similar thought is advanced in 1 Peter 1:18-19: "You know that you were ransomed from the futile ways inherited from your fathers, not with perishable things such as silver or gold, but with the precious blood of Christ" (RSV).

The ransom which Christ pays liberates from sin (Rom. 3:9; 7:23; 6:18-22). It releases humanity from bondage to the law, which bondage Paul ascribes to the power of sin (Rom. 7:1-6). It frees from slavery to the devil and to death (Col. 1:13; 2:14; 2 Tim. 1:10).

Sometimes in the history of Christian scholarship the idea of Christ's giving his life as a ransom has been interpreted most unfortunately. The payment of a ransom by Christ interested early Christian thinkers in the following intriguing question: To *whom* was the ransom paid? Some of the early Church Fathers replied that the ransom was paid to the devil. Origen (d. 245), for example, asked, "But to whom did He give His soul as a ransom for man? Certainly not to God: why not to the devil? For he had possession of us until there should be given to him the ransom for us, the soul of Jesus."[3]

Theologians who subscribed to this opinion argued that, through man's willing fall into sin, the devil had acquired certain rights over mankind. God redeemed man by paying to the devil the agreed-upon price of Christ's blood. Besides Origen, this view, with certain variations of treatment, was advocated by such outstanding scholars as Gregory of Nyssa and Jerome. It was rejected, however, by most of the Fathers, who would not concede that Christ's blood would be offered by the holy God to his evil adversary.

Another line of argument saw man's escape from the domination of the devil by reason of the devil's overreaching himself in bringing about the death of Jesus. When man sinned, it was thought, the devil acquired certain limited claims upon him. But when the devil attacked the Son of God, who was without sin, he forfeited these claims and overstepped the limits of his competence. God consequently liberated man from the devil's power.

In pursuit of this line of reasoning, there arose the "fishhook" and "mousetrap" theories, which seem bizarre to the modern mind. Some

---

[3]Cited in R. S. Franks, *The Work of Christ* (London, New York: Thomas Nelson and Sons Ltd., 1962), p. 40.

of the Fathers (as, for example, Rufinus of Aquileia), compared the devil to a fish which was attracted by the bait of Christ's humanity. Eagerly seizing this prize, he found himself ensnared on the hook of Christ's divinity. Even the great Augustine employed the "mousetrap" metaphor: "What," Augustine asked, "did our redeemer do to our captor? As our price, He held out His cross as a mousetrap and set as bait upon it His own blood."[4]

Theologians who employed this line of argument, however, did not concede that God paid a ransom to the devil. The devil was a usurper of power over man, not a legitimate possessor of it.

Perhaps the view that the giving of Christ's life was in a sense the payment of a ransom *to God* did not receive clear statement until Anselm (1093-1109). In Anselm's view, man by his sin acquires an infinite debt to God, for which God demands "satisfaction." Only Christ, the God-man, can pay the debt, and thus render to God the satisfaction which is due. Christ embraces his own death as a willing offering to the Father for the sins of man, and thus cancels man's indebtedness and achieves the full payment of God's required price.

To interpret the giving of Christ's life as a ransom, however, does not necessarily entail the consequence that the life of Christ was forfeited as a ransom offering either to the devil or to God. In line with the sacrifice of the Suffering Servant of Isaiah 53, we need not ask to whom the ransom was paid. The ransom metaphor was intended to show the *costliness* of our redemption. Christ's death was an act by means of which mankind is delivered from sin and from the ruin which sin brings in its train.[5]

God owes the devil nothing. The pretentious claims that this sinister figure exercises over human beings are not legitimate claims. He is a cheat, a usurper, an outlaw, a robber. This can be said whether the devil is considered to be a personal being or a personification of evil.

As far as the notion is concerned that God receives the blood of Christ as a ransom price for the redemption of human beings, great care must be exerted to exclude the thought that the Father exacts the

---

[4]Cited in Culpepper, *Interpreting the Atonement*, p. 77.

[5]A. R. Vidler, ed., *Soundings* (Cambridge: Cambridge University Press, 1963), p. 39.

blood of his Son as a payment for the price of our sins. The moral implications concerning the character of God that derive from this perspective on the atonement are simply intolerable. Whatever else Christ has taught us, we have learned from him that God is a "Christian" God. What we can say, and all we need to say, was well stated by James Denney:

> Whatever be the power which holds him, man is held in bondage somehow: it may be bondage to sin, or to death, or to demons, or to the devil, but he is indubitably a slave. The result of Christ's work, and especially of His Passion and death, is that man is set free, and he realises, as he looks at the cross, what his emancipation has cost. It has cost the death of the Son of God, who on the cross gave Himself a ransom for him.[6]

We need not allow the quaint or even repulsive thought forms of devout people of olden days to prevent our appreciating the acuteness of their insight. This insight was that God has given us Christ to redeem us from the Evil One, and to reclaim us as his own. By liberating and reclaiming us through Christ, he wins us back to that loving relationship to himself which has been his own yearning desire. The costliness of this reclamation has been perceptively expressed by Frank Stagg:

> Jesus *paid* to liberate us from our sin. Of course he paid no one, neither the Father nor the devil. He simply paid. He saved us at the cost of his own life. He paid in the humiliation of the Incarnation, in life and in death, in submitting to rejection, betrayal, and murder. The taunt at Golgotha, "He saved others, himself he cannot save" (Matt. 27:42), had far more meaning than his tormentors knew.[7]

Victory—Christ the Conqueror

The victory theme as a mode of expressing the redemptive work of God in Christ has received renewed interest and emphasis during the last fifty years. While this renewed interest was probably derived from

---

[6]James Denney, *The Christian Doctrine of Reconciliation* (New York: George H. Doran Company, 1918), p. 31.

[7]Stagg, *New Testament Theology*, p. 140.

an historical era of international tragedy marked by "wars and rumors of wars," an arresting book by Bishop Gustaf Aulén of Sweden in 1931 served to concentrate attention upon what Aulén called the "classic" theory of atonement. The book was called *Christus Victor*, and it won attention at a time when the Nazi threat was looming on the European horizon. It became apparent once again that in modern times also people might suffer martyrdom for their faith in God. When the World Council of Christian Youth met in Amsterdam in 1939, the theme was "Christus Victor."

Aulén argued that the victory theme had been the dominant interpretation of the Atonement for the first nine hundred years of Christian history, including the New Testament era itself. Two principal rival interpretations, Aulén acknowledged, were the "Latin" type, and the "ethical" type. The Latin theory received its most consummate formulation in Anselm (1033-1109), who understood atonement in a legalistic sense. Anselm's great contemporary, Peter Abelard (1079-1142), became the most famous proponent of the ethical type of understanding. He thought of redemption as something effected within man in response to the demonstration of God's love, powerfully enacted by Christ on his cross.

The "classic" or "dramatic" theme, Aulén believed, had been distorted by such interpretations as those which conceived Christ's death to have been a ransom paid to the devil, by "fishhook" and "mousetrap" theories, and so forth. The victory note, however, remained prominent particularly in popular Christian piety, until it was forced from the center of the stage by Anselm. Even then, it remained a subdominant note in the life of the church, and was reasserted in the strongest terms by Martin Luther.

The Christian world is much indebted to Bishop Aulén for calling attention to the prominence of the victory theme in the New Testament. But, while this theme is *prominent* in the New Testament, it is by no means certain that it is a *dominant* interpretation there. Atonement in the New Testament is looked at through many figures of speech, of which this is one. Their several values are best preserved when they are seen as corroborative of and supplementary to, rather than exclusive of, each other.[8]

---

[8]Cf. Culpepper, *Interpreting the Atonement*, pp. 120-21.

Aulén sees in the New Testament a warfare between God and Satan for the possession of mankind. There is thus a dualism in the New Testament itself, in which the forces of God are arrayed unrelentingly against the forces of Satan. This dualism, however, is a provisional, not an ultimate, dualism. The concept of ultimate dualism envisions God and Satan, supreme and sovereign in their own spheres, as eternally hostile towards each other and engaged in battle forever.

In a provisional dualism, God defeats Satan in the incarnation and particularly in the Atonement. God still battles against the powers of evil, yet at the same time he uses them as executants of his will against sin. The devil, sin, and death are evils, but God has set the limits of their operation. In effect, God has said to them, "Thus far shalt thou go and no farther." Evil is not good, of course, but it is held within the limits of good. It is made to serve the ultimate ends of good. Defeated in principle at the cross, evil and its hosts will be defeated finally and utterly by a sovereign God at the end of time.

While Aulén's thesis is stated pointedly, and with constant reference to Scripture and history, the central meaning of the victory theme is stated more succinctly by O. C. Quick:

> God's love by the cross and resurrection of Christ has won a great and final victory over all the powers of evil; these powers have been deprived of their dominion over man, and man by faith in Christ is henceforth established in a new and triumphant life of communion with God; even in this world "he tastes the powers of the world to come."[9]

Conflict and Conquest. In the gospels, the fight of Jesus against the forces of evil is a strong element in the interpretation of his life and ministry. Jesus is presented as one who took upon himself to the fullest extent the risk and actuality of battle against wrong. His acceptance of the conditions of human nature, in which he was involved as were all other men; his acceptance of a particular historical and cultural setting for his life; his acceptance of temptations and contested decisions—all of these and other factors brought him into a battle with the evils that flesh is heir to.

Jesus was "born of woman," "born under the law." He attacked, at

---

[9]Oliver Chase Quick, *Doctrines of the Creed* (London: Nisbet and Company, Ltd., 1938), pp. 224-25.

certain points, the religious establishment; he set aside time-honored authorities; he championed the cause of the weak against the strong, of "sinners" against the "righteous." The pious, the religious leaders, and the theologians among his own countrymen accused him and sought to accomplish his downfall. He was betrayed by one of his own disciples. His other disciples became cowards in the face of danger. A public with whom he had been popular turned against him. A Roman judge condemned him. Barabbas, a seditionist, and a third-rate one at that, was preferred to him by his own countrymen.

The New Testament, however, sees the conflict in which Jesus was engaged on a far larger scale than that of a mere power struggle between him and certain of his human contemporaries. This struggle is seen also as a battle between Christ and cosmic "powers." At the beginning of his public ministry he was driven into the desert to face the temptations of the devil concerning the nature of his messianic mission. He confronted and rejected the temptation to be a political messiah. He spurned the temptation to seize the reins of power over the kingdoms of the world. In the course of his ministry he fought and overcame demons, and he related this conflict to the coming of the kingdom of God: "But if I with the finger of God cast out devils, no doubt the kingdom of God is come upon you" (Luke 11:20, KJV). When the Pharisees charged that he cast out devils in the power of the prince of devils, he left no doubt in his reply concerning his relentless opposition to the prince of darkness: "When a strong man, fully armed, guards his own palace, his goods are in peace; but when one stronger than he assails him and overcomes him, he takes away his armor in which he trusted, and divides his spoil" (Luke 11:21-22, RSV).

Jesus' power over demons was considered by the early church to be a clear sign of his advancing conquest of Satan himself: "The seventy returned with joy, saying, 'Lord, even the demons are subject unto us in your name!' And he said to them, 'I saw Satan fall like lightning from heaven' " (Luke 10:17, RSV). John states the issue here: "The reason the Son of God appeared was to destroy the works of the devil" (1 John 3:8, RSV).

During the first three centuries of its existence, the triumph of the church over demons was such a conspicuous feature of the church's life that the distinguished historian, Adolph Harnack, penned a memorable paragraph on the subject:

It was as exorcizers that Christians went out into the great world, and exorcism formed one very powerful method of their mission and propaganda. It was a question not simply of exorcizing and vanquishing the demons that dwelt in individuals, but also of purifying all public life from them. For the age was ruled by the black one and his hordes . . .; it 'lieth in the evil one,'. . . Nor was this mere theory; it was a most vital conception of existence. The whole world and the circumambient atmosphere were filled with devils; not merely idolatry, but every phase and form of life was ruled by them. They sat on thrones, they hovered around cradles. The earth was literally a hell, though it continued to be a creation of God. To encounter this hell and all its devils, Christians had command of weapons that were invincible.[10]

Jesus' miracle-working power included not only the exorcism of demons. The forces of nature also were subject to him, as demonstrated in his stilling of the storm. Death was under his mastery, as shown in the raising of Jairus's daughter, and in the bringing of Lazarus back from the dead. He worked miracles of healing. The lame, the blind, the lepers, the ill, and the demented were cured by his healing word or touch. He alleviated suffering. He granted pardon. A particularly revealing story is the healing of the paralytic (Mark 2), in which Jesus showed that his power to heal was the same as his power to forgive sins.

Each miracle of healing was not only a compassionate act of grace, but also was a demonstration of the power of God over the evils of sin, disease, and death. Each incident was a confrontation between the power of cosmic forces of good and evil, and a living manifestation on the part of Jesus that in his own hands was the power of God to defeat the forces of evil and to bring in the healing reign of God's kingdom. A passage by Alan Richardson is worth quoting in full:

He was not concerned to impress His contemporaries with His marvelous power; but rather that He asked them by the same token to believe that He had authority upon earth to forgive sins. He not merely opened the eyes of the blind men,

---

[10]Cited in Alan Richardson, *Miracle Stories of the Gospels* (London: S.C.M. Press, 1941), p. 69.

but claimed by that sign the power to make men see the truth of God. He not merely healed the lepers, the diseased and the impotent, but demonstrated thereby His ability to break the power of sin and to enable men to fulfill the works of the Law. He not merely cast out demons, but saw in His victory over them the earnest of His triumph over the powers of evil, the binding of the Strong Man. He not merely fed hungry men in the desert, but claimed by that sign to be the dispenser of spiritual food by which men's souls are nourished upon their pilgrimage through a barren land. He not merely commanded the storm and trod upon the waves of the sea, but wished His disciples to see thereby in Him the restrainer alike of the forces of nature and of the madness of the people. And, finally, He not merely raised a child or a man from the dead, but claimed in doing so to be the resurrection and the life.[11]

With other people of his time, the apostle Paul shared a belief in the existence of supernatural evil beings which were too strong for human beings to combat in their own strength, and which could be mastered by God alone. He speaks of a constellation of hostile forces that he describes as "principalities," "powers," "thrones," and "dominions," all of which rule in "this present evil age" (Gal. 1:4).

Again and again, Paul speaks of sin and death together. Sin occupies the chief place among the powers which have enslaved humanity. Death, "the last enemy to be destroyed" (1 Cor. 15:26, RSV), is organically connected with sin. To be under the bondage of sin is also to be under the bondage of death. When Christ frees us from the dominion of sin, he delivers us also from the domination of death (Rom. 5:18).

Among the powers which have the capability of enslaving us, Paul believed, is the law. In one of its aspects, the law is a hostile power. Paul can say, on the one hand, that the law is "holy and just and good" (Rom. 7:12, RSV), and, on the other hand, that "the sting of death is sin, and the power of sin is the law" (1 Cor. 15:56, RSV). Again, he says, "For all who rely on the works of the law are under a curse" (Gal. 3:10, RSV).

---

[11] Ibid., pp. 131-32.

Although Paul speaks with relative infrequency about the devil, it is evident that to him Satan presides over the principalities and powers of evil. The purpose of Christ's coming into the world is to deliver us from the tyranny of the evils which collaborate with the devil in a veritable kingdom of evil.

Colossians 2:13-15 is a dramatic depiction of the battle-victory theme. In the cross, Paul writes, God "disarmed the principalities and powers and made a public example of them, triumphing over them in him" (v. 15, RSV). In this passage, Christ is likened to a great conqueror who made a victorious conquest of the forces of evil. He drags these evil powers as captives behind his chariot, as he makes a triumphal procession down the streets of (perhaps) his capital city. Paul wrote, "He has delivered us from the dominion of darkness and transferred us to the kingdom of his beloved Son, in whom we have redemption, the forgiveness of sins" (Col. 1:13-14, RSV).

Another Pauline passage states the great theme of divine victory as magnificently as any passage in the Bible:

> Who shall separate us from the love of Christ? Shall tribulation, or distress, or persecution, or famine, or nakedness, or peril, or sword? . . . No, in all these things we are more than conquerors through him who loved us. For I am sure that neither death, nor life, nor angels, nor principalities, nor things present, nor things to come, nor powers, nor height, nor depth, nor anything else in all creation, will be able to separate us from the love of God in Christ Jesus our Lord (Rom. 8:35, 37-38, RSV).

Although the theme of conflict and conquest is found in other parts of the New Testament besides the gospels and the Pauline writings, we have space here only to notice this theme further as it is elaborated in the book of Revelation. This writing, so highly figurative in the expression of its message, carries unmistakably the theme of God's battle against the forces of evil and of his eventual triumph. At the beginning of the writer's depiction of this theme, the risen and glorified Son of man appears, armed with a two-edged sword, and triumphant over Hades and death. Near the end of the book the Son of man appears again, riding at the head of his armies, and going forth to subdue the kingdoms of this world, and to destroy his enemies.

The Son of man is a conquering redeemer, who nevertheless shares the burdens and afflictions of his people. He is both a victor and a victim. The victorious Son of man makes his appearance in heaven as the Lamb of God. Although once slain, the Lamb is now the recipient of veneration and adoration by the redeemed and, indeed, of the whole creation: "And I heard every creature in heaven and on earth and under the earth and in the sea, and all therein, saying, 'To him who sits upon the throne and to the Lamb be blessing and honor and glory and might for ever and ever!' " (Rev. 5:13-14, RSV). The Lamb is adored, not just because he is a conquerer, but because he has triumphed over sin and death at the price of his own blood, at the cost of his own life. He has thus redeemed those who were held in servitude by these evil powers.

In the Apocalypse also appears the enemy of the Lamb, the Dragon, "that ancient serpent, who is called the Devil and Satan, the deceiver of the whole world" (Rev. 12:9, RSV). In the twelfth chapter, Satan stands ready to devour the child of the woman whose seed is to bruise his head, and who is destined to "rule the nations with a rod of iron." But when the child is born he is caught up to "God and to his throne," and Satan is robbed of his intended prey.

The Dragon, defeated finally at the ascension of the Messiah, is cast out of heaven with his angels. He renews upon earth his attacks against the rest of the woman's seed. Here too he is defeated, this time by the martyred Church which fights in the power of the Lamb who was slain. To celebrate the victory of a new and greater exodus, "they sing the song of Moses, the servant of God, and the song of the Lamb" (Rev. 15:3, RSV). Thus, the Lion of the tribe of Judah (Rev. 5:5) is also the Lamb, "and the Lamb will conquer them, for he is Lord of lords and King of kings" (Rev. 17:14, RSV).

The Character of Christ's Victory. The New Testament proclaims that God turned the cross of Christ into the instrument of the world's salvation. We do not isolate the cross from Christ's life, teaching, and ministry, but we see in the cross both the summit and the summary of what he was and did. The uniqueness of the cross lies not in the crucifixion as an instrument of torture and death, but in the identity of the Person who died upon it.

We should remark parenthetically that it was in the nature of Hebrew thinking not to envisage Christ's relation to God in metaphysical terms. Jewish Christians did not ask, "Is this person, in the fullest sense, the very being of God manifest in human form?" Nor did they ask, "How *much* of God is in him?" They did not ask, "Did he do this in his divine nature, and this in his human nature?" These were questions which emanated largely from the Gentile world.

When they thought of Jesus as the Messiah, Jewish Christians thought in terms of functional relationships. To them the *work* of Christ was the *work* of God. The emphasis was upon God's *action* in the ministry, death, and resurrection of Jesus. God *acted* in Christ. What impresses us as being the basis of the *kerygma* of the early church, says Friedrich Gogarten, is "not the portrait of the visible and individual personality of Jesus, but the figure of a man endowed with the divine power which rules the world."[12]

That God had acted in his true character in Christ was, to the New Testament writers, demonstrated by the triumphant events of the cross, the resurrection, the ascension, and the day of Pentecost. They believed that through the power of the Holy Spirit "God has made him both Lord and Christ, this Jesus whom you crucified" (Acts 2:36, RSV). The Christian life, they came to understand, was an experience of the life of Christ, crucified and risen. In the place of the hate and rejection which Jesus had experienced, and which they had gone through in his fellowship, they desired to return the love and obedience which they had seen in him, manifested supremely in the cross.[13]

The conflict which marked the life of Jesus, says Bishop Lightfoot, was, when seen in the light of faith, but a prelude to God's victory in Christ:

> Christ took upon himself our human nature with all its temptations (Heb. 4:15). The powers of evil gathered about him. Again and again they assailed him; but each fresh assault ended in a new defeat. . . . Then the last hour came. This was the great crisis of all, when "the power of darkness" made itself felt (Luke 22:53), when the prince of this world asserted his tyranny (John 12:30). The final act in the conflict began with the agony of Gethsemane; it ended with the Cross of Calvary. The victory was complete. The enemy of man was defeated. The powers of evil . . . were cast aside

---

[12]Friedrich Gogarten, *Christ the Crisis* (Richmond: John Knox Press, 1967), p. 54.

[13]Edith Lorna Kendall, *A Living Sacrifice* (London: S.C.M. Press, 1960), p. 29.

for ever. And the victory of mankind is involved in the victory of Christ.[14]

In assessing the victory of Christ over the forces of evil, the modern mind asks, inevitably, whether the demonic powers which were so real to Jesus and the early church actually have an ontological existence. Can disease or sin be attributed to demon possession? Modern man, who lives in the setting of Western civilization, has great difficulty in accepting the belief that these powers are personal entities.

Bishop Stephen Neill, speaking from a background of long experience as a missionary in technically less-advanced countries, calls attention to the fact that this problem cannot be discountenanced as easily as secular-minded Westerners would like. No missionary, he says, who has lived close to the people in India would dare contend that the spirit world is merely a realm of the imagination. Neill's observations on this point are both intriguing and incisive:

> In the Gospels Jesus is presented primarily as the conqueror of demons. He is a great many other things besides that; but there is no doubt at all, in much of the early preaching of the Gospel in New Testament times and after New Testament times, Jesus is proclaimed as the conqueror of demons. And that to a large extent is the way in which we ought to present Him today in the parts of the world inhabited by these simpler peoples who are still under the tyranny of evil spirits. It is no good telling them that the evil spirits don't exist; they know better. . . . But what these people have to learn is that whatever wicked spirits there may be in air and forest and stream and wilderness, Christ has conquered them all; He has triumphed over them, making them a spoil; and for those who trust in Him there is no more dominion or domination of the spirits.[15]

In many of the younger churches, Bishop Neill says, one of the gravest problems is the coexistence in the mind of the individual believer of a genuine, though simple belief in Christ, and at the same time a dread of the continuing power of evil spirits. The problem, he

---

[14]Cited in Richardson, ed., *A Theological Word Book of the Bible*, p. 274.

[15]Stephen Neill, *The Cross in the Church* (London: Independent Press, 1957), p. 46.

says, is to get Christians to see clearly that "a Christian can have no dealings whatsoever with the underworld of darkness. A Christian belongs to Christ, and Christ is the conqueror; and you cannot dwell simultaneously in the world of light and the world of darkness."[16]

With respect to other "powers," the mere disinclination to think of them in personal terms does not detract from our apprehension of their dread reality. Sin, death, and suffering are fearful "powers," the conquest of which Christ has accomplished in the power of God.

A temptation exists, however, to think of God's victory over the powers of evil in terms of a divine triumphalism which really serves to secularize the Christian note of victory. Christ defeats evil because he is the agent of God's power against the hosts of wickedness. This emphasis is likely to put us back into the "power game," in which we think of God's victory in terms of a preponderance of forces, a superior strategy, and an overwhelming weaponry. We are in danger of believing, in other words, that God uses the same kind of power as that possessed by his enemies, but that he wins because he has more of it and uses it to better advantage.

Here it is helpful to remember the claim of Gustaf Aulén that there is no statement which we can make about God, as Christians, that is not ultimately a judgment about his love.[17] If we keep this thought in our minds, it will qualify immeasurably our understanding of God's power and the nature of his triumph.

We must walk a ridge between two chasms—between thinking of God's power as cold, callous, and impersonal, on one hand, and thinking of his love as the largesse of a sentimentalized indulgence on the other. God's power is the power of the Creator, which not only brings into being, but also sustains and upholds the created order. The justice and wrath of God set limits to any human rebellion, however powerful, and the cosmic "powers," whatever the intensity of their defiance, are totally unable to dislodge him from his throne.

The justice and wrath of God show that there are limits beyond which a defiance of God cannot go, either on the part of individuals or on the part, indeed, of nations and civilizations. But, as Reinhold Niebuhr has well said, justice and wrath cannot reach the heart of the

---

[16]Ibid., p. 47.

[17]Aulén, *The Faith of the Christian Church*, p. 131.

offender: "There can be no repentance if love does not shine through justice. It shines through whenever it becomes apparent that the executor of judgment suffers willingly, as guiltless sufferer, with the guilty victim of punishment."[18] The "weakness" of God's love—which does not strike back at the offender and which takes upon itself the burdens and offences of the guilty into God's own heart—is the power of God which is effective unto salvation. "The crux of the cross," says Niebuhr, "is its revelation of the fact that the final power of God over man is derived from the self-imposed weakness of his love. This self-imposed weakness does not derogate from the majesty of God. His mercy is the final dimension of his majesty."[19]

The kingdom of God is not to be identified with the kingdoms of this world; the peace of God is not the peace of this world order; and the power of God is not the power of the world's dynamic forces. God's power has an ultimacy which transcends them, a character which is not akin to them, and which is, indeed, beyond their comprehension; but it has, everywhere and forever, a vital relevance to them. The victorious, redeeming power of God is the power of love, mercy, forgiveness, and service.

In his Son, God exposes himself to the full consequences of sin—its hatred, brutality, and destructive power—and he turns the cross, the instrument and symbol of man's hatred and estrangement, into the instrument of our redemption. All of the pious hypocrises, the tainted goodness, as well as the terror of the mailed fist, are exposed at the cross. On the other hand, as Emil Brunner reminds us, it is supremely at the cross that God "breaks through to show himself as he really is." The cross stands for the world's "No" to the powerful realities of God which Christ embodied in his own life. But the cross stands also for God's "Yes" and "Amen" to the Son, and to all the age-old promises of God which find their fulfillment in him.

Throughout his ministry, Jesus gave himself to the task of transforming evil into material for the construction of glory for God and good for human beings. Seen in the light of the cross, his works of mercy were not a mere accompaniment of his redemptive mission; they

---

[18]Reinhold Niebuhr, *Discerning the Signs of the Times* (New York: Charles Scribner's Sons, 1946), p. 146.

[19]Ibid., p. 134."

were of its essence. The compassionate self-sacrifice of his daily life prefigured his final sacrifice on Calvary. The signs of his triumphant march on the human scene were not the conquest of countless battalions and clashing arms, nor yet the intervention of "ten legions of angels." The signs of his triumph were that the blind received their sight, the lame walked, the lepers were cleansed, the deaf heard, the dead were raised, and the poor had the gospel preached to them. To this mission of love Jesus was obedient, even unto death. He broke the power of sin by opposing it with weapons drawn from the arsenal of God's own love, and used these weapons to fight the powers of evil at the point where they had wreaked their destructive havoc on human lives.

In fighting Christ, the forces of evil were not engaging themselves in combat merely against the forces of goodness which well-intentioned good men were able to deploy against them. They were, so to say, "fighting against the stars," fighting against the elemental, primeval, foundational realities of this world and of all worlds that may be. They were fighting against God.

Resurrection and Lordship. The victory theme cannot be discussed adequately without taking into full consideration the salient importance of the resurrection and the present lordship of Christ. Since, however, a separate chapter in this book is devoted to these topics, perhaps a brief discussion of them will suffice here.

The importance of the resurrection to the Christian faith was forcefully stated by the apostle Paul: "If Christ has not been raised, your faith is futile and you are still in your sins. . . . We are of all men most to be pitied" (1 Cor. 15:17-19, RSV). Jürgen Moltmann supports this Pauline conviction categorically: "Christianity stands or falls with the reality of the raising of Jesus from the dead by God."[20]

So crucial was the resurrection to Paul's gospel that he characteristically linked the resurrection with the cross. Cross-resurrection was a strong double accent in his thought concerning the redemptive work of Christ. In Romans 4:25, for example, Paul says that Christ "was put to death for our trespasses and raised for our justification" (RSV). In 2 Corinthians 5:15, he urges his readers not to

---

[20]Jürgen Moltmann, *Theology of Hope* (New York and Evanston, Harper and Row, 1965), p. 165.

live to themselves, but "unto him which died for them, and rose again" (KJV). Paul longed to experience both the "power of his resurrection, and the fellowship of his sufferings" (Phil. 3:10, KJV).

The resurrection is the consummation of Christ's redeeming work. Without it, his life as a whole would be not a triumph but humanity's supreme tragedy. On the other hand, the reality of the resurrection has determined that the mood of the Christian faith is not one of submission to death and despair, but one of life and joy. The resurrection stands not only for Christ's victory over death, and for the triumph of those who know in him "the power of an endless life," but also for a conclusive victory over sin.

Without the resurrection we are, in the words of C. H. Dodd, left wondering whether perhaps Christ "was a mere rebel against the universe, which, on the whole, stood for something quite different.... If, on the other hand, we hold the continued personal existence and activity of Jesus Christ to be an assured fact, then we know that what He wrought on our behalf is also wrought into the very fabric of the universe in which we live; and we are at home in it, even while we rebel against its wrongs."[21]

Christian insight has seen an indissoluble connection between the servant who "became obedient unto death," and the Lord whom God exalted, and gave "a name which is above every name" (Phil. 2:8-11). Richard R. Niebuhr has stated an essential truth precisely: "The apostolic confession was not simply a confession of a living Christ but of a living Christ who, as a crucified man, was raised from the dead." Again, Niebuhr says, "An exalted Christ who was not also crucified and raised may be confessed as Lord, but he is not a Lord who burst the gates of hell."[22]

The Dilemma of Continuing Conflict. Victory has been won in Christ, but sin, suffering, and death are continuing scourges. Perhaps no one has ever been more confident than Paul was of the ultimate victory of Christ. Nevertheless, Paul confessed, "We know that the

---

[21]C. H. Dodd, *The Meaning of Paul for Today* (London: George Allen and Unwin, Ltd., 1920), p. 105.

[22]R. R. Niebuhr, *Resurrection and Historical Reason* (New York: Charles Scribner's Sons, 1957), p. 30.

whole creation has been groaning in travail together until now; and not only the creation, but we ourselves, who have the first fruits of the Spirit, groan inwardly as we wait for adoption as sons, the redemption of our bodies" (Rom. 8:22-23, RSV). Both Paul and the author of Hebrews apply to Christ the words of Psalm 8:6: "Thou hast put all things under his feet." For each of these New Testament writers, however, this statement has to be stipulated as a future consummation as well as a present fact. "He must reign," said Paul, "until he has put all his enemies under his feet" (1 Cor. 15:25, RSV). Christ reigns, Paul seems to be saying, but he does not reign fully; his great enemies have not yet accepted their defeat at his hands.

The epistle to the Hebrews also enters what sounds like a kind of demurrer:

> Now in putting everything in subjection to him, he left nothing outside his control. As it is, *we do not yet see everything in subjection to him.* But we see Jesus, who for a little while was made lower than the angels, crowned with glory and honor because of the suffering of death, so that by the grace of God he might taste death for every one" (Heb. 2:8-9, RSV, italics added).

If the Christian views only the plain facts of the empirical world, there seems to be no relief from this painful dilemma between victory and continued conflict. Death is still universal and inexorable. Suffering is scarcely diminished by the palliatives of escapism or the sedatives of medicine. Ugliness is unrelieved by a civilization which is acutely addicted to cosmetic facades. Technology gives us "improved means towards unimproved ends." An ever-advancing, escalating civilization seems chronically surprised to discover that "the devil can climb."

Cullmann's metaphors of D-Day and V-Day do not speak with the same pungency to the contemporary generation that they had for those who lived through World War II. Yet they have a certain perennial relevance. The decisive engagement in God's war with the hosts of evil has already been fought and won in the crucifixion and resurrection of Christ. The victory, that is to say, has been won "in principle," but the war still goes on, and the enemy continues to be malevolent in his purposes and destructive in his unceasing efforts. While the ultimate outcome is not in doubt, the life-and-death struggle will continue to the end of time.[23]

Emil Brunner has stated with considerable illumination both the predicament and the promise of our situation:

> Only when "he hath put all His enemies under His feet," only then, when not only in principle, but also in actual experience, all resistance will have been broken . . ., only then will that actually become real, which since Good Friday and Easter has happened in principle and decisively: that to Him every knee shall bow, and He will really have all authority in heaven and on earth. Until then, however, the conflict between the Kingdom of the Son and the Kingdom of darkness will still go on, as a struggle which is, it is true, decided, but whose violence in the visible sphere of the earthly historical reality does not decrease, but rather increases. . . . In spite of all this, however, to believe in Jesus is also to believe in Christ, the Victor, because Easter is the guarantee of final victory.[24]

In the meantime, the Christian, and the Church, take their stand at "the place of overcoming," at the cross and resurrection of Christ. Here we can wait, here we can hope, here we can fight, here we can live, and here we die, in the mood of Paul, who said, "Thanks be to God, who gives us the victory through our Lord Jesus Christ" (1 Cor. 15:57, RSV).

---

[23]Cullmann, *Christ and Time*, p. 84; cf. Robert H. Culpepper, *Interpreting the Atonement*, pp. 149-50.

[24]Emil Brunner, *The Christian Doctrine of Creation and Redemption*, Olive Wyon, trans., Dogmatics, vol. 2 (London: Lutterworth Press, 1955), pp. 304-305.

--------- Chapter 7 ---------

Christ the Representative
of God and Man

The term *representative* is not used of Christ in the New Testament, although the idea for which it stands is widely prevalent there. The *doctrine* of Christ as representative, however, has had a place of considerable importance in Christian theology. Traditionally, this doctrine has been discussed in connection with the threefold office of Christ. This approach depicts Christ as prophet, priest, and king.

This threefold aspect of Christ's work reflects the Old Testament understanding that the will of God is carried out, in representative fashion, by prophets, priests, and kings. Each one of these offices, when applied to Christ, shows him in a mediatorial relationship between God and his people.

In his *prophetic* office, Christ in his teaching and preaching brings the Word of God to mankind. In his *priestly* office, he represents us in his redeeming sacrifice. In his *kingly* office, he represents God by manifesting and establishing the kingdom of God. These "offices" may be divided for study, but they were a seamless robe in Christ's life and ministry.

Oscar Cullmann makes a different approach in a notable and influential discussion found in his book, *Christ and Time*.[1] Cullmann develops his concept of Christ's representative role in the context of "salvation history" (*Heilsgeschichte*). Cullmann has been a protagonist of the view that the history of revelation and salvation is based on real events in history, of which Christ is both the center and the consummation.

Cullmann argues that, down to the advent of Christ, redemptive history unfolds successively from the many to the One—that is, from mankind, to the people of Israel, to the remnant in Israel, to Christ. In Christ, redemptive history reaches its focal point in that Christ becomes the redeemer of mankind and of all creation. In this movement, Christ is the culmination of God's redemptive action in human history, and he is the representative man in whom is crystallized God's redeeming efforts on behalf of all mankind.

From the time of Christ's coming there is a signal change, however, in the course of the redemptive movement. After the resurrection, the progression is no longer from the many to the One, but from the One to the many. By this is meant that redemptive history now proceeds from Christ to those who are redeemed by him. The line of advance leads from Christ to the apostles, and thence to the Church, the "body of Christ," whose task it is to fulfill for all people the role of a redeeming "remnant" of humanity. The task of the Church is therefore also representative. On the one hand, it represents Christ, whose body it is in the world. On the other hand, it represents the world, as that portion of the world which has experienced in Christ the redeeming power of God, and as that part of the world which understands what, in the plan of God, the world is meant to be.

Cullmann thus believes that the history of redemption is manifested in two movements. The first proceeds from the many to the One; this was history under the old covenant. The second proceeds from the One to the many; this is history under the new covenant. At the midpoint stands Christ, whose representative mission from God to the world receives its preeminent disclosure in Christ's ministry, death, and resurrection. He represents the old by fulfilling it. He represents the new by being its firstfruits and the continuing agent of its realization.

---

[1]Cullmann, *Christ and Time*.

Insofar as the above outline summarizes Cullmann's understanding of "salvation history," it is assumed here that his thesis is generally accurate. The main point of emphasis intended in this summary is that Christ was representative not merely in one or more of his "offices" or "roles," but that his whole ministry was a representative one. He was the representative of the old Israel, summing up in his person and in his mission the history and the God-intended destiny of the Jewish people. He was the representative of the new Israel, by being its inaugurator, norm, guide, inspiration, and goal.

Further, Christ represented all of humanity. He was the new man, the true man, the sinless representative of mankind. Lastly, he represented God. He was the Son of God, manifested in the flesh, the "image of the invisible God, the first-born of all creation" (Col. 1:15, RSV).

The church's early efforts to express its understanding of Christ in the doctrine of the "two natures" was, in part at least, an effort to preserve the integrity of Christ's mediatorial role as the representative of both God and man. No elaborate exposition of the doctrine of the two natures will be attempted here, but a statement by Nels F. S. Ferré outlines in contemporary terms both the intention of much early creedal Christology, and an understanding of the representative role of Christ which is found in early creedal formulations:

> In Jesus we have seen God truly and in him God has worked his mighty Christ-deed in history. In Jesus we have also seen true man, both in respect to his becoming man and to his being the flowering of manhood. Jesus was not some being who was more than human personality at its best nor less than human personality, but a personality that was made up of God's presence and man's in such organic and fulfilling togetherness as to be the kind of human personality that God intended, in the first place, by the creation of man, and such an intrinsic and inviolate involvement of God that apart from Him this personality could not be. Thus the creeds, in affirming one God, *of* God, not like God, *of* man, not like man, in one true personality, give the right positive pointers for Christology.[2]

---

[2]Nels F. S. Ferré, *Christ and the Christian* (New York: Harper and Brothers, 1958), pp. 64-65.

At the outset, it is important to distinguish between *representation* and *substitution*. The former term is much more adequate for setting forth the nature of the atonement than is the latter. "A substitute," says Alan Richardson, "takes or usurps our place, whereas a representative keeps it open for us, acts on our behalf and causes us to be present where in fact we cannot personally appear."[3] With this statement may be placed another by Vincent Taylor. The word *representative*, he says,

> does not indicate one whose activity lies apart from ourselves, or serves instead of our own, but one whose service leaves in our hands the decisive word in the affirmation of faith. Christ is our representative because in his self-offering He performs a work necessary to our approach to God.[4]

The work of Christ as representative, in other words, does not stand apart from us, but decisively involves us. Christ does what we cannot do for ourselves, but he takes us into his saving act. He is crucified *for* us, but *we* are also "crucified with Christ." He not only rose from the dead but also became "the first fruits of those who have fallen asleep" (1 Cor. 15:20, RSV).

We cannot cover in one chapter the multiple aspects of this large topic—the topic of representation. Therefore we shall deal in some detail with only two of the most prominent themes in the New Testament which give expression to Christ's representative role. The first theme deals with Christ as the Second Adam. The second theme is concerned with Christ's high priesthood and his vicarious sacrifice.

Christ the Second Adam

Paul tried in many ways to express the meaning of the transformation which he had undergone in his experience with Christ. Christ had brought him redemption from sin, reconciliation to God, liberation from the bondage of the law, and deliverance from the demonic forces of evil. Paul's epistles, says W. D. Davies,

---

[3]Richardson, ed., *A Dictionary of Christian Theology*, p. 290.

[4]Vincent Taylor, *Jesus and His Sacrifice* (London: Macmillan and Company, Limited, 1948), p. 306.

are full of antitheses setting forth the difference that Christ has made. He refers to an old man who was crucified with Christ, to the new man put on through Christ; bondage had given place to liberty; life in the flesh to life in the Spirit. He had been delivered from the power of darkness and translated into the Kingdom of His dear Son; delivered from the present evil age into the new age.[5]

One of the important ways in which Paul tried to express the difference which the coming of Christ had made in the world was by comparing and contrasting the first and second Adams. The main passages in which he deals with these images are Romans 5:12-21 and 1 Corinthians 15:20-22, 45-49. His discussion of the two Adams gives a striking picture of Christ's representative role.

We may first summarize the argument that Paul makes. In Romans, Paul claims that sin came into the world by the transgression of Adam, and death by sin. Thus Adam is the founder and head of the old humanity.

Paul was in line with contemporary rabbinic theology in his assertion that sin came into the world through Adam and that death resulted for him and for his posterity from Adam's sin. Both physical and moral evil, in fact, were explained usually by reference to Adam's disobedience. Adam, the head and symbol of the old and natural humanity, involved all human beings in sin, guilt, bondage, and death.

Just how the sin of Adam, and the death which supposedly resulted from it, were transmitted to all of humanity Paul nowhere says. He does not bother to answer many of the questions about this subject that a modern mind would ask. How, indeed, can all people sin "in Adam"? There seems to have been in Paul's mind here the ancient conception of corporate personality, or at least of some kind of corporate solidarity. The moral unit was not the individual, but the community, whether one means by this a clan, tribe, city, or nation. When Achan violated *taboo* (Josh. 7), his whole clan was cursed. Likewise, all of humanity could be considered to be members of the tribe of Adam, and Adam's sin was the sin of the whole race.

That Paul believed Adam to have been an historical personage seems evident. Yet he writes of Adam as if the name were more that of a

---

[5]Davies, *Paul and Rabbinic Judaism*, p. 36.

collective noun than that of an individual. Adam is mankind, everyman, and all men. Whether Adam was a single individual or not, he stands as a type, representing the rebellion of every person from the God who created him and loves him. Adam represents humanity, because all men have followed Adam's path of rebellion and alienation from God.

Whether Adam was an historical figure or not, the representative character of Adam's fall and its entail of death still have profound theological significance for a Christian interpretation of the human situation. John Whale has stated this position in memorable terms:

> Eden is on no map, and Adam's fall fits no historical calendar. Moses is not nearer to the Fall than we are, because he lived three thousand years before our time. The Fall refers not to some datable aboriginal calamity in the historic past of humanity, but to a dimension of human experience always present—namely, that we who have been created for fellowship with God repudiate it continually; and that the whole of mankind does this along with us. Everyman is his own 'Adam', and all men are solidarily Adam.[6]

Adam represents the whole of mankind. In his rebellion against God, and in his tragic destiny, the sins and deaths of all who came after his time are anticipated. While each person has lived his own life, sinned his own sins, and died his own death, each life has been a repetition of and a variation of Adam's life, sin, and death. Adam has been in us, and we have been in Adam.

As "Adam" is a name which stands in some sense for the "corporate personality" of mankind, so also a new "corporate personality" is found in Christ. While sin and death came through the disobedience of the first Adam, Paul affirms, the baleful influence of Adam's transgression is reversed in Christ: "Then as one man's trespass led to condemnation for all men, so one man's act of righteousness leads to acquittal for all men. For as by one man's disobedience many were made sinners, so by one man's obedience many will be made righteous" (Rom. 5:18-19, RSV).

In Paul's discussion of the first and second Adams in 1 Corinthians

---

[6]Whale, *Christian Doctrine*, p. 52.

15, we should notice that the context is a discussion of the resurrection. By the first Adam came death, Paul says, and by the second Adam has come the resurrection from the dead: "For as in Adam all die, so also in Christ shall all be made alive" (1 Cor. 15:22, RSV). The first Adam was a living being, but the last Adam was a "life-giving spirit." The first Adam was from earth, "a man of dust"; the second Adam came from heaven. "Just as we have borne the image of the man of dust, we shall also bear the image of the man of heaven" (1 Cor. 15:49, RSV).

Christ the Representative of God. In contrast to the first Adam, Christ the second Adam in a distinctive sense represents God in the human family. The claims of his oneness with all other persons must not be permitted to obscure the fact that he comes from and represents the divine side of reality. "He Himself," declares Emil Brunner, "is the bridge which God throws across to us, over which God comes to us."[7]

Not only does Christ identify himself with human beings, but also he comes as one who is wholly united with God. Brunner continues:

> His whole purpose and desire is directed towards the things of God: the Kingdom of God, the dominion and the glory of God, that is His "cause"; and all this not in the human ethical sense of an ideal towards which one aspires, but in the divine sense, of the sphere from which one comes. Christ does not act merely as One who is absolutely united with man, but also as One who is absolutely one with God, as the authorized representative of God, who makes an unconditional claim on man's obedience. The fact that He appears in the "form of a servant" is only the incognito of His royal state. The Kingdom, the dominion of God, is not merely the cause of God which He serves, but it is likewise the sphere in which He Himself reigns.[8]

Christ did the work of God; he brought to the point of human need the compassion, mercy, and healing of God. He forgave sins in the name of God. He conquered death by the power of God. "God shows by sending his Son," says Markus Barth, "that he is making man's

---

[7]Emil Brunner, *The Mediator*, Olive Wyon, trans. (Philadelphia: The Westminster Press, 1947), p. 491.

[8]Ibid., pp. 498-99.

business his business; he is giving away the best and dearest he has, his Son, for the redemption of men."[9]

Christ the Representative of Man. It is as important to a doctrine of the Atonement to assert Christ's humanity as to affirm his divine nature. Not only was he, in accordance with the Chalcedonian formula, "true God," but also he was "true man." This point is made emphatically by D. M. Baillie: "The gulf between Christ and us is not a gulf between human minds and a mind that was not human, for He was made in all things like unto His brethren. His psychical constitution was the same as ours."[10] Christ could represent us adequately only if, in the most literal sense, he were one of us, a fellow human being.

The New Testament affirms Jesus' humanity in unmistakable terms. The references to his human birth, his daily life as a boy and as a man, his death on a cross, the shedding of his blood—all show the deep connection of his life with the lives of other persons. He could take upon himself responsibility for them because he was one with them.

It is true that the New Testament claims Christ's humanity to have been sinless, and this sinlessness would seem to put him out of touch, so to say, with common humanity, "since all have sinned, and fall short of the glory of God" (Rom. 3:23, RSV). The New Testament claim for Jesus' sinlessness can be stated in the words of the book of·Hebrews. He was "one who in every respect has been tempted as we are, yet without sinning" (Heb. 4:15, RSV).

His sinlessness is to be viewed, not merely in a moral sense, as though his whole record were to be tested by his strict adherence to, let us say, a legalistic interpretation of the Ten Commandments. The ultimate evidence of his sinlessness was the harmony of his will with that of the Father, the unclouded fellowship which he had with God, and the free yet purposeful and sacrificial way in which he became an instrument of the Father's will.

In our battle against Satan, Karl Heim says, there is only one weapon in Satan's hands that can wound and destroy us. That weapon is forged from the sins which we have committed against God.[11] When

---

[9]Markus Barth, *Justification* (Grand Rapids, Michigan: William B. Eerdmans Publishing Company, 1971), p. 39.

[10]Baillie, *God Was in Christ*, p. 20.

[11]Heim, *Jesus the World's Perfecter*, pp. 75-76.

Christ presented himself in battle against Satan on our behalf, there was in Satan's hands no weapon with which he could destroy this man, for he was sinless. "The ruler of this world is coming," Christ could say. "He has no power over me" (John 14:30, RSV).

Even so, there was a battle of epic proportions for Jesus to fight. "He was in all points tempted. . . ." He faced and conquered the temptation to follow the road of politico-religious power. He resisted and denied the temptation for a fame that was cheap. He spurned the path that led to popular acclaim. At Gethsemane he measured with agony of soul the temptation to escape from suffering and death, against the will of the Father which pointed clearly to the cross.

The profound seriousness of the temptations can be grasped only if we appreciate the fact that his decisions were contested, that his temptations were real, that precisely here everything was at stake. He stood in a storm of temptations, but he did not yield.

Jesus' identification with the human plight did not stop short of his assuming the burden of the sins and afflictions of mankind. Here is where he showed himself most clearly to be the agent of God, and here he touched most sensitively and poignantly the raw nerve of the human condition. He asked no exemptions from human misery and woe. He carried none of the trappings of earthly power. He consorted with doubtful and repulsive characters, whose very existence was a cause for loathing among decent, godly people. Thus he embraced the cross in the daily course of his life as well as upon Golgotha's hill. And, says Harold DeWolf, "when we know God through the cross of Christ, we know him not as unrelated to the world but as involved in the most earthy and wretched hours of human life. There is no slum too full of stench, no riot or battle too saturated with hate, no bed of pain too heavily burdened with agony for his presence."[12]

As the second Adam who has taken upon himself to the fullest extent our human nature, Christ embraced vicariously the effects of sin which had brought suffering and death to mankind through the rebellion of the first Adam. He felt the alienation from the Father which was the common lot of all sinners. He drank the cup of suffering and death to its dregs. He felt and confessed the holy judgment of God upon our sin. He experienced that judgment willingly as iron in his own soul. He became obedient, even unto death.

---

[12]DeWolf, *A Hard Rain and a Cross*, p. 80.

No one ever plumbed the depths of vicarious suffering so deeply. And in it all, he represented us.

Christ's Priority to Adam. In his book on Romans 5:12-21, a book entitled *Christ and Adam,* Karl Barth shows that Christ, not Adam, is the "norm of all anthropology."[13] The first Adam was a "type" of the Adam who was to come (Rom. 5:14). Christ stands above Adam, superior to Adam. The essential nature of man is to be seen in Christ, not in Adam.

> Man's nature in Adam is not, as is usually assumed, his true and original nature; it is only truly human at all in so far as it reflects and corresponds to essential human nature as it is found in Christ. True human nature, therefore, can only be understood by Christians who look to Christ to discover the essential nature of man. Vv. 12-21 are revolutionary in their insistence that what is true of *Christians* must also be true of all men.[14]

As Adam's humanity was only a "provisional copy" of the genuine humanity that was in Christ, so our relationship to Adam is only a type, a "preliminary shadow" of our relationship to Christ. Adam can represent mankind only as one person among others. He has no essential priority over them. He is not their head and their lord. In his own life and destiny, to be sure, he anticipated the life and destiny of other men. He is the first man among others, but only in the sense that he is *primus inter pares.*

Christ, on the contrary, as true man, true Adam, is lord and head of mankind. Since he is also the sinless Son of God, he is true man in a unique and unrivaled sense. In his humanity we discover human nature in the character in which God created it, and intended for it.[15]

Man in Christ. Man's relationship to the first Adam is in no sense as decisive as his relationship to the second Adam. The obedience of Christ to the will of the Father overcomes the disobedience of the first Adam, and at the same time marks out the path which all people are to

---

[13]Karl Barth, *Christ and Adam* (New York: Harper and Brothers, 1956, 1957), p. 26.

[14]Ibid., p. 90.

[15]Ibid., pp. 93-94.

follow. In living under the law and subjecting himself to its demands, Christ fulfilled the law. He took upon himself the penalty and condemnation which result from the law's transgression, and thereby forfeited the destructive effects of sin for those who had disobeyed the law. He is the Righteous One, in whose healing and forgiving ministry our sins are taken away. In him the abounding grace of God proved itself to be stronger than sin. In Christ's resurrection, Paul saw convincing evidence that Christ not only had conquered death, but also had conquered the sin which was the cause of death and was the "sting" of death.

Any man who is "in Christ," said Paul, has become a "new creation," in which old things have passed away, and all has become new. For in Christ God created a new man, a new humanity (Rom. 5:12-21; 1 Cor. 15:20-23; Rom. 6:1-11; Col. 3:9). Of this new humanity, God was the creator, and Jesus was the prototype. In the obedience, righteousness, life, death, and resurrection of Christ, the grace of God was revealed, and the purpose of God was disclosed for all people who follow the one who, in another context, was called the "pioneer of life."

As the resurrected Lord, Christ is the "first fruits of those who have fallen asleep" (1 Cor. 15:20, RSV). When he died and rose from the dead, his followers also died and rose in him. Their aim thenceforth was to yield themselves to the grace of God which came to them in him, to make themselves in the human family the agents of the reconciliation which he had effected between them and God, and to allow the love of God which had flooded their hearts in his abiding presence to flow outward through them to others. They were to walk "in newness of life"—that newness of life which they had found in him.

Christ the High Priest and the Sacrificial Victim

Modern men and women have difficulty seeing the significance of sacrifice as it was practiced in Bible times. Today we are so far away from the Old Testament sacrificial system, and from the sacrificial ideas that we find in the New Testament, for that matter, that quite frequently we not only are puzzled by sacrificial rites and meanings, but also may be repulsed by them. We have an instinctual revulsion towards smoking altars, slain victims, and streams of blood.

For two reasons, however, we must consider the meaning of sacrifice, if we are to study the Christian interpretation of atonement: Sacrificial rites and ideas are indelibly fixed in the primary documents of the Christian faith—those which comprise the Bible—and there are spiritual values in these rites and ideas, values without which our faith would be greatly impoverished.

Rites of sacrifice have been a native ingredient of nearly all primitive religions. In the history of religion, the conduct of sacrificial worship has normally been placed in the hands of a regular priesthood. In its simplest forms, the observance of sacrifice has been carried out by the chief of the tribe or by the head of a household. In any case, certain persons have been designated to officiate in the celebration of the appropriate rites and ceremonies, and thus have occupied a mediating function between their people and the deity. With respect to the deity they acted on behalf of the people; with respect to the people they acted on behalf of the deity.

The purpose of sacrifice, despite its many variations of form, was to obtain and to maintain favorable access to the deity. This was true also with respect to the priestly system described in the Old Testament. The sacrificial cultus of Israel embraced many types of sacrifice, but we can attempt to give here only a brief general description of the sacrificial system.

The sacrificial offering, if it were an animal, sometimes was slain by the worshiper, sometimes by the priest. After it had been slaughtered, the offering of the slain victim was handled by the priest. His first task was to manipulate correctly and carefully the blood of the slain animal. The "life was in the blood," and was considered to be extremely valuable. In some cases the blood was devoted to God alone; in others it was directed to God and his worshipers.

The next task of the priest was to deal with the body of the slain animal. Both the type of sacrifice that was intended, and the nature of the dedicated offering, dictated the precise ritual form. In all cases the victim was given to God in some manner. The final stage occurred when certain specified parts of the animal were distributed among the people by the priests. Usually the ceremony ended with a feast in which both people and priests participated. Deeply germane to this part of the procedure was the belief that God himself was a participant in the feast. In a real sense it was a ceremony involving communion between God and his people.

Christ the Eternal High Priest. Outside the book of Hebrews, references to Christ as high priest are scanty. We shall recur to this book, therefore, for our principal source of insight on this topic.

In this epistle, the qualifications of Jesus to assume the office of eternal High Priest are closely joined with the concept of Christ's person. Christ is the "heir of all things" (Heb. 1:2, RSV). "He reflects the glory of God and bears the very stamp of his nature, upholding the universe by his word of power" (Heb. 1:3, RSV).

This high Christology is balanced by a strong emphasis upon Christ's humanity: "We have not a high priest who is unable to sympathize with our weaknesses, but one who in every respect has been tempted as we are, yet without sinning" (Heb. 4:15, RSV). "In the days of his flesh, Jesus offered up prayers and supplications, with loud cries and tears, to him who was able to save him from death, and he was heard for his godly fear" (Heb. 5:7, RSV). He was the Son of God, but "he learned obedience through what he suffered" (Heb. 5:8, RSV).[16]

Since Jesus was concerned not with angels but with the descendants of Abraham, "he had to be made like his brethren in every respect, so that he might become a merciful and faithful high priest in the service of God, to make expiation for the sins of the people" (Heb. 2:17, RSV).

In Hebrews, Christ is repeatedly declared to be a high priest "after the order of Melchizedek" (Heb. 5:6, RSV). In the book of Genesis, chapter 14, Melchizedek appears as a mysterious personage of unknown background. He was a king who also exercised priestly functions. He received from Abraham a tithe of goods which Abraham had taken in battle.

Melchizedek was both king and priest, so his priesthood was a royal priesthood. He blessed Abraham, and thereby demonstrated his right to exercise dominion over others. He is mentioned without any reference to his ancestors or descendants, or to his previous or subsequent history. The writer of Hebrews regarded him as a type of Christ, superior to the Mosaic priesthood of Aaron and his descendants.

Melchizedek is an important figure in the book of Hebrews, but it appears that the author of the book is not especially interested in Melchizedek as an historical figure. His real interest is to show that the

---

[16]Cf. Vincent Taylor, *The Cross of Christ* (London: Macmillan and Company, Ltd., 1956), pp. 53-54.

priesthood of Christ stands single, superior, and alone. Christ's priesthood is of a royal character. It is dependent, rather, upon a divine appointment to an office in which he has neither predecessors nor successors. The high priests of the old order were unable to continue in office because death overtook them one by one, but Christ is high priest forever "by the power of an indestructible life" (Heb. 7:16, RSV). As the true Melchizedek, Jesus stands incomparably above Abraham, and above all those who represent the Mosaic law and its priesthood.

This kind of argument is, of course, strange to the modern mind, but its content is a vital one. As Lionel Thornton points out, Christ

> is the true representative of the human race who offers to the Father the true sacrificial worship. He is the reality of which all ritual priesthoods were but shadowy symbols. He has an unchangeable, universal priesthood which will never pass away and which is efficacious in bringing men into the very presence of God.[17]

The contrast between the high priesthood of Jesus and that of the priests of Aaron's line is illustrated sharply by reference to the functions of the high priest on the annual Day of Atonement. The Jewish high priest offered sacrifices day by day, and the ritual of the Day of Atonement was observed once each year. The ministry of this priest, by the necessity of its constant repetition, showed at best its inadequacy and its ephemeral authority. The priesthood, moreover, was constantly changing: "The former priests were many in number, because they were prevented by death from continuing in office" (Heb. 7:23, RSV). The predicament of the high priest was shown by the fact that he himself, like the people whom he represented, was a sinner, who needed "to offer sacrifices daily, first for his own sins and then for those of the people" (Heb. 7:27, RSV). There was a necessity for sacrifice, for "almost everything is purified with blood, and without the shedding of blood there is no forgiveness of sins" (Heb. 9:22, RSV). At the same time, the necessity of sacrifice showed the inescapable dilemma of both priest and people, because the sacrifices which were

---

[17]Lionel Spencer Thornton, *The Doctrine of the Atonement* (London: The Unicorn Press, 1937), p. 102.

made were ultimately ineffective: "For it is impossible that the blood of bulls and goats should take away sins" (Heb. 10:4, RSV).

On the other hand, the priestly ministry of Christ was redemptively efficacious. He had no reason to offer sacrifices for himself, for he was "holy, guileless, and undefiled." The sacrifice which he made was perfect and final, "once for all," for it consisted in the offering of his sinless self. Unlike the Aaronic high priest, he, in his own person, "tasted death for every man." Unlike this priest, also, death could not hold him: "He suffered; and being made perfect he became the source of eternal salvation to all who obey him, being designated by God a high priest forever after the order of Melchizedek" (Heb. 5:8-10, RSV).

Christ the Sacrificial Victim. As developed in Hebrews, the image of sacrifice envisions a place where a sacrificial victim is being offered on the altar. A priest, whose function it is to go to God on behalf of man, consecrates and offers the victim. Yet *this priest* is different in that he does not offer the body and blood of an animal. Rather, he offers *his own* life on the altar. He gives himself that the sins of his people may be forgiven and that they may be restored to fellowship with God.

The parallel between the meaning of sacrifice in the Old Testament and that in the New receives illumination here, as well as differences that are striking. On the Day of Atonement, which is the subject of Leviticus 16, the hight priest made a sacrificial offering first for himself and then for his people. Entering then into the holy place within the veil, he presented the sacrifice to God in order to make atonement for the sins of those whom he represented: "But when Christ appeared as a high priest of the good things that have come, then through the greater and more perfect tent . . . he entered once for all into the Holy Place, taking not the blood of goats and calves but his own blood, thus securing an eternal redemption" (Heb. 9:11-12, RSV).

1. *A Vicarious Sacrifice.* As a sinless high priest, Christ had no need to offer sacrifice on his own behalf. His sacrifice was entirely vicarious. We see Jesus, "who for a little while was made lower than the angels, crowned with glory and honor because of the suffering of death, so that by the grace of God he might taste death for every one" (Heb. 2:9, RSV). Into the inner shrine behind the curtain (the holy of holies) Jesus has gone as a "forerunner" "on our behalf," and this act, the writer says in a beautiful metaphor, is "a sure and steadfast anchor of

the soul" (Heb. 6:19, RSV), to which we can moor our hope with certain confidence. Jesus had no need to offer daily sacrifices, for his one vicarious sacrifice was efficacious and adequate for all time and all people (Heb. 7:27).

2. *The Sacrificial Blood.* The clearest statement of the rationale of sacrifice in the Old Testament sacrificial system is found in Leviticus 17:11: "For the life of the flesh is in the blood; and I have given it for you upon the altar to make atonement for your souls; for it is the blood that makes atonement, by reason of the life" (RSV). When the blood of the sacrificial victim was released, it was believed that its life was released. The purpose of sacrifice was not to kill but to release life as an offering to God. Life was given through the death of the victim. The outpoured life of the victim was, presumably, taken up and absorbed, both into the life of God and into the life of the worshipers.

In a clarifying statement, Robert H. Culpepper shows both the Godward and the manward movement of sacrifice:

> The sacrifice is both given by God and offered to God. It is both God's movement to man and the vehicle of man's movement to God. It brings God to man that man might be brought to God. It is given by God, because it is the Father who did not spare his only Son but gave him up freely for us all (Rom. 8:32: cf. Gen. 22:8). It is the gift of his grace. But the sacrifice is also offered to God, and it is offered to God on man's behalf. "Christ loved us and gave himself up for us, a fragrant offering and sacrifice to God" (Eph. 5:2). . . . And the purpose for which Christ gave his life is accomplished when we make his sacrifice the vehicle of our approach to God and by faith-union with him die to sin and rise to newness of life.[18]

If the above explanation of the meaning of sacrifice is true, the representative character of sacrifice may be better understood. In Hebrews, Christ is the High Priest who makes the sacrificial offering to God on our behalf. He is also the sacrificial victim who represents both the dedication of our lives to God and God's own gift of mercy to us. He gave his own life to God for us, and in this offering we also give our lives to God.

---

[18]Culpepper, *Interpreting the Atonement*, p. 154.

3. *A Propitiatory Offering?* The word translated *propitiation* (*hilasterion*) in the New Testament appears only once in Hebrews, where it clearly means "mercy seat" (9:5, RSV). Other cognate words, whose root meaning in classical Greek is *to propitiate,* or *to appease,* are used in Luke 18:3, and in 1 John 2:2; 4:10. In Hebrews 2:17 (RSV), it is claimed that Christ, in the service of God, makes "expiation" for the sins of the people. Since in this case not God, but the sins of the people, are the object of Christ's atoning action, it is clear that expiation, the removal of the barrier between God and sinners, "a means by which guilt is annulled," is the intended meaning. In Romans 3:25, Paul used the word *hilasterion,* and the King James Version translates the verse as follows: "Whom God hath set forth to be a propitiation through faith in his blood, to declare his righteousness for the remission of sins that are past, through the forbearance of God."

The meaning of *propitiation* here has been a point of controversy among scholars. Some take it to mean simply the reconciling activity of Christ. Others contend that the word should be translated *expiation* instead of *propitiation.* Still others say that the meaning of the term is *mercy seat.*

In classical Greek, however, the word translated *propitiation* meant to placate or appease an angry deity. The problem posed in connection with a Christian doctrine of atonement is whether the sacrifice of Christ was intended to appease the wrath of God by the interposition of an offering on our behalf, which was acceptable to God.

This interpretation of the sacrifice of Christ poses serious questions about the intention and effect of Christ's atonement. In the concept of Christ's death which is found in the theory of "penal substitution," Christ interjects himself into our place, and receives the full punishment from the hand of God which was our due. He therefore appeased, made favorable, placated the vengeful anger of God, and satisfied God's demands for a just punishment. Thus he rendered God favorable to us by receiving in our place the blow which should have fallen on us.

In line with this interpretation is the belief that Christ has so identified himself with us that he has become "sin" for us and a "curse" for us: "For our sake he made him to be sin who knew no sin, so that in him we might become the righteousness of God" (2 Cor. 5:21, RSV). Again, in Galatians 3:13, Paul wrote, "Christ redeemed us from the curse of the law, having become a curse for us" (RSV).

While there is truth in the penal view, the truth being that Christ takes upon himself the penalty for our sins, the penal interpretation must be carefully handled, lest we allow it to distort the meaning of atonement. It is truer to say that Christ was crucified "for us" than to say that he was crucified "instead of us." He was crucified as our representative, on our behalf, not as our replacement. He gathers our own lives into his sacrificial offering. In the truest sense, his offering of his life to the Father represented and included our offering of our lives with his.

When we say that Christ "became sin" for us, we do not mean, of course, that Christ himself became a sinner. He took upon himself the consequences of our sin, but without himself becoming a sinner. When we say that Christ became a "curse" for us, we mean that he took upon himself on our behalf the curse that sin brings. We do not mean that God cursed Christ. We may say that Christ entered into the experience of the accursed, but we must not say that he endured the personal displeasure of God.

We should not say that Christ stands *for* us in mercy, while the Father stands *against* us as a God of stern, unbending justice who will not relent until all our "debts" to him are paid. Rather, we should say that the Son represented the Father in his sacrifice. The love of Christ is the love of God. The mercy of Christ is the mercy of God. God does not stand *aloof* from us, while Christ stands at our side. Instead, "God was *in* Christ, reconciling the world unto himself" (2 Cor. 5:19, KJV, italics added).

The meaning of the cross is not that God stood apart from it in vengeful anger, demanding restitution for a broken law or an offended honor, but the exact opposite. The cross means that, in infinite love and compassion, God involved himself in our plight, becoming the good Samaritan to us in Christ, while we were stricken and helpless in our sins. In Christ, he stepped into our destitute condition to take the penalty of our sins upon himself, gathering all our wrongs into his own great heart and consuming them in the fires of his own love. In *this* sense he bore the penalty for our sins, not in some kind of "mechanical substitution," but in the way of a profoundly personal love.

4. "*I Come to Do Thy Will, O God.*" The interpretation which we make of Christ's sacrifice must, of course, transcend the bloodletting

and physical slaughter of animals that belong to the Old Testament sacrificial system. These were "figures of the true," not the reality which Christ himself expressed and embodied. "Unless a grain of wheat falls into the earth and dies, it remains alone; but if it dies, it bears much fruit" (John 12:24, RSV). That is the principle of sacrifice. Life comes through the giving of life in the shedding of blood, the seat of life. F. C. N. Hicks has grasped this profound principle in the following statement: "Life, in the death of the sacrificial victim, was not ended, but surrendered; and surrendered in order that it might be accepted, and, in acceptance, lifted from its earthly limitations into full association with God in heaven."[19]

The true representative sacrifice was that of Christ himself, voluntarily offered, a giving of his life even to the uttermost limit, the limit of death: "Through the eternal Spirit [he] offered himself without blemish to God" (Heb. 9:14, RSV). "He entered once for all into the Holy Place, taking not the blood of goats and calves but his own blood, thus securing an eternal redemption" (Heb. 9:12, RSV). He did this for us, but with the giving of his life we have given our own.

The significance of Christ's sacrifice is missed if exclusive attention is given to the shedding of his blood. The giving of his blood meant the giving of his life, and the redemptive significance of blood is to be seen in the spiritual quality of his life which the blood symbolized. This quality is discovered in the consecration of Christ's will to the purpose of the Father in effecting the redemption of men:

> Sacrifices and offerings thou hast not desired, but a body hast thou prepared for me; in burnt offerings and sin offerings thou hast taken no pleasure. Then I said, "Lo, I have come to do thy will, O God," as it is written in the roll of the book (Heb. 10:6-7, RSV).

These words, McLeod Campbell observed, give the key to any true conception of a doctrine of atonement.[20] By Christ's obedience, said Paul, "many will be made righteous" (Rom. 5:19, RSV). Instead of exalting himself, Christ abased himself, taking the form of a servant. God exalted him because he was obedient unto death.

---

[19]F. C. N. Hicks, *The Fullness of Sacrifice* (London: S.P.C.K., 1959), p. 175.

[20]Cf. F. R. Barry, *The Atonement* (Philadelphia and New York: J. B. Lippincott Company, 1968), p. 92.

"I have come to do thy will, O God." "A body thou has prepared for me." In Christ the outreaching love of God received "a local habitation and a name." In him God's purpose did its work in the confines of flesh and blood, of time and space, in the stuff of everyday life, in the muck and mire of human squalor and human depravity, in the "grandeur and misery" of man. In the New Testament, the gospels clearly reveal the content and character of the obedience of Christ, and thus the content and character of his sacrifice. He caused the lame to walk, the blind to see, the deaf to hear, and the lepers to be cleansed. He proclaimed glad tidings to the poor. He defied and attacked the legalism, hypocrisy, mammonism, idolatrous nationalism, clerical despotism, acculturated religion, racism, and brutality of his age. This daily ministry put him on a collision course with the vested interests and entrenched powers of the world, and led to the terminus of the cross—and to the embarkation point which we call the resurrection.

5. *The Heavenly Temple.* The writer of the book of Hebrews affirms of Jesus: "When he had made purification for sins, he sat down at the right hand of the Majesty on high" (Heb. 1:3, RSV). In this position of honor and power, he is "a minister in the sanctuary and the true tent which is set up not by man but by the Lord" (Heb. 8:2, RSV). Other priests "offer gifts according to the law" (Heb. 8:4, RSV). "They serve a copy and shadow of the heavenly sanctuary" (Heb. 8:5, RSV). As High Priest, Christ, through the greater and more perfect tent not made with hands, "entered once for all into the Holy Place, taking not the blood of goats and calves but his own blood, thus securing an eternal redemption" (Heb. 9:11-12, RSV). In the heavenly sanctuary, Christ's ministry continues unchangeable. "Consequently he is able for all time to save those who draw near to God through him, since he always lives to make intercession for them" (Heb. 7:25, RSV).

Not surprisingly, students of the book of Hebrews have seen in such passages as those cited above the presence of Platonic concepts. The author of this book appears to have been not only a Christian Jew but also an Alexandrian. It might be expected that a cultured mind like his would show traces of a Platonism with which he was familiar. He accepts the view that there is a higher order of being which infuses meaning and purpose into the earthly order. On earth may be found only dim and inadequate reflections of this higher realm, and the different institutional forms of the Jewish sacrificial system are but imperfect copies or shadows of the heavenly realities.

Nevertheless, the writer believed that the earthly life and work of Christ were real and significant in the most profound sense. His coming was an expression in time and space of God's purpose and grace, in a solid particularity which was at the same time "the express image" of God's person. His position now at the right hand of God makes eternally efficacious what he did "once for all" on earth.

The Platonic overtones in Hebrews need not be more than scaffolding which the writer uses in the construction of his thought. When the scaffolding is taken away, the essential message remains. When the high priest entered into the holy place, all Israel, by virtue of his solidarity with his people, entered into the sanctuary with him. Also, when he entered within the veil with the atoning blood of the sacrificial victim, it was believed that God accepted all of Israel in the representative figure and ministry of the high priest.

"How much more," as this writer would say, is the above true of the high-priestly ministry of Christ. When Christ, nearly two thousand years ago, made his atoning sacrifice, we also died and rose with him and, representatively and preceptively, ascended into heaven with him. When he was raised "for our justification" to the right hand of God, God accepted and exalted us in him. John Calvin has said essentially this in a powerful passage:

> It is vain for men to seek God in His own majesty, for it is too far removed from them; but Christ stretches forth His hand to us, that He may lead us to heaven. And this was shadowed forth formerly under the Law; for the High Priest entered the Holy of Holies, not in His own name only, but also in that of the people, in as much as he had in a manner the twelve tribes on his breast and on his shoulders; for, as a memorial for them, twelve onyx stones were wrought on the breast plate, and on the two onyx stones on his shoulders were engraved their names, so that in the person of one man all entered into the sanctuary together. Rightly then does the Apostle speak when he says that our High Priest has entered into heaven; for He has entered not only for Himself, but also for us.[21]

---

[21]John Calvin, *Commentary on Hebrews*, 6:19; cited in T.H.L. Parker, ed., *Essays in Christology* (London: Lutterworth Press, 1956), p. 71.

Perhaps we cannot express precisely what is meant by Christ's priesthood in heaven. At least we can say, however falteringly, that Christ's atoning sacrifice is still powerful in human life because it lives on forever in the life and purpose of God. Our vital interests are represented in the heavenly and eternal realm by one who was and is one of us, and he represents us in glad harmony with the will of the Father. But we are able to say more than this. Without entering here into the debate over whether Christ's sacrifice was of a "once for all" character confined to Jesus' crucifixion under Pontius Pilate, or whether this event was a reflection of an atoning movement that goes on forever in the heart of God, we should say that God was, is, and will be an atoning God. If we do say the latter, we must conserve the historic Christian emphasis upon the sacrifice of Jesus on Golgotha's hill. The dual truth of both historical and eternal atonement is vividly portrayed by Henry Hughes:

> Not to age-long pain in heaven, but to one sharp immeasurable sacrifice of sorrow upon earth, we owe our deliverance in the blood of Christ. We were and are redeemed by Him who died for us to the glory of God and the Father. . . . (However), it is because we see the Lamb slain on Calvary that we know that in the midst of the throne there is a Lamb "slain from the foundation of the world." The Cross is the supreme actualization in time and history of the love and sacrifice that are eternally in the heart of God.[22]

Christ entered the heavenly temple when the veil of his flesh was rent asunder. He thus broke through the limitations of his earthly life, and became at the same time universally representative of all men and universally available for all mankind. To say that he is ministering in heaven at God's right hand does not mean that he is remote from earth. It means rather that he occupies the place of representative authority and power wherever God is carrying on his great work of redemption. That work proceeds not far away in some distant heaven, but here. Right here. Right now.

---

[22]Robert Mackintosh, *Historic Theories of Atonement*, p. 256; cited in Henry M. Hughes, *What is Atonement?* (London: James Clarke & Co., Limited, n.d.), p. 134.

Chapter 8

Christ the Servant of God

The interpretation of Christ as "Servant of God" is one of the great creative concepts of the New Testament. The principal foundation for this interpretation is a remarkable series of "Servant songs" in the book of Isaiah. These are: Isaiah 42:1-7; 49:1-7; 50:4-9; and 52:13 to 53:12. The last of these songs has been, in Christian thought, especially influential in the interpretation of the work of Christ.

Philippians 2:6-11 contains many echoes of the Servant passages of Isaiah, and makes a striking delineation of the atoning ministry of Christ with special reference to Christ's humiliation and exaltation.

In this chapter, we shall be considering the doctrine of atonement with an emphasis on Christ's servanthood. Although the above-mentioned passages are only a few of the many instances in the Scriptures which relate to this theme, they are of primary value in the assessment of its significance.

The Suffering Servant of God

The identity of the Servant in the Servant songs is a matter of controversy among scholars. Some passages in the Servant hymns seem to identify the Servant with all of Israel. Others appear to refer to just a part of the nation, a "righteous remnant." Other passages, again, appear to single out an individual person as the Servant. The identity of the Servant, at least in the intention of the writer of the Servant poems, cannot be determined for certain.

Another point of controversy among scholars is whether Jesus saw his own mission in terms of the Servant passages, and particularly in terms of the fourth one. We need not enter into this debate here. It is enough to cite the contrasting conclusions of two prominent New Testament scholars. Hans Conzelmann, on the one hand, contends: "Jesus did not refer Isaiah 53 to himself. This was done only by the community, because it found here the explanation of his death."[1] On the other hand, Oscar Cullmann says, "We conclude that the concept 'Jesus the *ebed Yahweh*' (Servant of Yahweh) has its origin with Jesus himself, just as does the concept 'Jesus the Son of Man.' Thus it is not the early Church which first established a connection between these two fundamental Christological concepts."[2]

Whether Jesus saw himself as the Servant of God in the light of Isaiah 53, the fact remains, says Lionel Thornton, that "the Servant-theology is rooted in the New Testament, and remains unaffected by questions as to how it originally entered the mind of the Church."[3]

The identification of Jesus with the Servant of God appears to go back early in the history of the church. In Acts 8:26-39, Philip informed the Ethiopian eunuch that Isaiah 53 referred to Jesus. In the sermon reported in Acts 3, a sermon attributed to Peter, the same identification is made. A similar claim may be made concerning the prayer of the Church mentioned in Acts 4:27, 30. Other examples may be seen in 1 Peter 2:22-25; Hebrews 9:28; and Matthew 8:17; 12:17-21. In Luke 24:46, the risen Christ echoes the servant concept when he says of his death and resurrection, "It behooved Christ to suffer, and to rise from the dead the third day" (KJV).

In the Gospel of Mark, Jesus says, "The Son of man also came not to be served but to serve, and to give his life as a ransom for many" (Mark 10:45, RSV). Some of the language here is close to that of Isaiah

---

[1]Conzelmann, *An Outline of the Theology of the New Testament*, p. 85.

[2]Oscar Cullmann, *The Christology of the New Testament*, Shirley Guthrie and Charles Hall, trans. (Philadelphia: The Westminster Press, 1959), pp. 68-69.

[3]Thornton, *The Doctrine of the Atonement*, p. 55.

53. The word *many* is expressed in the Isaiah passage three times, where it is said that the Servant of God gives his life for *many*. This important verse in Mark comes as a fitting climax to a lesson taught by Jesus on humility and service. In response to the request by James and John for preferential treatment, Jesus replies that whoever seeks to be great must become the bondservant of all. That Jesus himself had followed this way of service is made pointedly clear by the context, and the image of him which emerges fits, in large outline, that of the Suffering Servant.

In his study entitled *The Servant of God*, Jeremias admits that in the New Testament there are "strikingly few" passages in which, by specific quotation, a word relating to the Servant of God in Isaiah is applied to Jesus.[4] On the other hand, Jeremias says, this kind of numeration by itself would result in a distorted picture, for if, in addition to direct quotations, we add direct or indirect allusions, the result is an impressive array of corroborative evidence.[5]

Cullmann, who also undertakes to show at considerable length the part which the Servant concept of Jesus played in the New Testament, nevertheless calls attention to the fact that the Servant teaching virtually disappeared quite early in the history of the primitive church. Among the important reasons for this decline of prominence, Cullmann believes, was the fact that the title was misunderstood in the Gentile Christian community, which thought that to conceive of Jesus as a "bondslave" derogated from the kingly majesty which should be ascribed to him. Also, the resurrection of Jesus made the early Church much more conscious of his present lordship than of his former humiliation. "The early Christian and the early Church prayed to the present Lord; and in their breaking of bread, joy at his presence was more prominent than remembrance of his death." In view of their exultation over Christ's present lordship, says Cullmann, the title of *ebed Jahweh* as a designation of Jesus had to assume a "subordinate place."[6]

If only explicit quotations or provable evidence are considered,

---

[4]W. Zimmerli and J. Jeremias, *The Servant of God* (Naperville, Ill.: Alec R. Allenson, Inc., 1957), p. 88.

[5]Ibid., pp. 88-105.

[6]Cullmann, *The Christology of the New Testament*, p. 81.

Robert Culpepper's claim that the New Testament picture of Christ reflects "the dominance of the Servant ideal" would probably exaggerate the facts.[7] Culpepper himself remembers that the work of Christ is reflected in many titles and under many banners. The picture of Christ as Servant is only one of these. Yet, when we view the image of Christ in the New Testament in its totality, we are able to see with Culpepper how closely and creatively he followed the Servant pattern, how much the saying "I am among you as one who serves" (Luke 22:27, RSV) fits his whole life and his death, and, therefore, how superlatively valuable in interpreting the gospel it is to remember the profound significance of the Servant theme with respect to the question of who Jesus was and what he did.

The Servant and the Messiah. In the synoptic gospels, and also particularly in the gospel of John, Jesus is recognized both as the Messiah and as the Servant of God. But the Servant in the Servant songs had no direct relationship to the messianic hope of Israel. This hope envisioned typically an idealized and glorified Davidic king, whose work it would be to restore Israel to its ancient glory, to execute judgment on Israel's oppressors and enemies, and to set up a lasting kingdom marked by the reign of a just and peaceful government. The Messiah's authority and power were to be great, but he was essentially a human being, and his work was political and nationalistic.[8]

A somewhat different picture of the Messiah is found in the Similitudes of Enoch. Here the Messiah is a supernatural being who lives on high, and who, endowed with the power and glory of God, waits for the hour chosen of God to appear on earth.

In either case, the Messiah was expected to come as a regal figure, charged with a divine commission, endued with divine power, and endowed with divine authority. It was not envisioned that he would be a sufferer.

These figures of the Messiah and of the Servant appear to be mutually incompatible, and many scholars have contended that, before the Christian era, the two concepts were not combined. However, the book of Enoch, the Apocalypse of Ezra, and the

---

[7]Cf. Culpepper, *Interpreting the Atonement,* pp. 56-57.

[8]Taylor, *Forgiveness and Reconciliation,* pp. 16-17.

Apocalypse of Baruch do, in an indirect way, ascribe to the Messiah some of the attributes of the Servant. Even here, the Messiah was not conceived to be a *suffering* Messiah. Cullmann claims: "One can at best find faint traces of a suffering Messiah in Judaism."[9] That he *was* involved to some extent in the sufferings of his people is an inference that we made in chapter 6, page 93.

To say that this was a logical inference, however, cannot be promoted to a claim that this inference was supported in the common expectation of the Hebrew people. G. B. Caird sums up the situation well:

> We look in vain for Old Testament predictions that the Messiah must reach his appointed glory through suffering, unless we realize that the Old Testament is concerned from start to finish with the call and destiny of Israel, and that the Messiah, as King of Israel, must embody in his own person the character and vocation of the people of which he is leader and representative.[10]

The popular hesitation to ascribe humiliation and suffering to the Messiah is seen in the incident which describes Peter's confession of Jesus' messiahship at Caesarea Philippi. Jesus' disclosure to his disciples on this occasion that the Messiah "must" suffer and die was strongly controverted by Peter, who apparently thought that the Messiah's course would be one of constant and triumphant success (see Matt. 16:21-23).

The Servant and the Son of Man. On the basis of the gospel records, the title *Son of man* was Jesus' favorite designation of himself. This title is deeply imbedded in the Old Testament, and in Jewish history before the advent of Jesus. The term, however, had been given such varied interpretations in the Jewish heritage that its meaning was ambiguous. Perhaps its very ambiguity was one reason Jesus chose it as a self-designation, for the variety of interpretations allowed new meanings to be poured into it.

The Hebrew phrase *son of man* (*ben adam*) simply means "a member of the human race," a human being. In the book of Ezekiel, in

---

[9]Cullmann, *The Christology of the New Testament*, p. 56.

[10]G. B. Caird, *The Gospel of Luke* (New York: Seabury Press, 1968), p. 258.

which God frequently uses the phrase in addressing the prophet, the intention appears to have been that of contrasting the insignificance of the prophet with the majesty and greatness of God. At the same time, the term indicates the dignity which the prophet acquires by virtue of the great significance of the message which God has given him to deliver.

Whatever Jesus' purpose was in the employment of the *Son of man* title, the most decisive use of it in the synoptics connects it with Daniel 7:13f: "I saw in the night visions, and behold, with the clouds of heaven there came one like a son of man, and he came to the Ancient of Days . . . And to him was given dominion and glory and kingdom" (RSV).

Here to some extent the Son of man appears to be a corporate figure, embodying "the people of the saints of the Most High." In this passage, however, the Son of man is, if not himself a divine being, at least God's agent in the world for leading God's battle against the powers of evil. In Mark 2:10, Jesus associates this function with himself: " 'But that you may know that the Son of man has authority on earth to forgive sins,'—he said to the paralytic—'I say to you, rise, take up your pallet and go home' " (RSV).

The Son of man in Daniel 7 is also an eschatological figure, who in the last days will come to rule over God's kingdom with power, glory, and judgment. In what seems to be an obvious allusion to the passage in Daniel, Jesus addresses a reply to the high priest, who asks at Jesus' trial whether Jesus is "the Christ, the Son of the Blessed." "And Jesus said, 'I am; and you will see the Son of man sitting at the right hand of Power, and coming with the clouds of heaven' " (Mark 14:62, RSV. See Luke 22:67-71).[11]

In the Gospel of Mark, Jesus, while using the Son of man title about himself, gives it a fresh meaning in two respects. In the first place, the Son of man is no longer a figure of vague heavenly delineation, but a person of flesh and blood, Jesus himself. Secondly, this person who represents God with such august credentials must suffer and die. Only through suffering and death will his heavenly glory be revealed. Only so will his mission for the salvation of the world be accomplished. "To save," says Rudolph Otto, "is the calling and purpose of the Son of Man. To save, however, is also the purpose

---

[11]Cf. Green, *The Meaning of Salvation*, pp. 102-103.

of the suffering of the Servant of God. The Son of Man 'must' be the redemptively suffering Servant of God, if he is to fulfil his vocation as Son of Man, i.e., his vocation as Saviour."[12]

The picture of Jesus which we see in the gospels is that of a Messiah who explicitly rejected the messianic hope that Israel would become a world political power in line with the Jewish idealized retrospection concerning the kingdom of David and Solomon. Rather, Jesus is represented as interpreting his mission in terms of the picture of the Suffering Servant in Isaiah. Likewise, the figure of the Son of man is so blended with that of the Servant that the heavenly glory of the former is to be seen forever thereafter in the light of the humiliation of the Servant. Whether the author of the gospel of John owes his own interpretation of Christ to Isaiah's Servant, he sees the heavenly glory of the Son specifically in the Son's humiliation.

The fusion, in the New Testament picture of Jesus, of concepts embodied in terms like Messiah, Son of man, and suffering Servant, and of other concepts like the understanding of Christ as the Vine of Israel and the Priest-king at the right hand of God, is, in the words of C. H. Dodd, "an achievement of interpretative imagination which results in the creation of an entirely new figure."[13] National destiny, the role and mission of the nation as God's servant nation, the divinely appointed role of God's Messiah, the work of the heavenly Son of man who comes to earth embodying God's power and purpose to redeem— all of these were brought to a focus by the depiction of Christ as the Suffering Servant.

The Servant and the Lamb of God. The New Testament writers were convinced that Jesus died and rose for our salvation from sin, and that, in so doing, he fulfilled the Old Testament Scriptures. Paul asserts that the primitive Christian community believed that "Christ died for our sins in accordance with the scriptures, that he was buried, that he was raised on the third day in accordance with the scriptures" (1 Cor. 15:3-4, RSV). What these Scriptures were is unspecified, but they probably included Psalm 22, Psalm 16, and Hosea 6:2. No

---

[12]Rudolph Otto, *The Kingdom of God and the Son of Man* (London: The Lutterworth Press, 1938), p. 251.

[13]C. H. Dodd, *According to the Scriptures* (New York: Charles Scribner's Sons, 1953), p. 109.

passage in the Old Testament was so capable of immediate application to Jesus' death, burial, and resurrection, however, as was Isaiah 53.

The portrayal of Christ as the Lamb of God appears to be due to the association of the sacrifice of Jesus with the Lamb of Isaiah 53: "Like a lamb that is led to the slaughter, and like a sheep that before its shearers is dumb, so he opened not his mouth" (Isa. 53:7, RSV). In the fourth gospel, John the Baptist, representing the line of prophesy, gives the title, *Lamb of God* to Jesus. "Behold the Lamb of God," exclaimed John, "who takes away the sin of the world" (John 1:29, RSV). The saying of John would suggest that the sacrificial lamb is to be identified with the Servant, who "makes himself an offering for sin" (Isa. 53:10, RSV), who "bore the sins of many," and who "poured out his soul to death" (Isa. 53:12, RSV).

However, the fourth gospel *characteristically* sees the death of Jesus in comparison with the Passover lambs rather than in terms of the Suffering Servant. That this identification was made in the gospel of John is not surprising, since, according to John, Jesus was slain at the same time that the Passover lambs were being sacrificed.

The distinction between the Servant lamb and the Passover lamb is to be noted, for "the Paschal Lamb is not represented in the Old Testament as bearing away sin; its blood is a token which averts the judgment of Yahweh."[14] The difference may be noted by reference to Exodus 12:13, which shows the function of the blood of the Passover lamb: "The blood shall be a sign for you, upon the houses where you are; and when I see the blood, I will pass over you, and no plague shall fall upon you to destroy you, when I smite the land of Egypt" (RSV).

A similar distinction appears in 1 Peter 1:18-19. The writer affirms that Christians are redeemed, not with perishable things, "but with the precious blood of Christ, like that of a lamb without blemish or spot" (RSV). This verse identifies the sacrifice of Christ in the imagery of the Paschal lamb.

However, in chapter 2 of the same book, Jesus appears to be identified with the Servant lamb of Isaiah: "He committed no sin; no guile was found on his lips. When he was reviled, he did not revile in return; when he suffered, he did not threaten; but he trusted to him who judges justly." The Servant, this writer says, "bore our sins in his

---

[14]Taylor, *Jesus and His Sacrifice*, p. 227.

body on the tree, that we might die to sin and live to righteousness. By his wounds you have been healed" (1 Pet. 2:22-24, RSV).

In the book of Revelation, the term *lamb* is used with reference to Christ twenty-seven times. In some of these references, redemption through the blood of the Lamb is associated with the Passover story as recounted in Exodus 12 and in Exodus 24, the latter of which chapters describes the inauguration of the Mosaic covenant.[15]

Most references to the *Lamb* in the Apocalypse, however, are related to the Servant conception. In the fifth chapter the Lamb stands close to the throne of God, "as though it had been slain" (Rev. 5:6, RSV)—signifying that its glory has come through suffering. By his blood, the Lamb "didst ransom men for God" (Rev. 5:9, RSV). The salvation effected by his ransom included the Gentiles, for it applied to men "from every tribe and tongue and people and nation, and hast made them a kingdom and priests to our God, and they shall reign on earth" (Rev. 5:9-10, RSV). In Revelation 5:5-6, Christ is called both "the Lion of the tribe of Judah, the Root of David" and the "Lamb," indicating in this passage a fusion of ideas of the messianic King and the Suffering Servant.

In typical Jewish sacrifice, the sacrificial offering was not loaded with the sins of the people. Suffering on the part of the victim was not essential to the efficacy of the sacrifice; neither was it believed that the victim was being punished vicariously for the sins of the worshipers. The sacrificial animal was to be "without spot or blemish" in order that it might represent, in an ideal sense, the gift of the worshipers's life to God. This fact is what makes the offering of the Servant in Isaiah so striking, for "Isaiah 53 (verses 7 and 10) is the only passage in the Old Testament where a human figure is described in terms of the sacrificial cultus as a victim offered like a lamb for a sin-offering."[16]

The Servant in Isaiah 53 "bore the sins of many," was "wounded for our transgressions," and, by God's hand, has "laid on him the iniquity of us all." Advocates of penal substitution seize upon these statements as proof of their theory that penal substitution was the rationale of sacrifice. I do not believe that this thesis can be substantiated, yet we cannot dissolve away from the gospel message

---

[15]Thornton, *The Doctrine of the Atonement*, p. 59.

[16]Ibid., p. 58.

the truth that Christ, the Servant of God, bears our sins and our sorrows. This Lamb of God, so plainly shown to be without spot or blemish, was made an offering for sin.

Thus, in the Suffering Servant we see a picture of one in whom innocent and retributive suffering were joined. He accepted the judgment of God upon sin as a judgment upon himself, and he so identified himself with the sins and sufferings of his people that he poured out his soul unto death for them.

We can sharpen the point here. That Christ died as a Paschal lamb means that he died the death of an innocent victim. That he died as a Servant Lamb means that he died the death of a criminal victim. He, the innocent victim, vicariously accepted as his own the guilt and burden of our sins.

The Servant and God. The Servant in Isaiah is nowhere identified with God. He represents the will and purpose of God. He does the work of God. "It was the will of the Lord to bruise him," (Isa. 53:10, RSV) and "the Lord has laid on him the iniquity of us all" (Isa. 53:6, RSV). "The will of the Lord shall prosper in his hand; he shall see the fruit of the travail of his soul and be satisfied" (Isa. 53:10-11, RSV).

It is a Christian insight to go further, and to see in God himself a Suffering Servant on our behalf, who allows us to see him this way because Jesus revealed him to be this kind of God. This insightful thesis is advocated by G. A. A. Knight. Knight writes:

> It is quite beside the point for Jews and Christians to continue the recurring argument as to whether the Isaianic Servant passages refer to Israel or whether they refer to an individual. The passages may indeed refer to both, or to neither. But the belief that Jesus held was that they refer to *God*, to God immanent in a sinful world in the form of His *Shechinah.* As St. Paul points out: "It was *God* in Christ who was reconciling the world unto Himself." It was because *God* was like the Suffering Servant of Isaiah that Jesus identified Himself with that Old Testament figure.[17]

If this is true, then it is God himself who, in Christ, bears the burden of our sins and sorrows.

---

[17]G. A. A. Knight, *From Moses to Paul* (London: Lutterworth Press, 1949), p. 162.

The Kenotic Theme

Vincent Taylor quite properly observes that the Servant imagery with reference to Christ is used sparingly in the Pauline writings. A most striking exception is Philippians 2:5-11. Many scholars believe that Paul in this passage quoted a hymn which perhaps was already widely known and used in the primitive church. These scholars believe, in other words, that this hymn was not of Pauline composition, although Paul appears to have approved its teaching.

The indebtedness of this passage to Isaiah 53 is shown by technical evidence which need not be taken up here (See Jeremias and Zimmerli, *The Servant of God*, p. 97). Also, there is in the hymn a parallel to the Servant's meekness and subsequent exaltation, and to his willing obedience to the point of humiliation in death. The hymn to Christ found in 1 Peter 2:22-25 is capable of being interpreted as a short summary of Isaiah 53. Also, the song of praise of Simeon, found in Luke 2:29-32, takes up the theme of Isaiah 49:6, and refers this servant passage to Jesus.[18]

Christ Emptied Himself. The thought of the Philippian passage under consideration is as far as possible removed from an adoptionist concept of Christ, in which concept Jesus, in the fullest and most exclusive sense a human being, is elevated by God to a divine status. Rather, this passage appears to presuppose the preexistence of Christ, and perhaps a status of equality with God the Father.

The emphasis in the passage is upon Christ's self-abasement in assuming human flesh, with all the limitations of a human state, for the sake of redeeming men and women. The humiliation of his obedience in carrying out the will of the Father, in taking the form of a servant for our sakes, was steadfastly held onto until his death. The hymn appears in the context of a passage in which Paul is exhorting the church at Philippi to embrace a Christian unity which would preserve and exemplify a self-sacrificing Christian brotherliness. He appeals to Christ's example:

> Though he was in the form of God, [Christ] did not count equality with God a thing to be grasped, but emptied himself, taking the form of a servant, being born in the

---

[18]Zimmerli and Jeremias, *The Servant of God*, pp. 97-98.

likeness of men. And being found in human form he humbled himself and became obedient unto death, even death on a cross. Therefore God has highly exalted him and bestowed on him the name which is above every name, that at the name of Jesus every knee should bow, in heaven and on earth and under the earth, and every tongue confess that Jesus Christ is Lord, to the glory of God the Father (Phil. 2:6-11, RSV).

The strongly paradoxical character of the thought of this passage is evident, for it appears that, in becoming human, a divine person has laid aside his divinity in order to become a man. But we must not forget that this is a hymn, which does not bother to explain how Christ could so "empty himself" in becoming human that he could still remain divine. No doubt the interpretation which the passage makes was not intended to deny that some identity and continuity existed between the divine and human phases. There was a core of divinity which was preserved when Christ assumed human flesh. Without compromising his genuine humanity, this explains why he was able to conquer sin and to be in human flesh God's great agent of redemption.

No explanation of *how* this could be done is given, but the message, in its essential outlines, is clear. In a real sense, Christ renounced his divine prerogatives and became a man, radically sharing the limitations of our human life. Sin excepted, he participated profoundly in the human experience as a human being, from birth to bitter death. His exaltation was not just the resumption of a temporarily abandoned divinity. In some sense, God, because of Christ's obedience unto death, raised him to a glory even more resplendent than Christ enjoyed before his incarnate life.[19]

The self-emptying of Christ (from the Greek word *kenosis*, an emptying) described in this passage is the primary basis of the kenotic *theory* of the incarnation and atonement of Christ. This theory had few parallels in Christian thought prior to the nineteenth century. Some small gleamings of kenotic insight may be found in early Christian writings, but, according to Loofs, no developed theory of kenosis is to be found in early Christian thought. In the early church,

---

[19]Cf. John Knox, *The Man Christ Jesus* (Chicago, New York: Willett, Clark and Company, 1942), pp. 88-89.

Loofs says, "the usual exposition of the text sees in the 'self-emptying' of the Logos merely an equivalent for the 'taking the form of a servant,' and that again is merely an equivalent for becoming incarnate."[20]

Thomasius of Erlangen (1802-1875) has been called the founder of modern Kenoticism. Other European theologians gave the kenotic view prominence as they attempted to deal with the problem of harmonizing the Christological statements of the orthodox creeds with the portrait of Jesus which emerged from the historical-critical method of studying the Gospels.

Kenoticism became a prominent kind of interpretation of Christ's person and work in the latter part of the nineteenth century, particularly in British theology. It came out of the liberal tradition, and was an attempt to say that Jesus Christ was fully human and at the same time that he was in some sense the incarnation of God.

Although D. M. Baillie was a trenchant critic of kenotic Christology, he gave the following admirable statement of its essentials:

> Jesus was indeed identical with the eternal Son of God, one in essence with the Father and equal in power and glory. But in becoming incarnate He "emptied himself" of those attributes which essentially differentiate God from man; so that the life He lived on earth was a truly human life, without omnipotence or omnipresence or omniscience, a life subject to the conditions and limitations of humanity, as are the lives of all men. Thus we seem to get a real God-man, and an intelligible meaning of the Incarnation, thoroughly congruous both with the New Testament idea of the divine condescension and the self-emptying and with the modern treatment of the Gospel story and the rediscovery of the "Jesus of history."[21]

According to the interpretation of the kenoticists, Christ, while divesting himself of the attributes of majesty, such as omnipotence, omniscience, and omnipresence, in order to become man, still

---

[20]Friedrich Loofs, *The New Schaff-Herzog Encyclopedia of Religious Knowledge* (Grand Rapids: Baker Book House, 1950), 6:315.

[21]Baillie, *God Was in Christ*, p. 95.

perfectly embodied the attributes of God which were needed for his saving mission to mankind. These attributes were love, mercy, goodness, and compassion, among others.

While this view of the incarnation had and still has great devotional profundity, and was a powerful safeguard of the genuine humanity of Christ, in time it became involved in theological difficulties which many critics have thought to be insuperable. The view waned greatly in influence during the early part of this century, and has never regained its former prestige.

Norman Pittenger's assessment of kenoticism, made in 1959, advanced two damaging criticisms which are still pertinent:

> In the first place it supposes some sort of fancied transaction in the heavenly places by which the eternal Son of God divested himself of the so-called 'metaphysical' attributes of deity while retaining, for his incarnate life, the 'moral' attributes. And this leads to the second defect. It is doubtful whether or not a deity which is thus divided, and only one-half of which, so to say, is incarnate, can really be said to be deity at all.[22]

The theory, says Pittenger, "will not serve."

The problems which the critics of kenoticism raise about the kenotic view are probably unsolvable on the basis of the kenotic presuppositions of theologians like Gottfried Thomasius, Wolfgang Friedrich Gess, Charles Gore, and H. R. Mackintosh. This does not mean, however, that nothing can be said in favor of the kenotic *motif* as an *insight* as differentiated from a developed *theory*.

Sydney Cave observes that in the passage under consideration and its context, Paul was not trying to write with theological precision, or in an attempt to construct an erudite theory. He was not attempting to explain the mode of the incarnation. He was attempting to use the fact of the incarnation as a supreme incentive for the practice of an humble Christian love. "We have here," says Cave, "the mystery of the Incarnation and the Cross conveyed in the vivid picture-words of religion. It is useless to try to get from this passage answers to problems in which we have no evidence that Paul took any interest."[23]

---

[22]Pittenger, *The Word Incarnate*, p. 110.

[23]Sydney Cave, *The Doctrine of the Person of Christ* (London: Duckworth, 1947), p. 43.

Emil Brunner, whose aim was to preserve the "true God-true man" balance of Chalcedon, carefully avoided a subscription to some of the implications of modern kenotic theory, but he believed in a genuine kenosis.

Brunner believed that in Jesus God divested himself of the attributes of majesty. But, says Brunner, we cannot say *to what extent* and *in what manner* God "emptied himself" in order to become man. We cannot say, moreover, which elements in the life of Jesus belong to the human nature, and which belong to the divine. How divinity is combined with humanity in the person of Jesus is beyond our power of understanding. Yet, we must say that Jesus, in the wholeness of his person, not just in the divinity of his person, is the revelation of God. His flesh, the weakness which we see manifested in his creatureliness, are essential elements of God's revelation. We see Christ's divine glory specifically in his creatureliness. We see the wisdom of God in the folly and shame of the cross. We see the love of God in the sufferings and death of this man, Jesus Christ.[24]

Brunner's discussion may be used to show that some theologians who do not agree with the statements of kenosis found in what we may call kenotic theology still recognize the validity of the kenotic motif. The demurrers of the critics pertain to making this motif into a *theory*, rather than to preserving it as an *insight*. Moreover, there is a larger issue in the kenotic theme than the question of *how much* of God is in Christ, or of *how* the union of God and man actually occurred in him.

The reader should be referred to a book like Donald G. Dawe's *The Form of a Servant* for a study in depth of the kenotic theme as it appears in modern theology. The larger issue, says Dawe, concerns the kenosis *of God*. The question is no longer, Dawe adds, "How is kenosis possible in the light of God's nature? The question is rather: What is God's nature in the light of kenosis?" Dawe's answer is as follows:

> Kenosis is the characteristic of God's being and action in every aspect. God the Father is Creator by virtue of accepting the limitation of his creation. God the Son is Redeemer in accepting the limitations of the humanity he seeks to save. God the Spirit is the Perfecter of man by living in and through his history and accepting his suffering.

---

[24]Brunner, *The Christian Doctrine of Creation and Redemption*, pp. 357-63.

Kenosis is not an event in the life of the Trinity as the mediating theologians pictured it. Nor does it become possible because of certain rearrangements of person or attributes in the Trinity. Kenosis is a characteristic action of the divine love as it seeks and creates fellowship with men and the world. Kenosis is the key to the saving action of God. His characteristic act in salvation is not one of self-assertion but rather of self-negation. In contrast to all human attempts at self-salvation, God saves in a gesture of radical self-giving. God limits himself, taking upon himself the incompleteness, brokenness, and sin that separate men from him. Free self-limitation is the characteristic of God's every act, indeed, of God's own person.[25]

The Way of Obedience. Whatever it may mean to say that Christ did not consider equality with God a thing to be grasped, it is plain from the New Testament records that the ministry of Christ on earth was one of constant and creative obedience to the will of the Father.

Obedience is an unpopular concept in our contemporary era. Our emphasis is on freedom, not obedience. Any accent on obedience which threatens true freedom should, indeed, be adamantly opposed. Obedience, in the minds of long-subjugated people, has been leagued with oppression, colonialism, racism, caste, and obsequious subservience.

The obedience of Jesus of Nazareth to the will of God cannot be associated with these crippling evils. Indeed, the spirit of Christian obedience is an implacable enemy of all kinds and forms of subservience which rob men and women of their dignity and freedom as human beings. To obey God freely and truly is to set oneself against every form of tyranny which seeks to subjugate the minds and spirits of men and women.

What needs to be recovered is the truth that obedience and freedom are correlative, not mutually exclusive. Here let us engage in some legitimate surmise concerning what obedience meant for Jesus.

Jesus' obedience was not a slavish obedience; it involved a constant, prayerful effort on his part to find and follow the Father's

---

[25]Donald G. Dawe, *The Form of a Servant* (Philadelphia: The Westminster Press, 1963), p. 200.

will. The Father's will was not dictated to him, as by an audible voice. His life was not lived by a preconceived blueprint. His way was not one fixed by a road-map. His overall objective was clear: "I come to do thy will, O God." But many times the means by which he was to implement this objective were not so clear.

At every step there must have been human uncertainties, alternative paths which looked almost equally inviting or compelling, shades of gray in moral decisions, perhaps, instead of stark black and white. At times, Jesus had to decide whether to stand up to an issue by meeting it head-on or by meeting it by circumvention. Gethsemane was one of those crucial times, perhaps the most crucial of all, when there must have gone through his mind the question of whether *this* was the time to bring everything to a head, to risk all on "one turn of pitch and toss." In other words, Jesus did not see his way from start to finish all at once. Sometimes he saw it one step at a time.

The way of obedience was at the same time the way of heroic and creative freedom. Jesus showed freedom in his daring defiance of tradition when he believed that traditional ways and thought were stultifying. There was freedom, as well as creativity, in deciding how to match an objective with the exigencies of a particular situation. There was freedom to make his point in one way instead of in another. There were thought, pondering, brooding, ingenuity, courage, and prayer in the development of his teaching. There was tact, and at the same time firmness, in his dealing with persons. Arrogant persons felt the unbending quality of an iron will when they opposed him, as did some of the Pharisees. Persons who were at the "end of their rope" felt his vast compassion. He did not break bruised reeds, nor quench smoking flax (see Matt. 12:20), but he punctured the balloons of many timeservers and hypocrites.

Jesus did not become what he was, nor do what he did, by the overpowering fiat of the divine will. He was what he was in obedience, by the highest exercise of free decision: "And Jesus increased in wisdom and in stature, and in favor with God and man" (Luke 2:52, RSV). He did what he did by the seeking of divine guidance, by the weighing of alternatives, and (surely) by the seeking of counsel from his trusted friends. He learned from his disciples, not only they from him. And he learned from his enemies. "He knew what was in man" (John 2:25, KJV) not because an omniscience, ready-made, had been handed to him from heaven, but because, with the helping ministry of the Spirit, he had studied attentively and perceptively in the laboratory of human life.

The way of the servant which Jesus chose was the way of obedience. The saving power of Christ's atoning sacrifice was due, not primarily to the shedding of the blood of his body, but to the complete obedience to the Father's will which led to the cross. For this reason, the cross should be seen always in the closest relationship to the life of obedience which preceded it. His life was centered in the will of the Father, rather than in his own will. This was the decisive point. Perhaps nowhere in the New Testament is the willing outpouring of his life in obedience more graphically stated than at Gethsemane: "Father, if thou art willing, remove this cup from me; nevertheless not my will, but thine, be done" (Luke 22:42, RSV).

Obedience was the theme of the outpoured sacrifice of Jesus' life throughout its course. That "to obey is better than sacrifice" (1 Sam. 15:22, RSV) was everywhere recognized in the deepest levels of Old Testament thought. Is this not to say that, in its finest meaning, the essence of sacrifice is obedience? Both the priest and the prophet agreed on this truth. No sacrifice was efficacious *ex opere operato*. It was not effective unless it was done in humility of spirit, and in an act of dedication to the will of God. The self-sacrifice of Jesus nobly and decisively exemplified this principle.

The determination of Jesus to follow the course of obedience helps us to see the great significance of the wilderness temptation which occurred at the beginning of his ministry. He decided that he would not pander to the physical appetites of men in order to gain their approval. He embraced, rather, the decision that "man shall not live by bread alone, but by every word that proceeds from the mouth of God" (Matt. 4:4, RSV). For a time, many more persons would have followed him, if he had made his ministry a display of publicity-seeking sensationalism, but he resolved instead to follow a pathway of unostentatious service (Matt. 4:5). He might have risen to spectacular heights of popularity, if he had shaped his aspirations in the direction of a political messiahship which would have compromised with the power of the devil. But this he refused to do.

He renounced these false paths for the path of obedience. In turn, he embraced the way of love, truth, and righteousness which was in accord with the Father's will, and hence in faithful keeping with his vocation as Messiah and Servant of God.

The resolute decision to obey the Father, and to make obedience the steadfast pattern of his life, was far from being a cringing submission to the will of a superior power. It can be seen more truly as a bold defiance of the evil forces which had placed all mankind in bondage to sin and death. His decision to do the will of the Father placed him in conflict with these forces, and led to his death at their hands. John Howard Yoder writes:

> His very obedience unto death is in itself not only the sign but also the firstfruits of an authentic restored humanity. Here we have for the first time to do with a man who is not the slave of any power, of any law or custom, community or institution, value or theory. Not even to save his own life will he let himself be made a slave of these Powers. This authentic humanity included his free acceptance of death at their hands.[26]

The power of Jesus' Servant witness lay not in its ostentation, for God was in it, so to say, "incognito." Its power was in the fact that the obedience of Christ embodied the will, purpose, and presence of God himself, as God dedicated himself in Christ to the enterprise of human redemption. Through this particular man, in this particular time and place, God's redeeming grace reached out to all men, to all times, and to all places. The truth of this universal outreach has been captured by F. C. N. Hicks in an eloquent passage:

> Men are, like the prodigal son, exiles in the far country of their sins. They are like sheep wandering and lost upon the barren hills, wounded and sick from exposure and the attacks of their natural enemies. They are God's treasure, lost in dark corners and hidden beneath dust and dirt. . . . It is this Yahweh, so known and inherited by our Lord and by all those who had, or to whom He gave, the key to the history which He fulfilled, who is the Father of the Prodigal Son, the Shepherd who searches at whatever cost for the lost sheep, the householder who spares no pains for the recovery of His treasure. And as the teaching goes on, by word and by act, in the ministry of Jesus, the outlines of the unseen God

---

[26]John Howard Yoder, *The Politics of Jesus* (Grand Rapids, Michigan: William B. Eerdmans Publishing Company, 1972), p. 148.

take shape; as Jesus Himself is found seeking and saving and healing. . . . He has Himself gone into the far country of His people's sins. They come back, not alone but in His company, following Him, borne by Him. He has taught them that in doing this He must die; and that they must share His Cross; and that for Him and for them that means life.[27]

The ministry of Christ, so beset with toil and suffering, was steadied by a vision to which he adhered without faltering. This vision was defined on a sabbath at Nazareth at the beginning of his public ministry, when he read to his townsmen a passage from Isaiah:

The Spirit of the Lord is upon me, because he hath anointed me to preach the gospel to the poor; he hath sent me to heal the brokenhearted, to preach deliverance to the captives, and recovering of sight to the blind, to set at liberty them that are bruised, to preach the acceptable year of the Lord (Luke 4:18-19, KJV).

He made himself "of no reputation" by making common cause with the despised, the poor, the sick, the needy, and the lost. No matter who they were, or how much it cost him in time, energy, or anguish, he gave of himself to help and to heal.

The faithfulness of his obedience extended to the last extremity. He was faithful unto death: "With him they crucify two thieves; the one on his right hand, and the other on his left" (Mark 15:27, KJV). Thus, says the account which describes the scene, "he was numbered with the transgressors" (Mark 15:28, KJV). Thus he died the death of a common felon, an outcast from society, adjudged unfit for residence among decent people, a dangerous criminal whose deeds merited no less than capital punishment. "He had no form or comeliness that we should look at him, and no beauty that we should desire him" (Isa. 53:2, RSV).

The Way of Suffering. A universal datum of human and animal life, suffering has been a perennial enigma. Nothing is intrinsically redemptive about it; indeed, suffering frequently is debasing and destructive. The Old Testament belief that suffering is due to sin was

---

[27]Hicks, *The Fullness of Sacrifice*, pp. 150-51.

partially justified. Much suffering is caused by human wrongdoing. Yet the question, "Why do the righteous suffer?" was a question which was as clamorous for an answer as it was puzzling and insoluble.

The question of the meaning of suffering reached its most poignant and insistent form in the suffering of Jesus. The traditional answers here were, to Christian disciples, utterly inadequate. He did not suffer because he sinned; he was not, they believed, a sinner. In common opinion, the Messiah was not supposed to suffer. Prophets suffered in the fulfillment of their vocation, and Jesus was certainly a prophet. Yet there was something in the suffering and death of Jesus that transcended prophetic suffering.

The picture of Jesus which we see in the New Testament was a picture of a great sufferer. As H. Wheeler Robinson says, his ministry from first to last was one of suffering, both physical and spiritual:

> Some phases of it and some incidents in it doubtless brought
> joy to Him, but from the day of the temptation to that of the
> crucifixion, the quality of suffering was predominant. It was
> a life of poverty, of public scorn and private betrayal, of
> disappointed hopes and misunderstood aspirations, which
> was crowned by a shameful and agonizing death.[28]

By the world's standards, his life was a failure. His own people turned on him. He was crucified by a tolerably just government, at the instigation of the leaders of a religious system which to this day has been one of the highest in noble aspiration and in religious insight. He could not hold his own disciples together, and he was betrayed by one of them. And on the cross, he thought himself to be forsaken by the Father.

Even after the resurrection, the Christian community was baffled by the problem of a crucified Messiah. A man who was crucified bore the curse of God. How, then, could he be the "one who was to redeem Israel"?

Early in the history of the Church, however, the suffering of Jesus was interpreted in creative ways. Paul asserted that what seemed to be the folly of the cross was instead the veritable wisdom of God, who was working out through the death of his Son a justifying righteousness for

---

[28]H. Wheeler Robinson, *Suffering, Human and Divine* (London: Student Christian Movement Press, 1940), p. 162.

men and women. The writer of the book of Hebrews saw that the giving of Christ's life was a sacrifice, administered by an eternal High Priest, and efficacious forever. The author of the fourth gospel saw the glorification of Christ specifically in the cross itself, and discerned that in the cross, as nowhere else, there is to be found the measure of the love of God.[29]

Solid theological reasons permitted, and indeed constrained, the creative interpretations of Christ's sufferings which we find in the New Testament. One factor was the identity and character of this particular sufferer. He was one who embodied the "grace and truth" of the Father. He was the Son whom God's love gave for the *salvation* of the world. He was the Lamb of God whose divinely elected destiny was to bear away the *sins* of the world. As Priest and as Victim he offered himself in order that God might be glorified and men saved. The self-oblation of his whole life should not be forgotten in assessing the strength of his atoning sacrifice. Yet the cross was the summary and the sign of his entire life and ministry. The uniqueness of the crucifixion was not in the cross as the instrument of his agony, but in the Person who died upon it. Because he was the appointed agent and representative of God, a criminal's death was transformed into an atoning sacrifice.

Christ's obedience to his vocation was even more decisive than his sufferings. If we grasp this truth, we are relieved of the misconception that Christ had to suffer in an amount exactly equivalent to the penalty of suffering which our sins deserve, or that his sufferings for us effected an accumulation of supererogatory "merit" which can be transferred, in the manner of a commercial transaction, from him to us.

His suffering was obedience to a love which makes the commercial figure of merit not only extraneous, but also positively distorting. Obedience to his vocation gave purpose to his suffering; but suffering sanctified his obedience. The grace manifested here was not cheap grace. We see in the cross of Christ how seriously God regarded our dereliction, and how costly was the love that led him to bear our sins and our sorrows in Christ.

The suffering of Christ was a vicarious suffering; it was "for us" and "in our stead." But when we reflect that "God was in Christ reconciling

---

[29]Cf. ibid., pp. 162-63.

the world to himself" (2 Cor. 5:19, RSV), we are reminded that the principle of vicarious suffering goes back to the moral nature of God himself. This truth places the atoning work of God at the farthermost possible remove from any interpretation which separates the love of Christ from the love of God. The penal view holds that Christ was a victim sacrificed in order to turn a vengeful God into a God who comes to favor us because Christ's sacrifice has appeased his wrath. The love of the Son for us saves us from the wrath of the Father.

McLeod Campbell was much nearer the truth when he asserted that the cross of Christ was not the measure of what God inflicts, but a revelation of what God feels. We need not try to make a complete atonement theory of this insight in order to discern its penetrating truth. In the sufferings of Christ we perceive God's suffering love working for our salvation. "The cross of Christ does not stand for the idea that God laid on Christ, a third party, the burdens of the sins of man," said W. T. Conner. "It rather says that God in Christ takes that burden on himself."[30]

Many moderns are surprised when they discover that, although the most intense suffering has been acknowledged on the part of Christ, Christian theologians through much of Christian history have been exceedingly chary of admitting that God himself suffers. In fact, the belief in the impassibility of God—that God is *unable* to suffer—was the traditional teaching of the church for many centuries. This belief was strongly held by the Fathers, and Augustine's viewpoint was typical:

> Be it far from us to surmise that the impassible nature of God is liable to any molestation. But like as He is jealous without any darkening of spirit, wroth without any perturbation, pitiful without any pain, repenteth Him without any wrongness in Him to set right; so is He patient without aught of passion.[31]

The doctrine of the divine impassibility appears to have stemmed from Greek thought. Plato believed that the gods were exalted above

---

[30]W. T. Conner, *The Cross in the New Testament* (Nashville: Broadman Press, 1954), p. 85.

[31]Cited in Hughes, *What is Atonement?*, p. 86.

pleasure or pain. Aristotle believed that God lived in splendid isolation and self-contemplation beyond the reach of human pain or sorrow. Men should love and reverence the Deity, but they should expect no love in return. Ideas like these merged with views in late Judaism which asserted an exaggerated divine transcendence, and which placed God above pain.

Whatever the streams of influence which helped to produce the idea that God does not suffer, this idea became a tenet of orthodox Christian belief. Suffering in God, or emotion of any kind in God, for that matter, was considered to be an imperfection, and therefore was to be completely denied. Biblical ways of speaking about emotion in God were considered to be figures of speech—not to be taken literally. As for the sufferings of Christ himself, these were endured by his human nature, not by his divine nature. Some even held that when Christ went to the cross, his divine nature had departed from him, leaving only the human Christ to suffer the agony of Calvary.

Fortunately, in the modern world, this prejudice against the reality of divine suffering has given way to a view which, many Christians believe, is more in accord with the language and sentiment of the Bible. It is difficult to imagine a love which is incapable of suffering. Suffering in God which comes from compassion and mercy for his creatures is seen, not as an imperfection in love, but as love's crown. To say that Christ suffered in his human nature but not in his divine nature seems to be such an artificial division of his person as to merit an unqualified rejection.

If Christ is a genuine revelation of God, it is not easy to see how this "man of sorrows, acquainted with grief" can be so regarded without attributing sorrow and grief to the God whom he reveals and represents. It is therefore much more in keeping with the integrity of God, we believe, to say that the kenosis of Christ was a kenosis, not only of the Son, but also of the Godhead—Father, Son, and Spirit. The sufferings of Christ in his incarnate life, and preeminently in his passion and death, are to be given the paramount importance in Christian faith and devotion that they have given through the centuries. At the same time, it is just as important to say that the Father was present in, not separate from, what we sometimes call the *Christ-event* in its totality. We believe not only that God suffered in the atoning sufferings of Christ, but also that in the sufferings of Christ the very nature of the everlasting God is disclosed to us. This truth has seldom been given more eloquent or more forceful expression than in a passage by Charles Allen Dinsmore:

> What Jesus experienced in spiritual revulsion from sin, and his suffering on its behalf, is a revelation of an unchanging consciousness in God. As the flash of the volcano discloses for a few hours the elemental fires at the earth's center, so the light on Calvary was the bursting forth through historical conditions of the very nature of the Everlasting. There was a cross in the heart of God before there was one planted on the green hill outside of Jerusalem. And now that the cross of wood has been taken down, the one in the heart of God abides, and it will remain so long as there is one sinful soul for whom to suffer.[32]

Jesus died on the cross, not for himself, but in the place of sinners. The guilt and death which belonged to us he vicariously claimed as his own. But he was not a noble martyr, "standing starkly bright, against the void of cosmic night." His cross was the cross of God. "Only in the heart of God at last can the sin be taken, so as not only to be borne and forgiven but extinguished. Only the holy love of God can burn the sin to ashes, so that it is no more!"[33]

Exaltation. "Therefore God has highly exalted him and bestowed on him the name which is above every name" (Phil. 2:9, RSV). We shall give more attention to the exaltation of Christ in the following chapter. At this point, we must be brief, while acknowledging the central importance of the subject.

The resurrection and exaltation of Christ validated the life and ministry of Christ by the ultimate validation of a divine approval. This approval put the seal of God's authority upon Christ's suffering and obedience unto death for our salvation. It irradiated his sufferings with divine glory. The form of a sweating, bleeding, dying man on a cross was seen thereafter to be the embodiment of the power and wisdom of God. After the resurrection, people of faith could look the tragedies of

---

[32]Charles Allen Dinsmore, *Atonement in Literature and Life* (Boston and New York: Houghton, Mifflin and Company, 1906), pp. 232-33.

[33]William Manson, *The Way of the Cross* (Richmond, Va.: John Knox Press, 1958), p. 87.

life full in the face without evasion and without blinking, knowing that "in all these things we are more than conquerors through him who loved us" (Rom. 8:37, RSV). They could look upon the cross as God's sword of victory instead of as the white flag of surrender and defeat.

After his survey of the world's savior-heroes of the past, Arnold J. Toynbee states his conclusions in an arresting paragraph with which, making allowances for certain docetic implications in his imaginative treatment, we may bring this chapter to a fitting termination:

> This is the final result of our survey of saviours. When we first set out on this quest we found ourselves in the midst of a mighty marching host; but, as we have pressed forward on our way, the marchers, company by company, have been falling out of the race. The first to fall were the swordsmen, the next the archaists, the next the futurists, the next the philosophers, until at length there were no more human competitors left in the running. In the last stage of all, our motley host of would-be saviours, human and divine, has dwindled to a single company of none but gods; and now the strain has been testing the staying power of these last remaining runners, notwithstanding their superhuman strength. At the final ordeal of death, few, even of these would-be saviour gods, have dared to put their title to the test by plunging into the icy river. And now, as we stand and gaze with our eyes fixed upon the farther shore, a single figure rises from the flood and straightway fills the whole horizon. There is the Saviour; "and the pleasure of the Lord shall prosper in his hand; he shall see of the travail of his soul and shall be satisfied."[34]

---

[34]Arnold J. Toynbee, *A Study of History*, 6:278; cited in Dillistone, *The Christian Understanding of Atonement*, pp. 69-70.

—————————————— Chapter 9 ——————————————

Christ the Living Lord

That Jesus Christ rose from the dead is the conviction of every New Testament writer. Yet, to the modern mind, no other event in the New Testament is more problematic. There were no eyewitnesses to the resurrection. No "proof" for the resurrection, which would convince a determined sceptic, can be presented.

The earliest accounts of the resurrection do not fit into the categories of our common life. The event was not expected, even by Jesus' closest disciples. All of the accounts agree that Jesus died on a cross, and that his lifeless body was interred. All of the accounts agree that, on the third day after his death, he confronted the disciples again in a living form. But just what this form was is not clearly defined, and the accounts of the meetings that occurred between him and his disciples vary. Indeed, in certain respects the accounts seem to contradict one another.

The narratives testify to the reality of the risen Christ by telling of the empty tomb, of his visible body, and of his audible words. Yet there was a mystery about his appearances. He appeared suddenly through the barriers of closed doors and solid walls. Evidently he could appear at different places without having to travel the distances between them.

Even those who knew him best had difficulty in recognizing him. He talked, he walked, and he ate with them, yet the encounters with him were cloaked in a strangeness which was impenetrable. The experiences which came to the disciples removed all doubts that he was alive, but the event of the resurrection was unique and defied all their power to put it into words.

The reports of Jesus' appearances are central to the construction of any Christian doctrine of the resurrection. These reports do not agree, on all points, on *how* Jesus manifested himself; they do agree *that* he lived again. The conviction of those first witnesses that Jesus was risen from the dead transformed them from a group of dispirited, defeated persons to a fellowship of believers whose testimony "turned the world upside down." Their testimony is forever embodied in the living witness of the New Testament. Through the Holy Spirit, this conviction lives on in the church—that is, in those who not only believe the word of the first witnesses but also have confirmed the testimony of those witnesses by an encounter and a fellowship with the living Christ. There is an unbroken chain of witnesses whose own experiences cause them to repeat perennially the glad testimony of those early Christians who joined Paul in saying, "Now is Christ risen from the dead, and become the firstfruits of them that slept" (1 Cor. 15:20, KJV).

The Resurrection of Jesus Christ

The early church was the church of the risen Christ. An attentive reading of the book of Acts shows that in the earliest stages of Christian history, even more notice was given to the resurrection than to the cross. The reason for this fact was that, since the early church was principally Jewish, the resurrection was esteemed to be a conclusive guarantee that Jesus was the Messiah.

For Paul, the emphasis changed somewhat. While he exalted the cross, he saw the inseparable connection between the cross and the resurrection. Jesus was "put to death for our trespasses and raised for our justification" (Rom. 4:25, RSV). Christ was "crucified in weakness, but lives by the power of God" (2 Cor. 13:4, RSV). In Philippians, Paul speaks of the Christ who was humiliated unto death, but he affirmed that God "has highly exalted him and bestowed on him the name which is above every name" (Phil. 2:9, RSV). "Like as Christ was raised up from the dead by the glory of the Father," Paul says in Romans, "even so we also should walk in newness of life" (Rom. 6:4, KJV).

The synoptic gospels represent Jesus as seeing his cross in connection with his resurrection. Mark 8:31 may serve as an illustration: "The Son of man must suffer many things, and be rejected by the elders and chief priests and the scribes, and be killed, and after three days rise again" (RSV). To be sure, the synoptics contain critical problems concerning the origin of the resurrection. The point to be made here is that, in the synoptic interpretations, the cross and the resurrection are seen together, even though the disciples do not appear to have grasped prior to the event the fact that the resurrection would occur. Leonhard Goppelt states the central importance of the resurrection to the first Christian community when he affirms that the Easter *kerygma* "was the root of the whole original Christian proclamation."[1]

The Significance of the Resurrection. The appearances of the risen Christ, not the empty tomb, assumed the position of greatest importance in the earliest narratives. Paul, who wrote before any of the gospels was written, talked about the resurrection appearances, not about a tomb that was empty. In his account of the appearances in 1 Corinthians 15, Paul affirms that Jesus "was raised on the third day in accordance with the scriptures" (v. 4, RSV), but says nothing about the empty sepulcher. Jesus appeared, says Paul, to Cephas, then to the twelve, then to more than five hundred disciples at one time, "most of whom are still alive, though some have fallen asleep" (v. 6, RSV). He appeared to James, then to all the apostles. "Last of all, as to one untimely born, he appeared also to me" (1 Cor. 15:8, RSV).

The point which we seek to establish here concerns the question of priority. This point may be stated by saying that the most important fact for the resurrection faith was not that a tomb was empty, but that the disciples met the living Lord after his death.

It is true that the appearances were witnessed by believers only. They did not in any sense constitute proof to the unbeliever. Moreover, the initiative lay with the risen Christ himself. He "appeared" (Luke 24:34; Acts 1:3; 9:17; 13:31; 1 Cor. 15:5-9). He was "revealed" (John 21:1, 14). He "presented himself alive" (Acts 1:3, RSV). "God . . . made him manifest," and this "not to all the people but

---

[1]Leonhard Goppelt et al., *The Easter Message Today* (London, New York, Toronto: Thomas Nelson and Sons, 1964), p. 39.

to us who were chosen by God as witnesses" (Acts 10:40-41, RSV). "The appearances," John A. T. Robinson observes, "were assurances given to those who had previously accepted him, not proof to compel faith or confound doubt."[2]

If the risen Christ appeared to believers only, there would seem to be considerable plausibility to the charge that the appearances were merely subjective visions, hallucinations, in the minds of Peter, Mary Magdalene, and the other persons who claimed to have seen Jesus alive after his death. This charge would deny that there was any factual foundation for the claim that Jesus had risen.

On the basis of the empirical evidence available to us, of course, this charge cannot be either proved or disproved. In reply to the charge, however, it certainly can be said that the appearances completely reversed the expectations of Jesus' followers. They did not expect him to rise from the dead. Moreover, the charge assumes that the Church is founded upon an illusion. This claim has indeed been made repeatedly. It is remarkable, however, that this alleged illusion has lasted for two thousand years with such tenacity and with such creative power. Moreover, although the Church has treated as foundational to its very life the testimony of the original witnesses to the resurrected Christ, it has not rested its faith upon this testimony alone, but also upon a present experience with the living Lord, who was crucified, dead, buried, who was raised from the dead, who is our eternal contemporary and our present companion.

1. *Jesus Raised by God.* God raised Jesus from the dead: this is the way the New Testament speaks. Jesus did not raise himself. The resurrection was not the result of an inner divine power which resided in Jesus. He was dead, utterly and completely.

The resurrection, then, is not something that we first of all say about Jesus. It is something that we say about God. The resurrection of Jesus does not constitute a story analogous to the power of life in the seed which springs to bloom of itself when the sun warms the earth after the frigid dearth of winter. It is the story of a God who brings the dead to life. In Romans 1:4, as John Knox points out, we are told that Jesus was raised "from among" the dead. He was raised from the death which he suffered in accordance with the common lot of all other

---

[2]Buttrick, ed., *The Interpreters' Dictionary of the Bible*, R-Z:47.

human beings. "Here," says Knox, "in the assertion of his human mortality, is the decisive assertion that he was, not simply *like* us in all respects—if that be all, it would not be enough—but that he was of us in all respects, bone of our bone, flesh of our flesh, mind of our mind, heart of our heart. He could not now be the 'new man' in any relevant sense—that is, the saving man—if that were not true."[3]

That he was raised by the Father indicates that he, like all the rest of us, was radically dependent on God for his defeat of death. In his resurrection, too, he was the representative man, and in his restoration to life he became "the firstfruits of those who have fallen asleep" (1 Cor. 15:20, RSV).

The Christian faith loses its New Testament moorings if it conceives of the resurrection of Jesus apart from the initiative of the Father. Indeed, the Christian understanding of God received the capstone of its definition in this event. The vantage point from which everything was viewed thereafter was the vantage point of the resurrection. God was forever afterwards known as the God "who raised our Lord Jesus Christ from the dead."

2. The Christian Gospel Tied to the Resurrection. While the resurrection of Jesus was from the first a foundation stone of the Gospel, it is distorted hopelessly if it is separated from the person who walked on earth—from his life, his ministry, his sufferings, and his death. Without this indissoluble tie, resurrection can easily become a philosophical concept merely, a concept of the victory of life over death in a highly generalized sense. A decisive datum of Christianity is Jesus himself. In his words and deeds and person, Jesus in his earthly ministry was experienced as the *eschaton*, as a divine event. In connection with the Jesus of history, not in connection with a separately conceived "Christ of faith," the crucial importance of the resurrection is to be seen.

The difficulties in the belief that Jesus was raised from the dead in bodily form may be freely acknowledged. If a bodily resurrection is affirmed, we must grant that the resurrection was not the resuscitation of a corpse, but that the resurrected body was a transmuted, transfigured, "glorified" body.

---

[3]John Knox, *The Humanity and Divinity of Christ* (Cambridge: University Press, 1967), p. 90.

Sometimes an insistence on the bodily resurrection assumes an aspect of crass materialism. Rightly interpreted, however, the doctrine of the bodily resurrection preserves a truth of cherished value. Whatever the manner in which Jesus Christ was raised from the dead, or the form that his appearances took after the resurrection, it is crucially important to the Christian faith to say that God raised "this same Jesus" from the dead. The risen, triumphant Lord is no one else than the Servant of God who died on the cross for us.

On Good Friday it appeared that God's battle to judge and redeem the world had been lost on the ground on which God himself had chosen to fight it—on the battlefield of history, at the very place where sin, sorrow, pain, and death had oppressed and destroyed the bodies and seemingly the souls of men. The resurrection does not signify that God retreated from the battle by turning this world over to the conquering powers of darkness, while salvaging something from the battle by granting repose to the soul of Jesus in another world. The resurrection rather means that God won his battle exactly where he seemed to have lost it decisively—in time, in history, in the life that is lived amid tribulation and death, in the person of the crucified Jesus:

> On the basis of New Testament evidence we must say that the Christian faith includes at its heart the assertion that Jesus, though he died, is yet alive for ever more; and that he is alive, not in some vague sense of survival of the soul after death, but in the fullest and richest sense possible—namely, in the whole integrity of his human nature as well as in the divinity which is his by virtue of the intimate and "personal" relationship of the human nature with God.[4]

In the above statement, Norman Pittenger has captured a vital segment of the meaning of Jesus' resurrection.

3. The Resurrection as Vindication. In the resurrection, Christ received, at the hands of the Father, a complete vindication. There it was manifest that he, and not those political, religious, and cosmic forces which had opposed him, was in the right. These powers had fought against the will of God, and they were defeated by the Almighty Hand which raised Jesus from the dead:

---

[4]W. Norman Pittenger, *The Word Incarnate* (London: James Nisbet and Co., Ltd., 1959), p. 68.

The grain of the universe [says Culbert Rutenber] ran in Christ's direction, not Herod's or Caiaphas'. The things for which Christ stood, the truths of which he spoke, the love which he demonstrated—these were the enduring, living, powerful realities of the world; not the lust, the power-drive, the hate, the selfishness, the sin of men and nations. God's guarantee stood back of Christ's kind of life. He was right, forever right.[5]

The resurrection became and has been perennially the strongest possible assertion of the triumph of God over suffering, sin, and death. The resurrection was the divine reversal of the cross, as life is the reversal of death. Even in some of the primitive preaching of Acts, this theme of reversal from defeat to victory was sounded: "You crucified and killed [him] by the hands of lawless men. But God raised him up" (Acts 2:23-24, RSV).

Without the resurrection, the story of Christ's sufferings and death would convey a message of stark tragedy and of unrelieved pessimism. The import of this message would be that suffering, sin, and death— victors over the fairest and, spiritually speaking, the most powerful life ever lived—were relentlessly triumphant as the executors of the will of a malevolent world power, or that they reigned supreme in a mindless universe that divulges no meanings. If the disaster of Jesus' cruel death had not been reversed, not only for himself, but also on behalf of all mankind, it would be difficult to believe in a God who is just and good, for he would have answered an ultimate challenge with only a stony silence.

The radical good news of the New Testament is that the love and justice of God are stronger than death, and that this love and justice have received an open demonstration and vindication by the raising of Jesus from the dead. The resurrection of Jesus became, and for all time thereafter will be, a prophetic sign for mankind, the sunrise which dispels the darkness of the world. "The life of Jesus is condensed as a promise of God in the Resurrection. . . . God's promise, 'I live and you shall also live,' is fulfilled in Him."[6]

---

[5]Culbert Rutenber, *The Reconciling Gospel* (Philadelphia: Judson Press, 1960), p. 135.

[6]Goppelt et al., *The Easter Message Today*, p. 133.

4. Resurrection and Sacrifice. The meaning of the resurrection in the New Testament faith draws much of its profundity from its refusal to separate the resurrection from the cross. The scandal of a crucified Messiah is allowed to stand in all its starkness. Humiliation not only stands side by side with triumph, but also the glory of the resurrection is already disclosed in the suffering and disgrace of the cross. Victory for Jesus emerges from defeat, glory springs from disgrace, life rises from death. The grain of wheat falls into the ground and dies, and, dying, brings forth much fruit. Christ must lay down his life as a willing sacrifice, even unto death, in order that that life, transformed into a new glory and a new cleansing power, may be taken up again and shed abroad for the healing of the nations.

In the book of Revelation, the sacrificial Lamb has two marked characteristics. In the first place, though living, he appears as one who had been slain (Rev. 5:5-6). The risen Christ says, "I died, and behold I am alive for evermore" (1:18, RSV). In the second place, the Lamb who was slain has in his hands the lifegiving forces of God. He holds the keys of "Death and Hades" (1:18), The "four living creatures and the twenty-four elders" fall down before the Lamb, singing a new song:

> Worthy art thou to take the scroll and to open its seals, for thou wast slain and by thy blood didst ransom men for God from every tribe and tongue and people and nation, and hast made them a kingdom and priests to our God, and they shall reign on earth (Rev. 5:9-10, RSV).

The Exalted Lord

Philippians 2:5-10 ties together, in a way characteristic of much of the New Testament literature, the humiliation and exaltation of Christ. The one who became obedient unto death has been highly exalted by the Father, who has bestowed on him "the name which is above every name, that at the name of Jesus every knee should bow, in heaven and on earth and under the earth, and every tongue confess that Jesus Christ is Lord, to the glory of God the Father" (Phil. 2:9-10, RSV).

Paul repeatedly "rings the changes" on both the crucifixion and the resurrection of Jesus, yet even these central convictions are instrumental to Christ's exaltation to the right hand of the Father. The right hand of God is the position of authority. Christ is King of kings and Lord or lords. His lordship implies his subjugation of all other powers, both those of heaven and those of earth. Until his return at the *Parousia,* when his victory will be complete, "he must reign until he has put all his enemies under his feet" (1 Cor. 15:25, RSV). His reign at present is decisive but disputed. Although, in principle, all hostile powers have been subjected to his rule, the battle against these powers continues. Even though "God has put all things in subjection under his feet," we are told that "the last enemy to be destroyed is death"(1 Cor. 15:26-27, RSV). Despite the unfinished character of God's battle against evil, the unqualified lordship of Christ is powerfully and repeatedly asserted in the Pauline writings.

Little explicit reference to the resurrection occurs either in the gospel of John or in Hebrews; the resurrection is presupposed. What is emphasized is the exaltation and lordship to which the cross and resurrection have led. The emphasis is made in such a way as to interpret the cross in the light of the exaltation which follows.

In the fourth gospel, the focus of John's message is on Jesus' obedience to the will of the Father. As he envisioned the cross, which was imminent, Jesus reminded his disciples, "I do as the Father has commanded me, so that the world may know that I love the Father" (John 14:31, RSV).

From the perspective of Jesus' resurrection and exaltation, John can look upon the cross as Jesus' "glorification." The scandal and disgrace of a crucified Messiah, so repugnant to the Jewish orthodoxy of the time, is here dispelled by the light of divine glory which irradiates the cross. While Christ before his incarnation was already one with the Father, his incarnation, humiliation, and death brought heaven and earth together, and this was the objective of his earthly mission. The exaltation of Christ to lordship, therefore, was soteriological in purpose, as his whole life and ministry to the world had been. This purpose was graphically stated in Jesus' prayer in John 17:

> I do not pray for these only, but also for those who believe in me through their word, that they may all be one; even as thou, Father, art in me, and I in thee, that they also may be in us, *so that the world may believe* that thou hast sent me. The glory which thou hast given me I have given to them, that they may be one even as we are one, I in them and thou in me, that they may become perfectly one, *so that the world may know* that thou hast sent me and hast loved them even as thou hast loved me (John 17:20-23, RSV, italics added).

In the book of Hebrews, the exaltation of Christ to his place of honor at the side of the Father was not merely the restitution of a *status quo ante*. Because he suffered death he has been "crowned with glory and honor" (Heb. 2:9, RSV). His return to the Father, in the imagery of this book, was not that of a return to a royal authority and power which had been interrupted briefly by an earthly sojourn. His going into heaven is seen rather like the going of the high priest into the sanctuary. *This* High Priest takes the offering of his own blood, shed on Calvary's cross, into the sanctuary of heaven, where, through the intercessory offices of Christ, it remains a sacrifice of perpetual and efficacious validity. While the death of Jesus on earth provided the material for the sacrifice, the sacrifice itself was offered in heaven, where Christ "ever liveth to make intercession" for us (Heb. 7:25, KJV).

> Christ's expiatory sacrifice is valid precisely through what is living and eternal in all its elements: a living priest triumphing over death; an ever-living victim, whose vital, warm blood has the power of everlasting purification; a permanent and definitive sanctuary, heaven itself.[7]

The exaltation of Christ is seen in the New Testament under different aspects and through different metaphors. In all of these, however, the stress on Christ's authority is a marked feature. The resurrection does not make him Son, but it "designates" him "Son of God with power." To the risen Christ, "all authority" is given, both in heaven and on earth. He is the Lord of all lords and the King of all kings. Not only does he reign in the church, and in the hearts of individual believers, but also over all of creation. Though the world is still gripped by the powers of darkness, which hold men and nations in bondage, the resurrection has broken the dominance of these evil forces, and has effected a liberation of the world which will become manifest in the future subjection of all things to God in Christ. A magnificent passage in Ephesians asserts the lordship, present and future, of the Christ whom God raised from the dead. The writer of Ephesians prays that his Ephesian brethren may know

---

[7]Jose Maria Gonzalez-Ruiz, *Who Is Jesus of Nazareth?* (New York: Orbis Books, 1976), p. 399.

the immeasurable greatness of his power in us who believe, according to the working of his great might which he accomplished in Christ when he raised him from the dead and made him sit at his right hand in heavenly places, far above all rule and authority and power and dominion, and above every name that is named, not only in this age but also in that which is to come (Eph. 1:19-21, RSV).

The Coming of the Holy Spirit. The Holy Spirit stands in the Scriptures for the presence of God and the power of God. He is not an impersonal influence or emanation, but a personal presence. On the interrelationship between the Holy Spirit and God the Father, or between the Holy Spirit and Christ, the New Testament is not clear.

Sometimes there is a devotional equation between and an identification of the Holy Spirit with Christ, and with God the Father; sometimes there is a distinction and differentiation. Sometimes the Holy Spirit seems to be interpreted as the spiritual presence of the living Christ. In other passages, he appears to have come to take the place of Christ, in the sense that he is another being.

These differences of interpretation may be seen in a comparison between the gospel of John and the Pauline writings. In John the Spirit is called "another Paraclete." "It is to your advantage that I go away," Jesus said, "for if I do not go away, the Counselor will not come to you; but if I go, I will send him to you" (John 16:7, RSV).

On the other hand, the apostle Paul speaks of the Spirit of God, the Spirit of Jesus and the Spirit of Christ almost interchangeably. The Spirit appears at times to be the spiritual presence of the risen Christ.

In any case, the Holy Spirit does not come into our hearts apart from Christ; he brings Christ into our hearts. He does not take Christ's place while Christ is away. Christ is not away; he is present with us in the Holy Spirit.

The Holy Spirit turns the spotlight on Christ. He acts in the character of Christ. He does the work of Christ. He does not have a character that is ever alien to the character of Christ, nor is his work ever incompatible with the work of Christ. In a trenchant statement, C. F. Evans indicates the relationship between the Holy Spirit, the earthly Jesus, and the risen Christ:

The Spirit, as Christian faith understands it, takes the community not away from Jesus, earthly, crucified, risen, but ever nearer to him, expounding anew in each successive situation the meaning of the once-for-all revelation in the Christ event. This is why for the Fourth Evangelist the Spirit is the gift of the risen Christ. This insight of faith is as relevant and meaningful for the life of the believing community today as it was in the Evangelist's own time.[8]

Christ a Living Presence. One of the fundamental meanings of the coming of the Holy Spirit was that Christ was back again, although in spiritual presence only, in the lives of believers and in the life of the Church. The power of the presence of the resurrected Christ did not fade when the appearances ceased. The ground of the faith of even those who had shared the appearances was at least as much the continuing encounter with the invisible Lord as it was the experiences which they had had with the visible Lord in the past. Paul appealed to his vision of the risen Christ as the authority for his apostleship, but he did not require this vision for the support of his continuing faith. "Christ liveth in me," he said, and this abiding presence through the Holy Spirit gave power to his witness (Gal. 2:20). "I can do all things in him who strengthens me" (Phil. 4:13, RSV) was a testimony at least as effective as his assertion that he had met the Lord on the Damascus Road. The apostles called attention to the present signs of the living Christ, to "this which you see and hear" (Acts 2:33, RSV), to confirm the fact that Christ was still performing his saving works with great power.

In other words, the evidence of the resurrection continued to be shown, and continues to be shown today, in the testimony of the Church to the pervasive and sovereign presence of the Lord who died at Calvary. He was raised by the mighty hand of God, and he lives and reigns today at God's right hand, in the heart and life of the Church, and, although unacknowledged, in the saving ministry of Almighty God at the heart of the world.

The Resurrection Life

In the preresurrection lifetime of Jesus, his spirit was limited by his human life-structure. In him were the power and presence of God, but

---

[8]C. F. Evans, *Resurrection in the New Testament* (Naperville, Ill.: Alec R. Allenson Inc., 1970), pp. 174-75.

these, insofar as they were manifested in Jesus, were confined to a certain time and place. As G. C. Darton indicates, this limitation obtains no longer:

> He healed those whom he met in the road or in the Temple, or those who were brought to him (even, on occasion, "by proxy"); he taught those who were within reach of his lungs; he took his healing and his teaching as far as his legs would carry him. "God was in Christ"; all men needed God and the men within reach of him no more and no less than the others. The Gospel of the community is that the Spirit had been promised to it, to be received after Jesus had "returned to the Father." The Spirit has been shown in man and proceeding from man; now that manhood is assumed into Transcendence, and the Spirit will no longer be limited by the time and space of one man's life. The Spirit was released to the community, and known in the community, an all but visible presence. To be saved is "to have received" the Spirit; to know the power is to "be in" the Spirit.[9]

The Beginning of the New World. The coming of the Spirit, ushered in by the resurrection, was the beginning of the new world. After the coming of the Spirit, the disciples began to proclaim the "resurrection from the dead" (Acts 4:2). The "age to come" is no longer to be expected merely at the "last day." Even now Christ is the "resurrection and the life" (John 11:24-25).

The new order, however, has not arrived in its fullness with the resurrection and the coming of the Spirit. Christ is "the firstborn from the dead" (Col. 1:18), but men still have to die, and death, the last enemy, still has to be destroyed. Only Christ has risen to die no more. He is the first fruits and the guarantee of the new order which has come and is coming.

With the resurrection, however, there has been a reversal of the course of the world. This reversal has been seen, not indeed so clearly that it is beheld by all men. It is seen by men and women of Christian descernment, who know to be true the word of Jesus as given in John 11:25-26: "He who believes in me, though he die, yet shall he live, and

---

[9]G. C. Darton, *The Image of the Heavenly* (New York: Morehouse Barlow; London: Darton, Longman and Todd, 1961), p. 40.

whoever lives and believes in me shall never die" (RSV). Christians already have tasted "the powers of the age to come" (Heb. 6:5, RSV). Already, they have "passed from death to life" (John 5:24, RSV). Those who had the privilege of seeing the risen Christ sought to describe an experience that was to them unutterable. But, says Karl Heim, "they knew that in a small space for a little while they had been granted a view into the Reality which contained the destiny of the whole world to come, the future of nature and the world of men."[10]

The Overcoming of the Powers of Evil. The victory theme recurs again and again in the New Testament. This theme is sounded particularly in connection with the resurrection. When Christ went to his cross, Satan, "principalities and powers," sin, death, bondage to the law—all challenged in death struggle the mission which God was accomplishing in Christ. "All hell moved up to block the redemptive move that Heaven was making."[11] The new creation became possible and actual because, when Christ rose from the dead, the powers of evil met their "Waterloo." Sin, death, and the devil had their reign decisively broken. Christ "disarmed the principalities and powers and made a public example of them" (Col. 2:15, RSV).

But we live "between the times," and while Christ's victory over the forces of evil occurred at Easter, the final victory is postponed until the end of history. Hatred, injustice, brutality, lovelessness, and godlessness continue to ravage the lives of individuals, of nations, and of the world. Evil still must be taken seriously, and the Christian is eager to join God in his battle against it. The Christian knows from the resurrection that evil, though it is still powerful and is stronger than human beings, is not stronger than God. He knows that God, not evil, is going to have the last word. Already he sees that God is bringing reconciliation to replace alienation and hostility, love to conquer hate, and life to conquer death. Many times the situation seems hopeless, but the Christian knows a power at work which brings into the here and now a truth, a healing, and a redemption that evil cannot overcome. "If you have heard the Easter message," says Karl Barth, "you can no longer run around with a tragic face and lead a humourless existence of a man who has no hope."[12]

---

[10]Heim, *Jesus the World's Perfecter*, p. 171.

[11]Rutenber, *The Reconciling Gospel*, p. 80.

[12]Cited in Guthrie, *Christian Doctrine*, p. 279.

Life Transformed. The resurrection of Christ was to the New Testament Christians the beginning of the new creation and the pledge of the end. History now would move towards its consummation, with all its forces subordinate to the will of the risen Christ, who also would be the judge of the world order at last.

So close is the identification of the Christian with Christ that there is a close parallelism between the career of the Christian and that of his Lord. The Christian life is viewed as the unfolding of what is already complete in Christ. He has sanctified us to God by the offering of his own life for us (Heb. 10:14). When Christ died, we died with him. When he rose, we were raised with him. In his ascension, he has drawn us up to sit with him in heavenly places. We have been glorified together with him. We participate in the "newness of life" which is found in him, in the life of the new age, even though the life of the present age is still with us.

The resurrection life for Christ was followed almost immediately by his "exaltation," but this is not true for the Christian. While he lives in Christ, in the "age to come," he continues to live also in this world. He knows the subtle influence of daily temptations, of repeated failures, of daily sin and guilt, of burdens too heavy to bear, of sickness as well as health, of the infirmities of age, of the loss of friends and loved ones, and of demanding challenges to which he is not equal. He does not dare to imagine himself to be separated from the life of the present age. Indeed, he *must* not do so. For his life is daily one of cross-bearing as well as one of victory, of hope more than of present accomplishment, of anguished involvement in the needs and problems of his fellow human beings, as well as of rejoicing in the triumph which Christ has won in his resurrection.

The new life is not separated from the old life; rather, the old life is permeated and transformed by the new. The same life is lived, but to a new purpose. The same daily walk is followed, but to a different end. The same scenes abound, but they are viewed in a new light. The same multitudinous details exist, perhaps, but there is a new coherence. One has the same companions along the way, but they are seen with a new understanding and compassion. One has the same job, it may be, but a new witness within it. The old knowledge and competencies remain, but they are integrated into a new total vision.

The Christian lives in the consciousness that "the Lord is at hand" (Phil. 4:5, RSV). His citizenship is in heaven, from which he expects a

"Savior, the Lord Jesus Christ, who will change our lowly body to be like his glorious body, by the power which enables him even to subject all things to himself" (Phil. 3:20, RSV).

In the above passage Paul is saying that in the future resurrection the risen Christ will impart to Christians the same divine glory with which he (Christ) has been clothed in his own resurrection and exaltation. The resurrection, however, is also a matter of personal experience now, in the present, so that, in the same writing, Paul can say that his aim is to "know him [Christ] and the power of his resurrection," and to "share his sufferings, becoming like him in his death, that if possible I may attain the resurrection from the dead" (Phil. 3:10, RSV).

In other words, Paul brings into intimate union here both what he has experienced already of Christ's suffering, death, and resurrection, and what he confidently hopes to attain after his death. His hope is firmly based on what he has already experienced. What he has "experienced" is not just a subjective "feeling"; it is anchored in historical fact. This factual anchor is that Christ has risen from the dead, has been exalted to the right hand of God, and has made those who love him "more than conquerors" over all those powers which would enslave and destroy. The resurrection faith of all Christians is expressed succinctly by Paul in Romans 14:8: "If we live, we live to the Lord, and if we die, we die to the Lord; so then, whether we live or whether we die, we are the Lord's" (RSV).[13]

The Christian life must be viewed in a dual perspective. In the first place, it is a life which is hidden with Christ in God. In this life the victory of Christ for us over sin and death has been won and we have appropriated that victory by faith. In the second place, the Christian life is a life lived in the flesh. This is a life of struggle and growth, victory and defeat, sin and failure, advance and retreat, selfishness and unselfishness, discouragement and exhilaration, genuine service and (all too often) treachery to our Christian vocation.

These two aspects of the Christian life do not comprise two lives; they are one life. The life which we live in the flesh in the midst of perplexities and contradictions, toil and conflict, weakness and shameful compromise — is also the arena of our Christian witness, in

---

[13]Cf. Evans, *Resurrection in the New Testament*, pp. 163-64.

which arena our lives are brought into conformity with the will of Christ. The life which we live in the flesh is also the sphere of Christ's lordship. He will never leave us nor forsake us, and our onward march, through "mud and thunder," leads us, by the strengthening guidance of the Holy Spirit, to the "city which has foundations, whose builder and maker is God" (Heb. 11:10, RSV).

The New Humanity. We must not think of the resurrection life in merely individualistic terms. All of life in Christ is a life in fellowship with Christ and with his people. The new humanity which constitutes the Body of Christ is a community of the cross, and a community of the resurrection. This new humanity comprises a fellowship of the Holy Spirit in which both cross-bearing and newness of life are made real to the community of Christian disciples. The indwelling presence of the Spirit leads the whole fellowship to the tasks which Christ "has to accomplish for our time." Male and female, Jew and Greek, bond and free are made one in Christ, for the Holy Spirit batters down the walls of indifference, faithlessness, hostility, and lovelessness which divide us from one another.

One might almost claim, says John Knox, that the whole content of the preaching of Paul can be summarized under three terms: the *old man*, the *new man*, and *Christ Jesus our Lord*. The old man is actual fallen man, man in Adam. The new man is man who has been reconciled to God, who has been liberated from sin and death, and made free to live a life of love, fellowship, and witness. By raising Jesus Christ from the dead, God has brought this new humanity into being:

> The Spirit, the very Spirit of Christ, whose presence Paul knew within the community of faith, manifestly had its origin in "a better country, that is, an heavenly"; the love he found there was a divine love, "passing knowledge"; the peace was beyond "all understanding." God had brought within history what, at its source and in its fulness, belonged only beyond it. In the life of the Church he had given a foretaste, an earnest, of man's destiny—an advance installment of his inheritance. God had set on earth a colony of heaven.[14]

---

[14]Knox, *The Humanity and Divinity of Christ*, p. 82.

The End. Whoever looks upon the resurrection with discernment has seen the end, the *telos*, of the world. There is little reason here to discuss the consummation of all things when God rings down the curtain at the end (*finis*) of history. To set dates for the "second coming"; to construct a sequence of events which will accompany a millennial reign of Christ; to talk about the "rapture" of the church to meet the Lord; to envision the meaning and content of the "great tribulation"; to speak about whether there will be one resurrection, or two, or more; to describe how the last judgment will be conducted: these subjects need not be discussed here. The second coming of Christ, says A. M. Hunter, is not "an event in history but . . . the point at which (in C. H. Dodd's phrase) the race reaches its last frontier-post and encounters—not nothingness but God in Christ."[15]

The resurrection of Christ is the ground of our assurance; Jesus said, "Because I live, you will live also" (John 14:19, RSV). But the risen Christ is also the Lord who was crucified, and therefore our hope is of life through death. As it was the full humanity of Jesus that was restored on Easter morning, a humanity which bore still the marks of the cross, so the life of Christ's disciples will in their resurrection after death be an embodied life. Neville Clark's remarks on this subject give evidence of a shining faith which can be shared by all Christians:

> The life in this world of the man of Christ is destined not for destruction but for transfiguration; not for negation but for completion. Beyond the grave is the life embodied, the revelation of the fulness of our humanity which, in our life here in time, we have slowly and falteringly developed and matured. The unfinished tasks we have tried to do, the dreams and hopes and aspirations after which we have striven, the relationships we have vainly sought to perfect and complete, the experiences which have lifted us and laid us low, moulded us and made us—all these will not be lost or left behind, but will be the notes by which we render harmony to the music of the City of God. By the resurrection of Jesus Christ we know that all that is of good or can be made so will never perish, but will be exalted to the

---

[15]Hunter, *Interpreting Paul's Gospel*, p. 130.

heavenly places and clothed with the divine power, if only it be freely surrendered by us to that death which is the boundary line of our existence.[16]

As the resurrection life is an embodied life here, so will it be a corporate life hereafter. Those who are united with Christ in his death and resurrection will also be united forever with the people of Christ. The Body of Christ will receive its perfection and completion in the bonds of fellowship and love. While this in no sense means a loss of individual personhood, it does mean that individuality will be complemented by mutuality, that union will find its fulfillment in communion, both with God and with all the hosts of the redeemed.

In the meantime, the Church looks to the *parousia* not with folded hands but with a keen anticipation of the coming glory. The glow of the glory which is to come does not preempt a joyous and dedicated participation in the continuing ministry of Christ on earth. The Church is involved in the mission of God, which is the redemption of the world, not escape from, or denial of, the world. In expectation of the end, the Church, in the here and now—in the turmoil, terror, uncertainty, and hardship of this life—fights tyranny and injustice, feeds the hungry, clothes the naked, shelters the homeless, preaches the gospel to the poor, heals the brokenhearted, lifts up the fallen, reconciles the alienated, and rescues the lost. Thus, the risen Christ unleashes the power of his resurrection life in the world, and God's mission of redemption for the whole world is implemented by the daily testimony of his people.

---

[16]Neville Clark, *Interpreting the Resurrection* (Philadelphia: Westminster Press, 1967), pp. 114-15.

—————————————— Chapter 10 ——————————————

Atonement and the Church

In this last chapter, we can give close attention to only a few of the rich things that the New Testament says about the Church. In the New Testament, the Church is designated by various terms, such as sons, heirs, disciples, brothers, confessors, followers, witnesses, faithful ones, believers, ambassadors, free men, pilgrims, servants, stewards, friends, ministers, and sons of Abraham. The Church is called a holy nation, a chosen race, a commonwealth, a family of God, God's beloved, a colony of heaven, an *ecclesia*, a *koinonia*, and so forth. It is also called the Body of Christ, the temple, the new creation, the New Jerusalem, Israel, the building, the field, and the royal priesthood. In his book entitled *Images of the Church in the New Testament*, Paul S. Minear discusses nearly one hundred New Testament "images" of the Church.

In this chapter, our aim will be to concentrate upon several of the salient points which pertain to the relation of the Church to the Atonement.

In the Church, if anywhere, the atoning work and life of God—as wrought in history by Jesus Christ and as made existentially real by the ministry of the Holy Spirit—is luminously and powerfully demonstrated. In a sense, therefore, the doctrine of the Church should be a summation and an exemplification of the story of God's atoning work in the world. We may grant that the doctrine of the Church includes more than this; but if the Church is the Church indeed, the Atonement stands at its heart.

The Church as the People of God

Seeking to discover the exact historical point at which the Church began is a futile endeavor. Did Jesus *found* the Church? Not if we define the Church as essentially an "institution." No evidence exists in the New Testament that, upon a specific occasion, he "organized" the Church. The church was born in the comradeship of those whom Jesus had called to be with him. It received distinctness of outline and meaning at Pentecost. It began and matured not as an *institution* but as a *fellowship* of those who associated themselves with Jesus to accomplish with him the redemptive purposes for which he had dedicated his life. "The Christian Church," says Robert McAfee Brown, "is a response to the 'good news' of God, proclaimed and enacted by Jesus Christ. Strictly speaking, it is not only a response to the Gospel, it is a *part* of the Gospel, since God desires not only to save men but to have them in fellowship with one another."[1]

In Old Testament times, Israel was the "people of God." The covenant which God made with Abraham (Gen. 17:19) was reaffirmed a number of times in the history of the Hebrew people. The infidelity of Israel to the terms of their covenant relationship caused God to narrow the scope of the chosen people to a faithful remnant (Isa. 10:20-22), which became the predecessor of the church of the new covenant constituted by and in Christ (Gal. 6:16; Rom. 11:1-5; 1 Pet. 2:9-10).

In the first chapter, we called attention to the fact that the people of God in the Old Testament were an elect people. God chose Israel, not to be his pampered favorite among the nations, but to be the recipient of his revelation to the world, an exemplar and agent of his purpose, a witness to his saving grace.[2] "You are my witnesses, saith the Lord, and my servant whom I have chosen" (Isa. 43:10, RSV).

---

[1]Robert McAfee Brown, *The Significance of the Church* (Philadelphia: The Westminster Press, 1956), p. 39.

[2]Cf. Rowley, *The Biblical Doctrine of Election*, p. 164.

Christians of New Testament times believed in an organic continuity between themselves and the people of the old covenant. Christians also were in a covenant relationship with God, but with them this relationship was founded upon a "new" covenant. They were not dependent on national heritage, biological descent, or cultic observance as constitutive factors in their citizenship in a new Israel, an Israel not of the flesh but of the spirit. As the people of God, they were both a continuation and a consummation of God's covenant community.

However, this historical and organic continuity must be seen also in terms of a paradoxical discontinuity. To Christians, Jesus Christ was not only a consummation of what Israel at its best had been and had stood for but also a decisive break with the past. R. Newton Flew has stated this truth concisely: "The Church is old in the sense that it is a continuation of the life of Israel, the People of God. It is new in the sense that it is founded on the revelation made through Jesus Christ of God's final purpose for mankind."[3]

The electing love and purpose of God moved to the world in the Hebrew people. This love and purpose later came to a clear focus in Jesus Christ. God's saving mission then was taken up by a new nation, the Church, which now moves redemptively in the world through the indwelling power of the Holy Spirit.

In Jesus Christ the people of God have a new center. Christ not only fulfilled the mission of the Old Israel but also broke decisively with the Old Israel and its law. No one saw this break more clearly than did Paul: "But far be it from me to glory except in the cross of our Lord Jesus Christ, by which the world has been crucified to me, and I to the world. For neither circumcision counts for anything, nor uncircumcision, but a new creation. Peace and mercy be upon all who walk by this rule, upon the Israel of God" (Gal. 6:14-16, RSV).

The Old Israel, "Israel after the flesh," rejected the Messiah whom God had sent, and thus showed that it could no longer serve the purpose for which God had called it into being. The New Israel now carries on the tasks which Christ inaugurated during his incarnate life.

In terms of spiritual reality, the life of Christ is to be unfolded and

---

[3]Robert McAfee Brown, *The Significance of the Church*, p. 33; cited from Flew, *Jesus and His Church*.

reproduced in the people of God. It is a life given up on the cross, raised from the dead, and exalted to heavenly glory. The people of God are those people who are "re-made in the mould of the Christ-life."[4]

The Church as the Body of Christ

The image of the Church as the Body of Christ is one of the master-images of the New Testament. Unfortunately, it is also one of the most controversial.

Most Christians affirm an intimate relationship between Christ and his Church. But in *what sense* is the Church Christ's "body"? In the "Catholic" tradition, the use of the term quite often conveys the impression that the Church is Christ himself, as Christ lives now in the world. In illustrating this viewpoint, J. Robert Nelson quotes a statement from a Roman Catholic theologian, J. A. F. Gregg. "The Church," Gregg says, "is the extension in time and space of the Incarnate Word of God, crucified, ascended, glorified."[5]

Statements by Protestant writers also can be cited that seem just as explicit. The following characterizations of the Church were given by two Swedish Lutherans who were also distinguished theologians. Anders Nygren says: "The Body of Christ is Christ himself. The Church is Christ as He after the resurrection is present among us and meets us here on earth." Gustaf Aulen says, "The Body of Christ is Christ himself, the Risen Christ, alive and active on earth."[6]

Such statements should of course be carefully examined in context to see whether they actually mean what they seem to mean. In any case, any kind of divinization of the Church should be emphatically repudiated. To say that the Church is the Body of Christ is not to say that the Church is *the* presence of Christ on earth. Such an assignation of meaning makes an idol of the Church.

The Church is inseparable from Christ, but this does not mean that the Church is identical with Christ. As Lord of the Church, he stands over against the Church as Judge of the Church. The Church is the servant of Christ. It is an instrumental agent of Christ. It is a vehicle by

---

[4]Thornton, *The Doctrine of the Atonement*, p. 277.

[5]Cited in J. Robert Nelson, *The Realm of Redemption* (Greenwich Connecticut: The Seabury Press, 1951), p. 96.

[6]Cited in ibid., p. 90.

means of which Christ expresses himself in the world. It is a means of movement for Christ in the accomplishment of his redemptive purposes. It is Christ's body, insofar as it incarnates his spirit and his mission. Insofar as it does not do this, however, it is just another sociological entity in the world which exemplifies a spirit alien to the spirit of Christ.

However highly we estimate the Church, we ignore these distinctions at our peril. Preserving the distinctions between Christ and the Church is just as important as affirming their union. There is a union of fellowship, of service, and of spirit; there is no union of essence.

In the New Testament, the understanding of the Church as the Body of Christ is predominantly, though not exclusively, a Pauline conception. The most important passages are 1 Corinthians 12:27; Romans 12:5; Colossians 1:18; and Ephesians 4:12. (Many scholars doubt that Colossians and Ephesians are of Pauline authorship. The conception of the Church as Christ's body is more highly developed in these writings, perhaps, than in any other books of the New Testament.)

Closely related to the conception of the Church as the Body of Christ is the view that believers are "members" of Christ's body. A good illustration of this usage is Romans 12:4-5: "For as in one body we have many members, and all the members do not have the same function, so we, though many, are one body in Christ, and individually members one of another" (RSV).

Each Christian is a *member* of Christ, as one part of the body is a member of the whole body. Yet here again we must be careful not to say that the sum of the "members" is Christ himself. In the sense in which the Church constitutes Christ's "body," each member does not belong to himself, but is rather a functioning part of the whole. In the body all the members are knit together into one unit; they belong profoundly to each other. The common life is a life in union—union with Christ and union among the members. This union transcends differences of gifts and functions, while at the same time these gifts and functions complement and support each other. This membership in Christ, and this belonging to each other, is a union in love, service, purpose, and suffering.

Closely related to the metaphor of the Church as the Body of Christ is that of Christ as the head of the Church. This figure can well be construed as a corrective of the view that the body is identical with Christ. For, to call Christ head of the Church means that the Church draws its direction and nourishment from him. "As 'Head,' " says Norman Pittenger, "Christ was the controlling power, the informing presence, and the inspiring mind of the Church; he was alive in his Church, known and apprehended through the corporate life of the fellowship."[7]

From the head the body draws the capacity and actuality of spiritual growth. Growth proceeds as the Church draws many elements of nourishment from Christ, such as thanksgiving, peace (Col. 3:15-16), patience, forgiveness, compassion, and love. Ephesians 4:15-16 is a beautiful expression of this truth: "Speaking the truth in love, we are to grow up in every way into him who is the head, into Christ, from whom the whole body, joined and knit together by every joint with which it is supplied, when each part is working properly, makes bodily growth and upbuilds itself in love" (RSV).

In interpreting the Church as the Body of Christ, there is a dangerous temptation to draw from this metaphor the fallacious conviction that the Church is the principal object of God's love and care. If this conviction is held by the Church, the Church gives itself to the sustenance and protection of its own life above all. The body may become a fortress into which its members withdraw in order to defend themselves against the onslaughts of the world's hostile forces. The Church then becomes a religious ghetto withdrawn from the world and useless to the world.

The Church must keep in the forefront of its attention the fact that it is not only an object but also an instrument of God's redeeming purpose in the world. God so loved the *world* that he gave his Son. The Church faces outward towards the world, not inward for the protection of its own life and interests.

The British theologian P. T. Forsyth has said that the Church is not so much a continuation of the incarnation as it is a continuation of the atonement. This is a profound insight, for the Church in its daily life bears forward through history the dying and rising of the Lord. It is that community which, in the service of Christ, pours out its life for the world's salvation.

---

[7]Pittenger, *The Word Incarnate*, p. 271.

The Church as the Fellowship of the Holy Spirit

The presence of Christ in the Church must be conceived in terms of spirit as well as of body. For this reason it is important to think of the Church as the "fellowship of the Holy Spirit." "The Holy Spirit may be the last article of the Creed but in the New Testament it is the first fact of experience."

The Church may have existed in a "preceptive" state before Pentecost, but at Pentecost the Church emerged into the clear light of day. With the Spirit's coming, there emerged clearly, also, what the New Testament calls the *koinonia*, the fellowship. *Koinonia* is one of the great New Testament words that characterize the Church. In the one body is a unity of fellowship which is marked by a common sharing in the life of the Spirit. This fellowship is not just a feeling of affability among like-minded people. It is a spiritual unity that binds men and women into a common life across divisions of race, of religious tradition, and of cultural, social, and economic background. It is not just a feeling that "the more we get together, the happier we'll be." It is a togetherness *in the Spirit.* It is a spiritual oneness that embraces the burden of the gospel as well as its glory, the fellowship of Christ's sufferings as well as the power of his resurrection. It is a "common life in the body of Christ" that allows for varieties of gifts and varieties of service.

The function of the Spirit in the Church is to witness to Christ. The presence of the Spirit in the Church is the presence of Christ. The work of the Spirit in the *koinonia* produces in the Church "the fruits of the Spirit: love, joy, peace, patience, kindness, goodness, faithfulness, gentleness, self-control" (Gal. 5:22-23, RSV). These are the virtues of Christ.

If the task of the Spirit is to witness to Christ, crucified and risen, one of the great creative works of the Spirit is to make the Church a fellowship of witness. Pentecost was the occasion on which the worldwide missionary task of the Church was launched. The descent of the Spirit transformed the disciples into apostles and missionaries. Pentecost was the fulfillment of the promise, "But you shall receive power when the Holy Spirit has come upon you; and you shall be my witnesses" (Acts 1:8, RSV).

The Spirit creates the supernatural birth by which men and women are made children of God (John 3:5-6). He gives effectiveness to Christian preaching, which is futile without the Spirit's empowering

(1 Cor. 2:4). The Spirit guides the Church in its activity and its daily life (Acts 6:3). He directs the Church's missionary endeavor (Acts 8:29; 10:19-20). He supplies the gifts that diversify and enrich the Church's ministry (1 Cor. 12:4-30). He leads the Church into all truth (John 16:13).

To say that the Spirit is the "Holy" Spirit is to say that he is the sanctifying Spirit. He sets apart his people for the work which Christ came to do. He places on their shoulders the burdens that Christ came to bear. The light of God that shone in the face of Christ shines from their lives by an enkindling radiance that comes from the Holy Spirit. The Holy Spirit sheds the love of God abroad in their hearts, and they pass this love on to the world with the same compassion that filled the heart of Jesus.

The Church as the Community of the Cross and Resurrection

Some years ago, Paul Scherer painted a graphic picture of what happens to the Church when it withdraws from a real and profound participation in the epic realities of the Christian life. When the Church follows Christ from such a great distance that it loses sight of the cross of Christ, said Scherer, it wanders

> from room to room of humanity's tragic house, wringing its hands, mumbling its creeds, its best wishes and kindest regards, making its distant gestures toward eternity; not even meeting man's need, let alone shaping anything; apologizing for man's poverty; fawning on its governments at war; stroking a cross, but never getting itself crucified because it is not worth crucifying.[8]

The Church must incorporate in its life the cross principle in emulation of its Lord. Unfortunately, the Church has embraced all too affectionately and naively the success standards of the environment in which it lives. It has been enamored with the "edifice complex," which measures achievement in terms of large, commodious, comfortable, and efficiently used buildings. It is preoccupied with large budgets, with large crowds in attendance at its various functions, with shrewdly conceived and diligently promoted programs, and with the production

---

[8]Paul Scherer, *For We Have This Treasure* (New York and London: Harper and Row, Publishers, 1944), p. 122.

and use of a plethora of religious literature on an astonishing variety of subjects. Much is said in its teaching and preaching about the Christ who bore the burdens of the poor, who healed the brokenhearted, who fought evil at the expense of great risk and suffering, and who finally gave his life on a hideously cruel cross for the salvation of all men.

Such subjects are tolerable to the Church if they are discussed in air-conditioned comfort, if they are not dwelt on past the noon hour on Sundays, and if allegiance to the Christ-life demands little more than a lip-service adherence.

We need not belittle the need for budgets, buildings, and programs. But if the Church does not embrace the cross, it is not the Church at all. The Church is not necessarily the Church even if it works hard in humanitarian endeavors to alleviate the sufferings of damaged and broken lives within the reach of its ministry. The Church is of course thankful for any person or group engaged in this kind of activity. The Church, however, does its own work "in the name of Christ." Its labor for human betterment is animated by the compassion *of Christ*. The suffering, forgiveness, hope, and triumph *of Christ* inform the church's witness. This means that the Church is tied forever to the crucifixion and resurrection of Jesus, to those specific historical events which occurred during the governorship of Pontius Pilate. In all of its service, the Church gives account of these events, and repeats the story of what happened in the ministry, death, and resurrection of its Lord.

This does not mean, however, that the Church is anchored merely to a past series of events, which recede farther and farther from us on the coursing river of time. The death and resurrection of Christ, to be sure, had their time, their historical finality, their once-for-allness. Christ, having died once, dies no more (Rom. 6:9). The life of the Church, however, stems from the present effect of Christ's death and continuing life. "The death he died," says Paul, "he died to sin, once for all, but the life he lives he lives to God. So you also must consider yourselves dead to sin and alive to God in Christ Jesus" (Rom. 6:10-11, RSV).

In its worship the Church communes with its Lord, but it does not forget that its Lord was crucified and now is risen. All of these factors—the death, the resurrection, and the present Lordship—are indispensable factors in true Christian worship. Christ crucified and risen is the church's Lord, and communion with the Father through him shapes the purpose and pattern of the church's life.

In his book entitled *The Atonement and the Sacraments*, Robert S. Paul describes a special celebration held at Christmas in the churches of Indonesia. Each church member is given a candle. At a certain spoken signal—"Arise, shine, for thy light is come"—the members go forward and, one by one, light their candles from a large, central candle. With their candles still burning, the worshipers then kneel around a crib to pay homage to the coming of Christ, the Light of the world. Later, the whole congregation, with candles alight, form a large cross as a reminder that the incarnation was for the purpose of atonement. By forming themselves into the shape of a cross, they signify that they have become a part of Christ's sacrifice, giving their lives in the giving of Christ's life. At the end of the service, they leave the house of worship with their candles aflame to take the Light of the world to the dark world outside.

In vivid picture, they thus proclaim their recognition that they are the community of the cross and of the resurrection, and that, as such, they derive the burning flame of their own witness from him who was, and is, the Light of the world.[9]

The Church's Sacraments

The sacraments were called by Augustine a *verbum visible*, a visible word. They were so called because they made intensely evident the central proclamation of the Christian faith.

In his book entitled *The Spirit of Protestantism*, Robert McAfee Brown repeats a basic conviction of Christianity when he says that, in a preeminent way, God spoke his word to us in Christ. "We 'hear'," Brown says, "in Scripture and sermon that he gave up his life for us, but we 'see' in the breaking of the bread that his body was broken on our behalf. He it is who is 'made visible' in the sacraments, and they exist to witness to him and to his saving power."[10] P. T. Forsyth was pointing in the same direction when he stated that there is only one sacrament, "the sacrament of the Word," which is conveyed through the media of Scripture, sermon, Lord's Supper, and baptism. All of

---

[9]Robert S. Paul, *The Atonement and the Sacraments* (New York, Nashville: Abingdon Press, 1960), p. 387.

[10]Robert McAfee Brown, *The Spirit of Protestantism* (New York: Oxford University Press, 1961), p. 145.

these media are important in the life of the church because they witness to the Word.

The grace of God, says Forsyth, does not flow from the sacraments—that is, grace does not originate in them or with them; grace is not inherent in them. Grace flows through them. They are vehicles of grace. In *this* sense, they are "means of grace."[11]

The Anglican *Book of Common Prayer* states that a sacrament is "an outward and visible sign of an inward and spiritual grace." In this wide sense of the term, anything can have sacramental significance, if it is a medium of God's self-communication to us. If the heavens declare the glory of God, then we have what William Temple called a "sacramental universe." If sunsets and rainbows bring to us a communion with God, they are to us sacramental media.

The Church has been wise, however, to observe a stated number of sacraments. Roman Catholicism and Eastern Orthodoxy observe seven sacraments: baptism, the eucharist (or mass), penance, confirmation, matrimony, ordination, and extreme unction. Protestants, on the other hand, characteristically observe two sacraments, baptism and the Lord's Supper. McAfee Brown says that the Protestant insistence on only two sacraments is based on the conviction that only baptism and the Lord's Supper are given explicit warrant in the teachings of Jesus. Hence, Protestants refer to these two rites as "dominical" sacraments—sacraments established by the Lord.

The wisdom of having two sacraments only, however, is deeper than this. For, in sanctioning two sacraments, the Church ever and again is recalled to the basis of its life, namely, God's redemptive act which he accomplished in Christ. By viewing all things from this vantage point and by drawing all the elements of its life into this center, the Church sees all things as sacramental. More than anywhere else, these two sacraments make vivid, in powerful symbol, the fact that the community of faith is centered on God's saving action in Christ. From this event the Church springs into being, is sustained, and is recreated.

A sacrament is a *church* rite. It has corporate and social meaning for the *community* of faith. It is not individualistic or atomistic in its significance. For example, baptism—where, in a manner of speaking,

---

[11]Cf. P. T. Forsyth, *The Church and the Sacraments* (London: Independent Press Ltd., 1917), pp. 130-53.

attention is centered on the individual who is being baptized—is performed by the *church* and before the *church*, and incorporates the individual formally into the membership of the *church*.

Baptism and the Lord's Supper are symbols of God's work of redemption in Christ Jesus, and of the faith response of those who embrace this saving deed. We should remember, however, Paul Tillich's insight that a symbol participates in the reality which it represents. To say that the sacraments are "mere symbols" reflects an anti-sacramental bias that is too radical. What is a "mere" symbol? It is true that the sacraments are not converting ordinances; they are ordinances for the converted. They do not induce the experience of regeneration; they celebrate a Christian experience which has already entered deeply into the heart of the believer. But they are themselves profound experiences in which the saving power of God, already manifested to the believer, is lived through again in joyful and, for some, ecstatic remembrance. By "remembrance" we do not mean mere "recollection." We mean rather that God's redemptive deed, appropriated by faith, is vivified again with a deepening and enlarging power, not only for the individual but also for the whole assembled congregation.

This corporate and individual experience far transcends the sheer memorialism which some denominations have inherited from the tradition of Zwingli. The doctrine of the "real presence" does not have to be a subscription to the view that the body and blood of Christ are present in the consecrated wafer and wine. It should mean, rather, that the living Christ is present at the feast, that he presides at its celebration, that he is the same Christ who lived and died for us, and rose again, and that together we enter into communion with him in full recognition of his atoning deed on our behalf. The first Christians "brake bread with gladness" because they knew that the risen Lord was with them, triumphant over sin and death, and because they knew that his triumph was theirs also.

At the Lord's Supper, the Church celebrates not only what Christ has done to atone but also what the Church is. It acknowledges that it is that body of people in the world that incorporates daily the dying and rising of the Lord. It is the community whose life is broken, whose dedicated service is poured out in order that the redeeming ministry of Christ might be carried on in the world to the end of time.

At the Lord's Supper, John A. T. Robinson reminds us, the risen Christ presides over the service: "It is he that takes, he that blesses, he that breaks, he that gives."

> Here at this service we enter the very workshop of the new world. Here the master carpenter is in action, refashioning matter and men, forming and tooling the Body which is the instrument of his mission. When we have been to communion we have been present at the changing of the world, present at the carpenter's bench, yes, and on the carpenter's bench, so that our whole lives come out chiselled and renewed.[12]

While in the Lord's Supper the emphasis is on the fact that the individual and the Church must be united with Christ ever anew, baptism emphasizes that this incorporation is an initial act which takes place once for all. In this rite the individual Christian makes a public declaration that he is separating himself from the world, in a spiritual sense, decisively. He belongs to the world no more; he belongs rather to Christ. He proclaims that he has died with Christ, has been buried with Christ, has risen with Christ, and that, thenceforth, he will live "in Christ." He pledges allegiance to the community of faith into which he is formally incorporated by the act of baptism. He joins the chorus of the whole Church which, with him, says as one body, "for me to live is Christ."

The Church's Ministry

Theologically speaking, the Church has only one ministry: the ministry of the love which God shared with mankind in the life, death, and resurrection of Christ. This ministry of God, ablaze in Jesus, determines the ministry of the Church. "To take up one's cross and follow Jesus . . . is not to set up a smaller cross alongside his greater one. It is to grasp the cruciform nature of all existence in the light which Christ has shed upon it. It is to participate in the work of crossbearing, to identify ourselves with Christ in his costly caring for mankind."[13]

---

[12]John A. T. Robinson, *Liturgy Coming to Life* (Philadelphia: The Westminster Press, 1960), p. 59.

[13]The quotation is from Robert McAfee Brown, but I have been unable to relocate the source.

The Church's Authority for Ministry. The Church's authority for ministry is the risen Christ. This truth is stated nowhere more clearly than in Matthew 28:18-20: "And Jesus came and said to them, 'All authority in heaven and on earth has been given to me. Go therefore and make disciples of all nations, baptizing them in the name of the Father and of the Son and of the Holy Spirit, teaching them to observe all that I have commanded you; and lo, I am with you always, to the close of the age" (RSV).

This great imperative must be seen by the Church as more than and other than a legalistic requirement. It must be seen in terms of God's purpose to raise up for himself a people who will be one people in Christ, and who, through suffering and tribulation, will devote themselves to the work which God sent Christ into the world to do.

The Message of Ministry. The Church's message must be expressed in the thought forms of the particular historical era to which it is addressed. In all eras, however, the Church's essential message is the *kerygma*—which was and is proclaimed in the New Testament. Professor C. H. Dodd has summarized the substance of the New Testament proclamation, and his summary shows the relevance of the atonement to this proclamation. First,

> the age of fulfilment has dawned. . . . Secondly, this has taken place through the ministry, death, and resurrection of Jesus. . . . Thirdly, by virtue of the resurrection, Jesus has been exalted at the right hand of God, as Messianic head of the New Israel. . . . Fourthly, the Holy Spirit in the Church is the sign of Christ's present power and glory. . . . Fifthly, the Messianic age will shortly reach its consummation in the return of Christ. . . . Finally the kerygma closes with an appeal for repentance, the offer of forgiveness and of the Holy Spirit, and the promise of "salvation," that is of "the life of the Age to Come" to those who enter the elect community.[14]

The Church's Ministry of Witness. There is little space here for describing the wide-ranging, multifarious, and changing techniques of

---

[14]Cited in Flew, *Jesus and His Church*, p. 121, from C. H. Dodd, *The Apostolic Preaching and Its Developments* (New York and London: Harper & Brothers Publishers, 1936), pp. 38-43.

the Church's witness in the modern world. The principle to be observed is always, as Paul Tillich pointed out, that the eternal gospel must constantly be related to the ever-changing situation. It is all too easy to think of witness only in terms of "winning souls," or of mass evangelism, or as Christian social action, or as "carrying the gospel to the heathen" across the seas. No one of these modes of witness should be neglected; every one of them should be emphasized; and all of them together should be brought into a concert of life and action by the Church. If evangelism is "relating the gospel to the torments of the world," the Church must fight entrenched powers of evil wherever they are, proclaim and apply the gospel message both to individual lives and to the structures of society, conceive its strategy of witness intelligently and prosecute it boldly, exulting in the present signs of the coming of the kingdom, but never imagining that utopia is just around some eschatological corner, or that the millennium is thundering at our doorsteps.

Preparatory to witness, the Church must participate in Christ's incarnate life. The Church has nothing to say to the world unless it worships the God who revealed himself in Christ. It cannot illuminate the world's darkness unless it reflects the light which God caused to shine in Christ's face. It has no healing power unless it has embraced the "healing cross." Unless the Church proclaims "Christ, and him crucified" in its varied ministries, its proclamation finally is little more than "a noisy gong or a clanging cymbal." Yet its true proclamation is filled with the exhilarating good news that God has raised Christ from the dead, has made him Lord to the glory of God the Father, and has sent him back in the Holy Spirit to be the companion of our daily walk "even to the end of the world."

The Church's Priestly Ministry. In a former chapter we have discussed the role of Christ as our eternal High Priest, who makes an offering of his own life for the salvation of the world. Here we should notice the priestly role of the Church as it identifies itself with the priestly work of Christ.

Along with the high-priesthood of Christ, the priesthood of Christians is affirmed in the New Testament. Although there is no record that Jesus called his disciples priests, he did call them to share in his own life of self-sacrifice. The discipleship which becomes the privilege and challenge of the Church is such a profound identification with the life of Christ that the Church shares in Christ's priestly ministry. Paul calls upon the members of the church at Rome to offer their bodies (that is, their total selves) as living sacrifices, holy and acceptable to God (Rom. 12:1). The book of Hebrews urges Christians to offer to God an acceptable service. Through Christ, the author of this epistle says, "Let us continually offer up a sacrifice of praise to God, that is, the fruit of lips that acknowledge his name. Do not neglect to do good and to share what you have, for such sacrifices are pleasing to God" (Heb. 13:15-16, RSV).

The writer of the First Epistle of Peter calls the Church a "royal priesthood" (2:9). The writer of Revelation ascribes praise "to him who loves us and has freed us from our sins by his blood and made us a kingdom, priests to his God and Father, to him be glory and dominion for ever and ever" (Rev. 1:5-6, RSV).

The Church carries out its priestly role when it offers to God a true worship, obedience, witness, thanksgiving, suffering, and dedication, in the name of Christ, and for the sake of the ministry of Christ. In so doing, it does not forget its vicarious and representative role. As Christ's sacrifice was for the sake of the world, so the Church in the power of Christ's risen life makes its own sacrifice as the new humanity which God has created in Christ. It seeks to do this by penetrating and transforming the world so that the world itself is drawn into becoming the "new world" of which the Church is herald, harbinger, and representative.

Few Christians, however, are so euphoric in their faith that they believe that, in the present world era, "the kingdom of the world has become the kingdom of our Lord and of his Christ" (Rev. 11:15, RSV). Dorothee Soelle's comment about the Church's vicarious offering on the world's behalf is a true one. "The Church exists," she says, "wherever it emerges as the world's champion, not as its accuser; as its true spokesman, not as its denigrator. It accordingly knows and promotes the interests of its client."

To "promote the interests of its client" certainly does not mean that the Church redeems the world by its own priestly sacrifice. It rather means that the Church mediates to the world the saving efficacy of the priestly ministry of Christ by identifying itself with that ministry. It identifies itself as the follower of, not the replacement of, the crucified and risen Servant and Savior. The priesthood of all believers, says William Manson, "lies in the fact that each believer offers himself as a sacrifice according to the pattern laid down by Christ; and—what is equally essential—that all these individual offerings are taken up into one perpetual offering made by the one eternal high priest of the New Covenant."[15]

The whole Church, not just a special clerical class, exercises a priestly ministry. The whole Church is a servant people; every member is a minister. Every Christian is called to be a *saint* in the sense that he or she is set aside for God's use. There is in the New Testament no concept of "full-time Christian service," except as this concept applies to every Christian and to all Christians. The doctrine of the "priesthood of all believers" means more than the right of every person to go to God for himself. The greater truth is that the believer's priesthood involves a responsibility to go to God on behalf of other persons as well. As a priest, the layman is a minister in the Christian community, the Church. His primary responsibility is to aid the Church to realize its God-given redemptive role in the world.

Not much of the Church's priesthood is exercised in the church building, in the church "gathered." This can be said without minimizing in the least the indispensable importance of the congregation's gathering for worship, fellowship, and training. But the Church's priesthood is exercised most frequently and perhaps most effectively in the ministry of the church "scattered," as the members of the church serve in home, market, factory, field, classroom, and legislative chamber. A well-known passage by George McLeod is a telling statement of this aspect of the Church's ministry:

> I simply argue that the Cross be raised again at the center of the market place as well as on the steeple of the church. I am recovering the claim that Jesus was not crucified in a cathedral between two candles, but on a cross between two thieves; on the town garbage heap; at a crossroad so cosmopolitan that they had to write his title in Hebrew and in Latin and in Greek; . . . at the kind of place where cynics talk smut, and thieves curse, and soldiers gamble. Because that is where he died, and that is what he died about. And that is where churchmen should be and what churchmen should be about.[16]

---

[15]William Manson, *Ministry and Priesthood: Christ's and Ours* (London: The Epworth Press, 1958), p. 64.

[16]George McLeod, *Only One Way Left* (Glasgow: Iona Community, 1958), p. 40.

The priest, it has been said, is the man who "stands on the Godward side." As Christ, the High Priest of our salvation, stands on the Godward side of our humanity, so the Church stands in its priestly role on the Godward side of our race. It makes its offerings and its intercessions, and it endures its sufferings, for the sake of its fellow human beings, but in obedience to the will of God.

The Church's Ministry of Reconciliation. The reconciling ministry of Christ is carried on by the Church at the world's center, and out to its far frontiers. Wherever the Church batters down the walls of hostility between Jew and Greek; wherever it battles against the ignorance, poverty, sickness, suffering, and alienation that form the breeding grounds of hatred, malice, and envy between races, classes, and nations; wherever the Church steps in to shoulder, in the name of Christ, the burdens of sick, lost, discouraged, dispirited men and women; wherever it proclaims the good news of the forgiveness of sin, of healing for the brokenhearted, of mercy and love for all men, it carries on its Lord's ministry of reconciliation. Wherever the Church abases itself to be a community of penitent and forgiven sinners, recognizing itself to be, in a paraphrased version of D. T. Niles's striking statement, "beggars who tell other beggars where they can get bread"; wherever the Church is willing to be cleansed and equipped to carry on Christ's saving work—"His eyes to see where the Father's work is waiting to be done, His feet to speed on His errands, His mouth to speak His words, His hands to do His deeds"[17]—then it carries on its ministry of reconciliation.

The ministry of reconciliation is a task given to the Church, to be shared by every member of Christ's body. This task cannot be delegated exclusively or even primarily to a professional clergy. The whole Church is to be the salt of the earth, permeative in its seasoning and preservative power. The whole Church is to be the light of the world, working at its redemptive mission until the clean, awakening light of God overspreads the world. The Church does not seek to dominate the world. Like leaven, it rather permeates the world's life. No ministry is too low for it. No troubled or broken life is beyond the reach of its compassion. No area of human enterprise is beyond its

---

[17]Leonard Hodgson, *The Doctrine of the Atonement* (New York: Charles Scribner's Sons, 1951), p. 96.

concern. The Church sees and heeds the basic insight of the Christian faith which was enunciated with power by the apostle Paul: "God was in Christ reconciling the world to himself, not counting their trespasses against them, and entrusting to us the message of reconciliation" (2 Cor. 5:19, RSV).

The Church as Eschatological Community. Eschatology concerns our confrontation with ultimate reality—that is, with God. It is concerned with the end of all things. The end, however, is to be conceived not only as *finis*, but also as *telos*, aim, purpose. Eschatology has an already dimension, a now dimension, and a not yet dimension. It comprises the past, the present, and the future, as these are seen in the light of the purpose and activity of God. God the Father Almighty, Maker of heaven and earth, is the unifying factor in all eschatology. He is the Alpha, who was before all things, and the Omega, the divine creative power who brings all things to their consummation. To pre-Christian Jews, as A. M. Hunter says, "eschatology meant the doctrine of the End—the End conceived as God's age-long and final purpose destined to be realized in the future and to give meaning to the whole travail of history."[18] In Christian interpretation, eschatology also deals with God's age-long and final purpose. In Christian understanding, however, God's purpose is Christologically centered. God reveals, implements, and consummates his purpose in Jesus Christ.

The Church, living in the dynamic life of the present world, lives also in the world which is to come. Its situation in the world is one of immersion in the world's life and of vicarious suffering for it. At the same time, while it does not seek an avenue of cowardly escape from the world, it experiences deliverance from the evil powers of the world. Jesus Christ has given "himself for our sins to deliver us from the present evil age, according to the will of our God and Father"(Gal. 1:4, RSV). God "has delivered us from the dominion of darkness and transferred us to the kingdom of his beloved Son" (Col. 1:13, RSV).

As the eschatological community, the Church remembers the Word which God has given to the world in history, in the Scriptures, and preeminently in Jesus Christ. It is the community of the cross,

---

[18]A. M. Hunter, *Introducing New Testament Theology* (London: S.C.M. Press, 1957), p. 26.

because it has been baptized into Christ's death. It is the community of the resurrection, because it has been raised to newness of life. It is the community which lives in hope; it has "tasted the goodness of the word of God and the powers of the age to come" (Heb. 6:5, RSV). Its life is lived in and shaped by the end towards which it sees the creating and redeeming God directing all things: "For he has made known to us in all wisdom and insight the mystery of his will, according to his purpose which he set forth in Christ as a plan for the fulness of time, to unite all things in him, things in heaven and things on earth" (Eph. 1:9-10, RSV).

The Church in the world must always address itself with understanding and with power to the profound, perennial, ultimate problems of human life, and of the human spirit—the problem of sin, the problem of suffering, the problem of meaninglessness (called by some contemporary thinkers the paramount problem of the late twentieth century), and the problem of death. Whatever else the Church does, it must come to grips with these problems, illuminate them with searching Christian insight, and answer them with the adequate resources which are available in the authentic Christian gospel.

A striking passage by Jürgen Moltmann sets these problems in a true Christian perspective:

> The raising of Christ . . . is also God's contradiction of suffering and death, of humiliation and offence, and of the wickedness of evil. Hope finds in Christ not only a consolation *in* suffering, but also the protest of the divine promise *against* suffering. If Paul calls death the "last enemy" (1 Cor. 15:26), then the opposite is also true: that the risen Christ, and with him the resurrection hope, must be declared to be the enemy of death and of a world that puts up with death. . . . That is why faith, whenever it develops into hope, causes not rest but unrest, not patience but impatience. It does not calm the unquiet heart, but is itself this unquiet heart in man. Those who hope in Christ can no longer put up with reality as it is, but begin to suffer under it, to contradict it. Peace with God means conflict with the world, for the goad of the promised future stabs inexorably into the flesh of every unfulfilled present. . . . This hope makes the Christian Church a constant disturbance in

human society, seeking as the latter does to stabilize itself into a 'continuing city.' It makes the Church the source of continual new impulses towards the realization of righteousness, freedom and humanity here in the light of the promised future that is to come.[19]

The Church lives a pilgrim life in the land of promise, seeing through clouds of darkness only occasionally, perhaps, the gleaming spires of the heavenly city which is its goal. But as it travels, it seeks to bring the eternal gospel to bear upon the issues, the hurts, and the torments of the world. The needs of the world define the scope of its witness and its ministry. It moves forward in the sure conviction that the God of yesterday and today is also the God of tomorrow. It cherishes and proclaims its message, that Christ died for our sins, that God has raised him from the dead, has brought life and immortality to light through him, has made him Lord over all thrones and dominions and eras of history, and has purposed to sum up all things in him. In the midst of uncertainty and travail, the Church remembers that "to know Him is to be at home on every continent and in every sea."[20]

---

[19]Moltmann, *Theology of Hope*, pp. 21-22.

[20]Nels F. S. Ferré, *The Atonement and Mission* (London: London Missionary Society, 1960), p. 30.

Indexes

(For the location of subjects, see the extensive listing of contents, pages vii-x above.)

1. Text Index

2. Author Index